William Mason Cornell

Recollections

William Mason Cornell

Recollections

ISBN/EAN: 9783744730280

Printed in Europe, USA, Canada, Australia, Japan

Cover: Foto ©ninafisch / pixelio.de

More available books at **www.hansebooks.com**

RECOLLECTIONS

OF

"Yᴇ OLDEN TIME,"

WITH

BIOGRAPHICAL SKETCHES

OF

EMINENT CLERGYMEN, STATESMEN, MERCHANTS, PHYSICIANS, LAWYERS, PRESIDENTS OF COLLEGES, TEACHERS, ETC., IN MASSACHUSETTS, RHODE ISLAND, CONNECTICUT, NEW HAMPSHIRE, AND PENNSYLVANIA.

Illustrated with numerous Steel Plates and Wood-Cuts.

BY

WILLIAM MASON CORNELL, D.D., LL.D.,

Author of "The History of Pennsylvania," "How to Enjoy Life," "Life of Horace Greeley," "Memoir of Charles Sumner," etc., etc.

BOSTON:
LEE AND SHEPARD, PUBLISHERS.
NEW YORK:
CHARLES T. DILLINGHAM.
1878.

CONTENTS.

CHAPTER I.
                                                PAGE.

Use of History — Settlement of Quincy, then Braintree — Revs. John Codman and Daniel Dow — Famous for Presidents — Birthplace of John, and John Quincy Adams — John Adams Ditching — Anecdote of Adams and Judge Niles — John Adams's Speech before King George — The Old King's Reply — John Adams in Troublous Times — The Political Pot . 3

CHAPTER II.

John Quincy Adams — His Mother — Parson Smith, of Weymouth — He goes abroad with his Father — His Economy — Punctuality — Love of Education — Morality — Temperance — Reverence for the Bible — Filial Affection — A Walker — Regard for the Sabbath — His Poetic Talent — A Man of Prayer — Of Strong Feelings 17

CHAPTER III.

John Quincy Adams as a Statesman — His thorough Training in his Profession — His Historical Knowledge — Dealing with Henry A. Wise — Letter to Dutty J. Pierce — His Personal Appearance in Age — What he did when he left the Presidency — A Representative in Congress — Address to his Constituents — Superior to Party — Advocates the Right of Petition — Holds the House at Bay for Four Days — How he managed the rebellious Clerk — His Death in the Harness . 35

CONTENTS.

CHAPTER IV.

The Old Unitarian and the Episcopal Churches — Rev. Dr. Cutler — Efforts for a Trinitarian Church — The Council and its Organization — Names of Members — "Chief Women" in the Church — Decease of the First Member, Mrs. Mary Baxter — A Part of the Sermon on that Occasion . . . 53

CHAPTER V.

Rev. Daniel D. Smith — Rev. Elias Smith — Father of Daniel — A Wonderful Man — A Scourge of all the Learned Professions — A Member of some half-dozen Religious Denominations 68

CHAPTER VI.

Hereditary Descent — Daniel D. Smith's Subtlety — George W. Beal and Josiah Brigham — The Town Meeting — The Results — John Quincy Adams in a Petty Parish Quarrel — Lucius Manlius Sargent and Dr. Cutler — Kind Treatment by John Quincy Adams — Matthew Hale Smith and Temperance in Quincy. 99

CHAPTER VII.

My School in Quincy — Rev. John Gregory — His Temperance and Trouble — The Little Church — Its Various Pastors — A Reign of Peace 111

CHAPTER VIII.

Rev. Edward T. Taylor — Dedication of the Methodist Church in Quincy — Father Taylor's Temperance Addresses — His Dedication Sermon — His laying us all on the Shelf — His Prayer for the Bigots of Albany, N.Y. — Getting the Railroad — J. Q. Adams's Funeral — The Turnpike — Deacon Newcomb and John Tappan — Quincy Then and Now — The Doctors of Quincy then — Wollaston Heights . . . 123

CHAPTER IX.

The Lyceum in Quincy — Lectures — J. Q. Adams, his Themes — Peter Parley — Debates — New Science of Phrenology — Its Wonderful Popularity — My Lecture, exposing its Fallacies

— Prediction fulfilled — The Records of the defunct Phrenological Society of Boston in one of the Pigeon-Holes of the N. E. H. Genealogical Society 137

CHAPTER X.

The Cause of Temperance, 1836 — John Quincy Adams's Address on Temperance — Rev. E. Taylor's — The Address of the Writer on Temperance. 164

CHAPTER XI.

The Neighboring Ministers of Quincy in 1834: Rev. John Codman, D.D., Rev. Richard S. Storrs, D.D., Rev. Jonas Perkins, Rev. David Sanford, Rev. Dr. Gile, Rev. John Phillipps, Rev. Ebenezer Burgess, D.D., Rev. Wm. M. Rogers . . 184

CHAPTER XII.

Visit to Boston in 1816 — Jesse Smith's Stages — Stop in "Bromfield Lane" — Boston Then and Now — Value of Land Then and Now — Central Court and Winter Street — Benjamin Russell — Rev. C. G. Finney — Rev. Mr. Dodd, the Mesmerizer — The Old Winter-Street Church and Rev. Wm. M. Rogers — Millerism and the End of the World — Old Relics of Boston — The Common, and its Fences — The Ministers of Boston — The Public Schools. 215

CHAPTER XIII.

Matters relating to the Health of Boston — The Professors of Harvard and Jefferson Medical Colleges, and the Doctors of Boston — Dr. J. C. Warren — Visit from the Legislature — Dr. John Ware — Dr. George Hayward — Dr. Walter Channing — The Medical and Clerical Professions combined — Practice in Boston — Fifty Years ago — Then and Now . 241

CHAPTER XIV.

First Visit to the Quaker City — Camden and Amboy Railroad — Contrast in the Streets of Boston and Philadelphia — Second Visit to that City — Our Boarding-House — Medical College — Clinton-Street Church — Lecturing in Private

Schools — Visiting Public Places — The Place of Penn's Treaty with the Indians — His Second Purchase — Independence Hall — Fairmount Water-Works — Fightings in 1852-3 in Philadelphia — Medical Colleges of that City . . 261

CHAPTER XV.

Girard College — Removal to Philadelphia — The Private Schools of that City — The Public Schools and the School-Boards — Comparison between them and the Schools in Boston — Mischief of Choosing Directors there by Politicians: the same as in Boston — Ladies at the Head of the Grammar Schools — Voting-Places in Philadelphia — Liquor-Selling and Tobacco — Sabbath Schools, and Two Sessions in Philadelphia — The Squirrels, the Worms, and the Birds of Philadelphia. 273

CHAPTER XVI.

Things and Prominent Men of Philadelphia — The Methodists and Education — The City Pro-Slavery — Southern Newspapers — The Union League — The Ladies' Work for the Soldiers — Rev. Albert Barnes — Revs. Drs. John McDowell, Henry A. Boardman, Henry Steele Clarke, George W. Musgrave, William Blackwood, Elias R. Beadle, Alfred Nevin, Jonathan Edwards, Charles Wadsworth, Edwin N. Nevin, John Chambers, James M. Crowell, Richard Newton, William P. Breed — Laymen: Matthew Newkirk, Alexander Whilldin, Matthias W. Baldwin, Stephen Colwell, George H. Stuart, George W. Childs, William H. Allen . . . 286

CHAPTER XVII.

The Centennial Exhibition — Opening Day — Concourse of People — Philadelphia the Right Place — Bishop Simpson's Prayer — Whittier's Centennial Hymn — John Welch's Address — Cantata by Sydney Lanier — Address by Gen. Hawley — President Grant speaks — Concluding Ceremonies — Starting the Great Engine — Sabbath Law of Pennsylvania — Some of the Centennial Buildings 307

CHAPTER XVIII.

Brown University Fifty Years ago — Recollections of College-Life — President Messer — Professors at that Time — Dr.

Messer's coming to the Point — Dr. Wayland's Advent — Inspection of him — The New Order of Things — One Mistake — Tristam Burgess and Professor DeWolf — Dr. Wayland's Success — The Manner of his Teaching, and his Interest in the Pupils — His Compliments to our Class — Our Regard for him 333

CHAPTER XIX.

Recollections of Cape Cod — The Name — Not to be altered — King Charles defeated — Early Settlement of — Marshpee Indians — Anecdotes of — Provincetown of Old — Improved — Churches and Ministers on the Cape Fifty Years ago — Progress in Union — Language peculiar to Themselves — Their Language — Good Citizens and Honest Men . . . 350

CHAPTER XX.

Recollections of New Hampshire — Newmarket — Mr. Broadhead — Bishop Heading — The Quaker — The Fat Man — The Coe Family — Boarding there — The Candle-Mould — Newington — John N. Maffit — Effect of his Preaching — Mrs. Maffit — Rev. Mr. Roland — Rev. Mr. Hurd — Mr. Belden and Judge Smith — Visit to Pembroke, and Rev. Mr. Burnham — Visit to Gilmanton — Gass's Hotel — Dr. Shattuck of Boston 364

CHAPTER XXI.

History and Recollections of Woodstock, Conn. — History of the Town — Settled by a Colony from Roxbury — King Philip's War — Rev. Mr. Lyman — The Old Major — My Advent to Woodstock — Four Quarts of Oats sent me there — Rev. Mr. Williams of Dudley — Muddy Brook — The Parish Quarrel — Capt. Walker and Daughters — Emily's Criticisms — Removal to South Woodstock — Father Lyman — His Settlement — Mr. Lyman's Kindness — Dr. Jedediah Morse — Dr. Abiel Holmes — William Bowen, Esq., and his Grandson Henry C. Bowen — Effects of Anti-Masonry — Deacon Chandler and Wife — Mr. Barsto laughing in Meeting — The Lions — Deacon Walter Paine — State of Religion in Woodstock — — Protracted Meetings — How conducted — Results — Protracted Meeting in Providence — Rev. Dr. Dow — Rev. Mr.

Wilson — Rev. Charles G. Finney — His First Visit to New England — His Preaching — Rev. Dr. Wisner — Endurance of the Converts — The McClellan Family — Gen. George B. — Lorenzo Dow 374

CHAPTER XXII.

Amos Lawrence — Birth, Death, Countenance, Manner of Giving, Contrast of Givers — Mother — Letter to Her — Delicate Constitution — Studying Astronomy — Education — Integrity — Temperance — Tobacco — Esquire Brazer's Store — Beginning just right — Recognition of Providence — Little Doctor — Catholicity — Debility — Diet — Letter to President Hopkins — Advice to One in pursuit of a Wife — Letter to his Daughter — Letter to his Sister — General Characteristics and Advice — His Sons 420

ILLUSTRATIONS.

Steel.

W. M. CORNELL	*Frontispiece.*

	PAGE.
JOSIAH QUINCY	5
JOHN ADAMS	12
JOHN QUINCY ADAMS	19
DR. JOHN C. WARREN	241
WILLIAM H. ALLEN	307
AMOS LAWRENCE	420

Wood Engravings at End of Book.

PENN'S TREATY WITH THE INDIANS.
FAIRMOUNT PARK FROM PENNSYLVANIA BRIDGE.
FAIRMOUNT WATER-WORKS FROM CALLOW-HILL BRIDGE.
GIRARD COLLEGE.
LEDGER BUILDING.
CENTENNIAL BUILDINGS: THE MAIN BUILDING.
THE HORTICULTURAL HALL.
THE ART GALLERY.
THE AGRICULTURAL BUILDING.

RECOLLECTIONS AND SKETCHES OF QUINCY. MASS.

As an introduction to some things I have to say of Quincy, both of a curious and ludicrous character, it may be well to preface them by remarking that thirty years have now elapsed—the life-time of a generation, since I removed from that town. Most of the men, who were then in active, middle or advanced age, have now passed away. A race that knew me not has arisen to take their places; and, consequently, some things recorded in these Recollections and Sketches will be new to them. Then there was no rail road, I mean for passengers or cars carried by steam. There was, however, the first rail road ever built in America, namely, one from the granite ledges to the water, for the purpose of taking that material from the ledge to the vessels for transportation to Boston, New York, and even to New Orleans. This short road, traversed by horses, gave the name to the Railroad Village, (a very singular name now, when every village, and almost every house, has a railroad) in Milton and Quincy. "The Old Colony Railroad" brought some people into Quincy, and others have moved into the place from other towns, so that with the deaths that have taken place, and the change of population in the time, but few, comparatively, are now there who were the active population when the writer went there, forty years ago; still, in these Recollections and Sketches I expect to draw a portrait that will be recognized by some now living, and by some, who were then children.

"They will see their own likeness in their fathers' faces."

It is sometimes useful to retrace our former steps, and Virgil made his Hero say, "I have seen sorer troubles than these; and, perhaps, God will grant an end to these also." At all events, *Deo Volento*, I purpose to give some personal Recollections of Men, Manners and Things of this "large and highly respectable town;" and, I doubt not, I shall have some readers. So then, I commence my story.

CHAPTER I.

CONTENTS.—Use of History—Settlement of Quincy, then Braintree—Revs. John Codman and Daniel Dow—Famous for Presidents — Birth-place of John, and John Quincy Adams — John Adams Ditching — Anecdote of Adams and Judge Niles—John Adams speech before King George—The Old King's reply—John Adams in troublous times. The Political Pot.

I now come back to Massachusetts, my native State; left Woodstock, Aug. 12th, 1834, and was installed in Quincy, the next week, Aug 20th. Revs. Drs. Dow, of Thompson, and John Codman, of Dorchester, arguing two hours on Congregationalism in Massachusetts, and in Connecticut, at the Council.

Some account of this town may interest those of my readers who are unacquainted with it. It was once a part of Boston; and, probably, will be again at some future time. In 1640, Braintree was set off as a separate town. Braintree included Quincy, what is now Braintree, and Randolph and Holbrook. In 1792, Quincy was incorporated as a separate town. It included what was once called "Dorchester Farms," Squantum, Mount Wallaston, or "Merry Mount;" and is now bounded north by Boston, east by Boston Harbor, south by Weymouth and Braintree, and west by Milton. It received the name of Quincy in honor of one of its patriots who died at sea in the early part of the Revolution, and whose worthy descendants still own the Old Quincy estate.

This town has been remarkable for producing Presidents. John Hancock, President of the first Congress, and John Adams and his son, John Quincy Adams, two Presidents of the United States, were all natives of this town. It may hence be inferred, there was considerable aristocracy in Quincy, the workings of which will be seen as we proceed.

The first church was gathered in 1639, only nine years after the settlement of Boston.

The following were the ministers or pastors in succession:

Revs.	Set.	Died or Dis.	Aged.
Wm. Thompson,	1639,	1668,	68.
Henry Flint,	1640,	1668,	66.
Moses Fiske,	1672,	1708,	66.
Joseph Marsh,	1709,	1726,	41.
John Hancock,	1726,	1744,	42.
Lemuel Bryant,	1745,	1753,	00.
Anthony Wibird,	1755,	1800,	72.
Peter Whitney,	1800,	1843,	73.

Mr. Whitney was pastor when I went to Quincy, and the next year, 1835, Rev. Wm. P. Lunt was installed as his colleague. The church was Unitarian. There had been an Episcopal church in this town for many years; indeed, I do not know from what date. At the time I went there, the Universalists also had a church.

It may be appropriate to give a sketch of some of the eminent men of this town, as I recollect them.

THE QUINCY FAMILY.

[As the town received its name from the Quincy family, it seems appropriate that this should be the one first named. It was suitable that the name should be given it, as Josiah Quincy, jun. (as he has ever been called), was a leading man; and, from his early decease, well worthy to have such a respectable town named for him.]

EDMUND QUINCY was the first of the name who came to New England. He landed in Boston, Sept. 4, 1633, and was accompanied by Rev. John Cotton. He and William Coddington — afterward Governor of Rhode Island — bought of the sachem Chickalabat a tract of land at Mount Wollaston, afterward called Braintree, now Quincy. Soon this acquired the name of Merry Mount, from the revels of Morton, because of their "setting up a Maypole, drinking and dancing about it, like so many fairies or furies rather."

This Edmund Quincy died the next year, after making the purchase in 1637. He left a son, also named Edmund. He was a magistrate and a quiet man.

He also left a daughter, named Judith, who was married to John Hull, who became famous and rich by coining money before King Charles II. put a stop to it. It is said, Hull gave the name of "Point Judith" to that stormy point, after that of his wife.

Lieut.-Col. Edmund Quincy, who was a child when he was brought to New England, died in 1698, and left two sons, Daniel and Edmund. Daniel died before his father, leaving an only son John, who graduated at Cambridge in 1708. He died in 1767, the day his great-grandson John Quincy Adams was born. Edmund, the other son, graduated in 1699. He was a magistrate, and one of the judges of the supreme court. He died Feb. 23 (O.S.), 1737.

Judge Edmund Quincy had two sons, Edmund and Josiah. Edmund graduated at Cambridge in 1722, and lived at Braintree and Boston. Josiah graduated in 1728. For some time he was engaged in ship-building in Boston. When he was forty years old he retired from business, and removed to Braintree, where he lived for thirty years a country gentleman. In 1755, during the old French war, he was sent to Pennsylvania as a commissioner.

Col. Josiah Quincy, had three sons, Edmund, Samuel, and Josiah. Edmund graduated in 1752, and died at sea in 1768. The second son, Samuel, graduated in 1754. Josiah Quincy bore the name of his father, and was called Josiah Quincy, jun. He was born Feb. 23, 1744, and graduated in 1763. He studied law with Oxenbridge Thacher. He ranked high in his profession. He died the 16th of March, 1775.

My personal acquaintance with the family commenced with the Josiah Quincy who was born in Boston the 4th of February, 1772. He was not quite three years old when his father went away to die. In 1793 he was admitted to the bar. Party politics ran high between the Federalists and Republicans during Mr. Quincy's youth. Edmund Quincy, his son, says, "Political lying was never carried to greater perfection than it was at that time." In 1800 he was a candidate for Congress, being twenty-eight years old. This was then considered so young for a man to be a candidate for Congress, that the Democrats called "for a cradle in which to rock the baby-candidate of the Federalists." He was defeated in consequence of a division among the Federalists. In 1804, in the Senate of Massachusetts, Mr. Quincy showed his first opposition to slavery. He was elected a member of Congress in 1804.

His son Edmund, in the life of his father, says, "The moment when Mr. Quincy took his seat in the House of Representatives was a very critical one in regard both to the foreign and the domestic affairs of the United States. Mr. Jefferson was in the first year of his second term, and had an unquestionable and unquestioning majority in both houses at his beck. The Federalists were in a hopeless minority in Congress and in the nation. They had but seven senators, counting John Quincy Adams, who soon went out from among them, and barely twenty-five members of the lower house. A majority even of the Massachusetts delegation (ten out of seventeen) were Democrats. Of course, all that the minority could do was to watch the administration, to expose its shortcomings and excesses, to resist mischievous measures as well as they could, and record a protest against them when resistance was in vain."

Mr. Quincy, while in Congress, though the youngest, was the leading spirit of the then dying Federal party; but even when so eminent a man as John Quincy Adams turned from a Federalist to a Republican, or, as they were then called, Democrats, Mr. Quincy still held on to his Federal principles.

Mr. Quincy was about all the New-England man who maintained a long and pleasant correspondence with John Randolph of Roanoke.

The author has the following recollections of Josiah Quincy. After retiring from Congress, Mr. Quincy did good service in the State Senate of Massachusetts. When dropped from the Senate, 1820, he was sent to the House, and made Speaker of that body. From the Speakership he became Judge of the Municipal Court of Boston, and was on the bench in the trial of the famous John N. Maffit against Joseph T. Buckingham for libel upon Maffit.

Mr. Quincy was the second mayor of Boston, and for many years President of Harvard College; and it may be truly said, no man in either of these positions has exceeded him in energy and efficiency in managing either the finances and order of the city, or the oldest university in the United States.

John Adams was born, at the foot of "Penn's Hill," October 19th, 1735.

This engraving represents the birth-place of two Presidents of the United States. John Adams was born in the house represented on the right, and his son in the other. In the attic of the latter, John Quincy Adams stowed away his valuable library, while U. S. minister in Russia. In the rear, is a meadow in which John Adams once worked. He says, "when I was a boy I had to study the Latin grammar, but it was dull and I hated it. My father was anxious to send me to college; and, therefore, I studied grammar till I could bear it no longer; and, going to my father I told him I did not like study, and asked for some other employment. It was opposing his wishes, and he was quick in his answer. 'Well, John, if Latin grammar does not suit, you may try ditching, perhaps that will. My meadow needs a ditch and you may put by Latin and try that.' This seemed a delightful change, and to the meadow I went. But I soon found ditching harder than Latin, and the first forenoon was the longest I ever experienced. That day I ate the bread of labor and glad was I when night came on. That night I made some comparison between Latin grammar and ditching, but said not a word about it. I dug the next forenoon and wanted to return to Latin at dinner, but it was humiliating and I could not do it. At night toil conquered pride, and I told my father — one of the severest trials of my life

— that if he chose I would go back to Latin grammar. He was glad of it, and, if I have since gained any distinction, it has been owing to the two day's labor in that abominable ditch."

His courtship and marriage with Miss Smith, the Parson's daughter, of Weymouth, presents another anecdote of his youthful life, which has passed into history, and will appear when we come to speak of John Quincy Adams.

I never saw John Adams but twice, and then he was an old man, nearly ninety. He died on the 4th of July, 1826, with the words on his lips, which 50 years before he had uttered on the floor of Congress, "Independence forever."

He was not a believer in the Calvinistic doctrines, and especially in divine foreordination. Old Judge Niles, of Vermont, was a class-mate of John Adams, at college. He used to visit his brother, Old Parson Niles, at Abington, (nobody who has lived in Abington for the last seventy-five years, or will live there till the millenium, will ever see the like of Parson Niles) and on his journey, always called upon his class-mate, Adams.

Adams, being liberal in his views, and Niles a stiff old Calvinist, (as they were called in those days, for, as the Unitarians now say, with truth, they neither believe nor preach as they once did) used to hold long arguments on these deep things, and never the one convinced the other. The last visit Judge

Niles made to see John Adams, Mr. Adams' legs were very sore and troublesome, and he said, "Judge, I suppose I ought to be resigned to this, as it was foreordained."

The old Judge, with a merry twinkle of his eye, for which he was famed, replied, "Well, not unless it is of as much importance as the fall of a sparrow."

Of course, I cannot enter fully into the life of John Adams in these sketches; I may be allowed, however, to give one of his speeches. It is Mr. A's own representation of his meeting with King George, when he presented his credentials as the first Minister Plenipotentiary from the U. S. to the Court of St. James, and to the King, from whom our Independence had been wrenched, by an eight year's war.—Mr. Adams gives the following account in a letter to a friend — " Here stood the stern monarch who had expended more than six-hundred millions of dollars, and the lives of two-hundred thousand of his subjects, in a vain attempt to subjugate freeman; and by his side stood the man, who, in the language of Jefferson, was the great pillar of support to the Declaration of Independence, and its ablest advocate and champion on the floor of Congress." Mr. Adams says : — At one o'clock on Wednesday, the first of June, 1785, the master of ceremonies called at my house, and went with me to the Secretary of State's office, in Cleaveland Row, where the Marquis of Carmarthen received and introduced me to Mr. Frazier, his under-secretary, who had been, as his lordship said, uninterruptedly in that office through all the changes in administration for thirty years. After a short conversation, Lord Carmarthen invited me to go with him in his coach to court. When we arrived in the ante-chambers, the master of ceremonies introduced him and attended me, while the Secretary of State went to take the commands of the King. While I stood in this place, where it seems all the ministers stand upon such occasions, always attended by the master of ceremonies, the room was very full of ministers of state, bishops, and all other sorts of courtiers, as well as the next room, which is the King's bed-chamber. You may well suppose, I was the focus of all eyes. I was relieved, however, from the embarrassment of it by the Sweedish and Dutch ministers, who came to me and entertained me with a very agreeable conversation the whole time. Some other gentlemen whom I had seen before, came to make their compliments to me, until the Marqius of Carmarthen returned and desired me to go with him to his majesty. I went with his lordship through the levee room, into the King's closet. The door was shut, and I was left with his majesty and Secretary of State alone. I made three reverences; one at the door, another about half way, and another before the presence, according to the usage established at this and all the northern courts of Europe, and then I addressed myself to his majesty in the following words:

"Sire, the United States have appointed me Minister Plenipotentiary to your majesty, and have directed me to deliver to your majesty this letter, which contains the evidence of it. It is in obedience to their express commands that I have the honor to assure your majesty of their unanimous disposition and desire to cultivate the most friendly and liberal intercourse between your majesty's subjects and their citizens, and of their best wishes for your majesty's health and happiness, and for that of your family. The appointment of a minister from the United States to your majesty's court will form an epoch in the history of England and America. I think myself more fortunate than all my fellow-citizens in having the distinguished honor to be the first to stand in your majesty's royal presence in a diplomatic character; and I shall esteem myself the happiest of men, if I can be instrumental in reccomending my country more and more to your majesty's royal benevolence, and of restoring an entire esteem, confidence, and affection; or, in better words, the old good nature, and the good old humor, between people, who, though separated by an ocean (and under different governments) have the same language, a similar religion, a kindred blood. I beg your majesty's permission to add, that although I have sometimes before been instructed by my country, it was never in my whole life in a manner so agreeable to myself." The King listened to every word I said, with dignity it is true, but with apparent emotion. Whether it was my visible agitation, (for I felt more than I could express,) that touched him, I cannot say; but he was much affected, and answered me with more tremor than I had spoken with, and said "Sir; The circumstances of this audience are so extraordinary, the language you have now held is so extremely proper, and the feelings you have discovered so justly adapted to the occasion, that I not only receive with pleasure the assurance of the friendly disposition of the United States, but I am glad the choice has fallen upon you to be their minister. I wish you, sir, to believe, and that it may be understood in America that I have done nothing in the late contest but what I thought myself indispensably bound to do, by the duty which I owed my people. I will be frank with you. I was the last to conform to the separation: but the separation having become inevitable, I have always said, as I now say, that I would be the first to meet the friendship of the United States as an independent power. The moment I see such sentiments and language as yours prevail, and a disposition to give this country the preference, that moment I shall say, let the circumstances of language, religion and blood, have their natural full effect. I dare not say that these were the King's precise words, and it is even possible that I may have, in some particulars, mistaken his meaning; for, although his pronunciation is as distinct as I ever heard, he hesitated sometimes between members of the same period. He was indeed much affected, and I was not less so; and, therefore, I cannot be certain that I was so attentive, heard so clearly and understood so perfectly, as to be confident of all his words or sense. This, I do say, that the foregoing is his majesty's meaning, as I then understood it, and his own words, as nearly as I can recollect them. The King then asked me whether I came last from France; and upon my answering in the affirmative, he put on an air of familiarity, and, smiling, or rather laughing, said, "There is an opinion among some people that you are not the most attached of all your countrymen to the manners of France." I was surprised at this, because I thought it an indiscretion and a descent from his dignity. I was a little embarrassed, but, determined not to deny the truth on the one hand, nor lead him to infer from it any attachment to England on the other, I threw off as much gravity as I could, and assumed as much gaiety, and one of decision, as far as was decent, and said, That opinion, sir, is not mistaken; I must avow to your majesty, I have no attachment, but to my own country. The King replied as quick as lightning, "An honest man will never have any other." The King then said a word or two to the Secretary of State, which being between them, I did not hear, and then turned round and bowed to me, as is customary with all kings and princes when they give the signal to retire. I retreated, stepping backwards as is the etiquette; and, making my last reverence at the door of the chamber, I went to my carriage."

John Adams lived in troublous times. He was

a true patriot, and served his country in many important offices with great fidelity. He was a Federalist of the first water, and it is reported that when his son J. Q. Adams had somewhat departed from the principles of the Federal party, his father relished it so little, that, when it was announced to him that his son was chosen President of the U. S., John Adams replied "That is no pleasure to me."

Political lying was never carried to greater perfection, and party spirit was never more rampant than in the days of John Adams and Thomas Jefferson. The political pot boiled when Andrew Jackson was elected President; but it was ten fold hotter in the rage between the Federalists and Republicans of those days.

People talk about ministers preaching politics in our day; but such preaching as we have heard upon this subject for the past forty years would bear no comparison with the old Federal ministers of those days. Compared with that, delivered with the head and heart on fire, to what we have since heard, "much as it has been talked of, has been like a dose of Mrs. Winslow's Soothing Syrup"

"There were giants in those days" among the clergy, and they wielded their political battle-axes with the strength and power of Sons of Anak, and made the hair on the heads of their parishioners stand on end, especially, if any of them happened to be Republicans for the clergy were all Federalists.

CHAPTER II.

CONTENTS.—John Quincy Adams—His Mother—Parson Smith, of Weymouth—He goes abroad with his father—His Economy—Punctuality—Love of Education—Morality—Temperance—Reverence for the Bible—Filial Affection—A Walker—Regard for the Sabbath—His Poetic Talent—A Man of Prayer—Of Strong Feelings.

Napoleon Bonaparte, born but two years after the man of whom I am to write, never uttered a grander or more sublime truth than when he said, "Great men have had great mothers. What France needs most is mothers."

No man, in any measure acquainted with John Quincy Adams, can deny that he was great. To whom, under God, did he owe that greatness? Not so much to JOHN ADAMS, his father, the second President of the United States, as to ABIGAL SMITH, the second daughter of a country clergyman, his mother.

If a man have a " grandmother LOIS, and a mother EUNICE, " in whom dwelt the unfeigned faith of the gospel, it may make but little difference, as was the cause with young TIMOTHY, "though his father were a Greek."

The Rev. Mr. SMITH, of Weymouth, Massachusetts, was an eccentric but good man; and neither he nor his parishioners approved of the marriage of his daughter with JOHN ADAMS, the son of a farmer, and above all, himself a *Lawyer*—which profession the earlier settlers of New England considered quite unnecessary; while they approved of the marriage of the eldest daughter, MARY, with Mr. CRANCH, a neighbor of Mr. ADAMS.

When MARY was married, the father preached a wedding sermon from the text, "Mary hath chosen the good part, which shall not be taken away from her." When ABIGAL was to be married, her father told her, she might select her own text, and he would preach her a wedding sermon. She selected, "John came neither eating, nor drinking, and they said he had a devil." This was merely a specimen of her youthful independence.

It is true, female education at that day was not what it is at the present time; and yet in some respects, it was more substantial. With the writings of MILTON, DRYDEN, SHAKESPEARE, ADDISON, TILLOTSON, BUTLER, LOCKE, YOUNG, and the whole class of writers of that golden age of English literature, MISS SMITH, afterwards the mother of JOHN QUINCY ADAMS, was well acquainted. The letters of this remarkable woman to her son, JOHN QUINCY ADAMS, have been published by her grandson, CHARLES FRANCIS ADAMS, and are well worthy the perusal of all mothers and all sons. They, undoubtedly, had a powerful influence in making JOHN QUINCY ADAMS, the man he was. They abound with sentiments like the following, written to him when at Paris:—"My anxieties have been, and still are great, lest the numerous temptations and snares to vice should vitiate your early habits of virtue, and destroy those

principles which you are now capable of reasoning upon, and discerning the utility of, as the only rational source of happiness here, or foundation of felicity hereafter. Placed, as we, are in a transitory scene of probation, drawing nigher and still nigher, day by day, to that important crisis, which must introduce us into a new system of things, it ought certainly to be our principal concern to become qualified for our expected dignity."

Thus made acquainted with the mother, the daughter of a prophet, educated in the family of a prophet, rooted and grounded in christian principle, you are now prepared to be introduced to her son, JOHN QUINCY ADAMS. He was born in the town of Braintree, in the part now called Quincy, July 11th, 1767. The house in which he was born is still standing. It is about nine miles from Boston, on a plat of level land at the foot of Penn's Hill," so called, about a mile from the old mansion afterwards built by JOHN ADAMS; then occupied by JOHN QUINCY ADAMS, and now owned by his son, CHARLES F. ADAMS.

The house of his birth is two stories in front and one story back, and sits half side-wise to the street, as the old Pilgrims often located their dwellings, as has been already seen in the Plate. One may have some idea of this Puritanic taste, if he has ever visited the "old Pilgrim city, of Boston, which is conspicuous in sharp angles, narrow, crooked streets, zigzag lanes, crossings and turnings.

I have been in every room of that old house in

which JOHN QUINCY ADAMS first breathed the vital air. Here, one of the best of mothers watched over the childhood of one of the greatest of men. Here he attended the village school, and learned the first rudiments of education. Here, according to his own description, the Dame who first taught him to spell, flattered him with the idea that he would one day become a scholar. Here he looked on nature with a lover's eye and, in after years wrote from Europe, " Penn's Hill and Braintree North Common Rocks never looked and never felt to me like any other rocks."

Standing on this hill, at the age of ten years, he heard the cannon booming from the battle of Bunker's Hill, saw the smoke and flames of burning Charlestown, and watched the shells and rockets during the seige of Boston.

At the age of eleven years, he went to Europe with his Father, and studied in the schools of Paris, of Amsterdam, at the University at Leyden, at St. Petersburg, and at Stockholm. At the age of nineteen he entered the junior class of Harvard University. He became an active member of all the literary societies in college; and though he entered late, took the second part at graduation. His habits of punctuality and industry then, were what they were sixty years afterwards, when a member of the house of Representatives remarked, it was time to call the House to order, and another replied: "No, Mr. ADAMS is not in his seat." The clock was actually three minutes too fast, and before these three minutes elapsed Mr. A. *was* in his seat.

In summing up Mr. A's private character it may be remarked ;

1. *He was economical of time.* He said "I feel nothing like *ennui.* Time is too short for me, rather than too long. If the day were forty-eight hours long instead of twenty-four, I could employ them all, if I had but eyes and ears to read and write." While at St. Petersburg he complained bitterly of the great loss of his time, from the civilities and visits of his friends and associates. "I have been engaged," he wrote, "the whole forenoon, and though I rise at six o'clock, I am sometimes unable to write only a part of a private letter in the course of the day." FRANKLIN became what he was by industry; Mr. ADAMS became what he was by economizing time.

There is not a young man who cannot imitate him in this respect.

To redeem time, he *rose early.* I have met him when riding out on horseback myself, more than two miles from his home, on his return from his morning walk, and this was before sunrise. Perhaps it should be added, he retired early, when practicable.

2. Mr. ADAMS *was remarkable for punctuality.* He was never known to be late. One instance has already been given in the halls of Congress. He always attended to a previous appointment, whatever were the intervening circumstances. He had appointed an evening to see a young man of his native town, and myself, relative to the young man's application to be admitted to the "West Point Military Academy.

The old servant, said to us, "I think Mr. A. cannot see you to-night." "Will you tell him we are here," said I Mr. ADAMS immediately left his company—some members of Congress, from a distance—and spent half an hour with the young man. What young man cannot imitate Mr. A. in punctuality.

3. Mr. ADAMS *encouraged education.* He visited the public schools. He visited my own school and examined a class in the Greek Reader, when he was seventy-six years old, and wore no glasses; while on either hand of him sat a clergyman, more than twenty years his junior, with glasses on. In the interview with Mr WOOD, the young man alluded to, Mr. A. inspired him with an interest in, and a love of study which he never lost; and, when I saw him, one of the teachers of West Point, some years since, he referred to that evening's conversation with Mr. A. as the mainspring of his eminence or success in life.

4. MR. ADAMS' *morality was worthy of all imitation.* There have been comparatively few men, who have been public men, that have so strictly observed all the laws and rules of society as he did. What an example, coming from one who had filled the highest office in the gift of the people,—the nation—the highest office in the gift of the world!

He was a faithful husband, a kind father, an exemplary magistrate, and a friend of every young man and young woman. What a vast difference between him, in these respects, and multitudes of the smaller politicians of our day! Who will follow his example in these matters?

5. MR. ADAMS *was a temperate man.* I have heard him give a noble lecture on temperance. He did not wholly dispense with the use of wine; but his address was most interesting. He, of course, did not come fully up to the ultra temperance measures of to-day.

6. Mr. ADAMS' *reverence for the Bible was striking.* He was a great reader of this sacred book. While studying the various languages of the world, and the most abtruse sciences — while preparing and delivering lectures on *belles letters*, in Harvard University —when retired in the family circle, where restraint is thrown off, and the man appears in his true character —while in the whirl of political excitement and filling high posts of trust — in each and all of these conditions he was a constant reader of the Bible. Four or five chapters every day, he read. In a letter to his son, as early as 1811, he says :—" I have many years made it a practice to read through the Bible once a year. My custom is to read four or five chapters every morning after rising from my bed. It employs an hour of my time, and seems to me the most suitable way of beginning the day. In what light soever we regard the Bible, whether with reference to revelation, to history, or to morality, it is an invaluable and inexhaustable mine of knowledge and virtue."

What a lesson to those whom "a little learning has

made mad," and whom a slight political elevation has so far turned their heads, that they despise the Bible! To such we would say, go learn a lesson from the example of one who excelled you in learning and honors, "as far as light excelleth darkness!" Indeed, so familiar was he with the sacred scriptures, and so well did he understand their power and application to the affairs of life, that he often *clinched* his own opinions in his private conversation and in public addresses with some appropriate passage from the Bible.

7. Mr. ADAMS' *filial affection was strong, especially towards his mother.* In this, he was a pattern worthy of imitation. Upon her death, Mr. A. said:—"This is one of the severest afflictions to which human nature is liable. The silver cord is broken—the tenderest of natural ties is dissolved—life is no longer to me what it was. My home is no longer the abode of my mother. While she lived, whenever I returned to the parental roof I felt the joys and charms of childhood returned to make me happy. All was kindness and affection. At once silent and active, as the movement of the orbs of heaven, one of the links which connects me with former ages is no more."

How many hearts can respond to this language? It reminds us of the pious and subdued Poet's appeal —"My mother, when I learned that thou wast dead," &c.

8. Mr. ADAMS *was a great Walker.* He never rode to church, though his family always did. He used to

walk, when seventy-five years old, from his residence in Quincy into Boston, a distance of eight miles, when he had horses and carriages enough in his stable. He used to say, he " noticed that those had the best legs who used them the most." Would it not be better for them, if some younger people, of both sexes, would walk more and ride less?

I might expatiate largely on Mr. A's private habits, and show the wisdom and sagacity manifested in them; but will content myself with this one—his habit of *walking*.

We have seen him walking home before sunrise, a distance of two miles from his house.

This is one of the most healthful exercises that can be practised. It brings into action all the muscles of the body and strengthens them. For many years, the writer has largely practised walking, as he believes, greatly to his benefit. The old adage is true,—"those have the best legs who use them most"—but the benefit is not confined to the lower extremities, for the whole body is invigorated.

Some suppose riding on horseback is a more healthful exercise. But, they are mistaken. There may be cases where the person is too debilitated to walk far; or where the lungs are diseased, in which gentle exercise on horse-back may do good; but, in all cases, where there is strength enough to walk any distance, the exercise had better be taken upon the feet. This statement is made from long experience.

When the writer was about twenty years old, he taught a public school in the town of Dighton; and, as the custom then was, he "boarded round." He was feeble, dyspeptic, liver torpid, eyes bad; and on the whole, not fit for anything. Rev. Mr. Gushe, the old minister, (he looked old to a young person, then being about three score) said to the debilitated young man, "I advise you to walk, you will find it a healthy exercise. I have practised taking long walks for many years, and it has been of great service to me." Mr. Gushe continued to walk till he was over ninety years of age.

A quarter of a century ago, Richard H. Dana removed from "Dana Hill," in Cambridge, into Boston, that he might have a better opportunity to walk, being more sheltered in winter, and having better sidewalks, in the latter, than in the first named city. Yesterday, the writer met him in his walk, and said to him "Mr. Dana, more than forty years ago, I spent a night at your house, and I have not spoken to you since. I see you still walk. Are you in good health?" "Yes," he replied: "my health is good, though I am not so strong as I once was."

What is your age? "I am nearly eighty-six—shall be, in less than a month."

Do you walk every day?

"Nearly every day, unless the weather is very severe."

Have you continued thus to walk ever since you moved into Boston?

"O yes, and for many years previous."

The writer knows another gentleman, who has resided in Dorchester, and who has walked into, and out of Boston, to State street, for forty years, daily, being connected with an Insurance company. Now, as a "Guardian of health," we say to every one, especially, to every invalid, walk. If you can walk but five rods at first, begin; and prolong the walk as you gain strength. You will become more healthy, and live longer by adopting such a course.

Mr. Adams thus lived more than four score years, and continued his activity as long as he lived. Most old men have been like him great walkers. Read Milton's Epitaph on the death of old "Hobson, the University-carrier," or, that of old Parr, at the Palace: like him, many die when just beginning to live easy: i. e. living easy kills them quickly:—

"Here lies old Hobson; Death hath broke his girt,
And here, alas! hath laid him in the dirt;
Time's such a shifter, that if truth were known,
Death was half glad when he had got him down;
And surely Death could never have prevailed,
Had not his weekly course of carriage failed.
Here lieth one who did most truly prove
That he could never die while he could move.
Time numbers motion; yet, without a crime
Gains't old truth, motion numbered out his time.
Rest, that gives all men life, gave him his death,
And too much breathing, put him out of breath."

This is the case of multitudes, having retired from active life, and nothing to do but eat and fatten, they soon die.

9. Mr. ADAMS *had much poetic talent.* He wrote several hymns, which are sung in public worship. He had a wonderful tact in writing poetry upon the spur of the occasion. Near the close of his eventful life, when he had been to Cincinnati to give his memorable address at the laying of the corner-stone of the Astronomical Observatory, on his return from that city to Pittsburgh, he was accommpanied in a steamboat by a young lady of Pennsylvania, and the following beautiful piece of poetry was presented to her by MR. ADAMS, on the passage :

"If in life's dull and toilsome way,
  The pilgrim chance to meet,
On some rare, bright, auspicious day,
  A jewel at his feet ;
The memory of that gem shall give
  A balsam to the heart ;
And, while hereafter he shall live,
  Unnumbered joys impart.
That pilgrim's fortune now is mine—
  And this the day of joy ;
I see the precious jewel shine—
  Pure gold without alloy ;
And memory brooding o'er the past,
  Shall ever bless the day,
When fortune, in her kindness, cast
  The jewel in my way."

The above, and the Poem on the " Wants of Man," were both written by Mr. Adams for young ladies of Pennsylvania. I give the first verse of the latter here, and will give another under the *religious* head of Mr. ADAMS' character:

> "Man wants but little here below,
>   Nor wants that little long
> 'Tis not with me exactly so—
>   But 'tis so in the song.
> *My* wants are many, and if told
>   Would muster many a score;
> And were each wish a mint of gold,
>   I still should wish for more."

10. Mr. ADAMS *kept the sabbath.* He attended public worship, not *half*, but *all day.* He did not, like many political men and others, too, go to church half a day, and spend the other half in secular business. He was a noble example to others in his attendance upon God's house.

When Minister to the Court of Holland, he joined a society of men of learning, which met once a week for mutual improvement. Mr. ADAMS was one of the youngest members. His polished manners, well-cultivated and well-stored intellect, and his ready conversational powers, soon endeared him very much to his colleagues. He both gave and received enjoyment, and was always present, and *punctually so.*

On one occasion, the meeting was adjourned to a Sabbath evening. Mr ADAMS was not there. It was appointed on the next Sabbath evening. Mr. ADAMS was not there. The members noticed and regretted his absence. They met again on the third Sabbath evening. Mr. ADAMS' chair was still vacant. Many were surprised that *he,* who was formerly so constant and punctual, should so suddenly disappear. How did it happen? Press of business, it was supposed. At last the meetings were returned to a weekday evening, and, lo! there was Mr. ADAMS in his place, punctual to the moment, brilliant and pleasant as ever.

The members gave him a hearty welcome, expressed their regret that press of business, or the duties of his office, had so long deprived them of his company. But he did not let that go as the reason. " *Not* business engagements hindered me," he replied; " you met on the Lord's day. That is a day devoted to religion by me."

Noble declaration! well worthy of the son of a mother EUNICE and a grandmother LOIS! He then told his companions, he had been brought up in New England, where the Sabbath was kept as holy time, and under the instruction of a mother, who was not of Puritan descent only, but also the daughter of one minister and nearly related to another. He had always kept the day; and from all that he had felt and seen, he was convinced of the unspeakable advantages arising from a due observance of it. Let every young man maintain the religious views in which he has been educated, and few among us will make shipwreck of their religion.

11. Mr. ADAMS *was a man of prayer*. It was characteristic of him; he maintained secret devotion: and it has already been said, he was a constant attendant in the sanctuary.

In the poem, already alluded to, the last two verses are as follows: and if we all have what he asks in them, it will be well with us forever:

> "These are the wants of mortal man;
>   I cannot want them long;
> For life itself is but a span,
>   And earthly bliss a song.
> My last great want, absorbing all,
>   Is, when beneath the sod,
> And summoned to my final call,
>   *The mercy of my God.*"

> "And oh! while circles in my veins
>   Of life the purple stream,
> And yet a fragment small remains
>   Of nature's transient dream,
> My soul, in humble hope unscared,
>   Forget not thou to pray
> That this, thy *want* may be prepared
>   *To meet the Judgment Day.*"

12. Mr. ADAMS *was a man of strong feelings and prejudices.* Theodore Parker, in writing of him said, "he counted every political opponent his personal enemy, and trampled upon him with an iron heel, and never forgave him". This language was too strong. It was not true; yet it must be confessed, his feelings were very strong, and he sometimes allowed them to run to excess, as in the case of Andrew Jackson, when he was chosen President. But we know better things of Mr. Adams personally.

13. *Mr. Adams' memory was so tenacious that he was never known to be mistaken upon a matter of fact.* He was the most accurate man in this country. The

following from recollections of an old stager, in Harper, is in point upon *extemporaneous efforts:*

"Marshall of Kentucky, one of the most brilliant orators of his time, and a man of large scholarly attainments, who had as much of that mystical quality called genius as any of his contemporaries in Congress, was full of affectation in this regard. He spoke readily without preparation, his ideas following each other consecutively and with uncommon force; but he never trusted to the inspiration of the moment, when there was an opportunity for studying up the subject and arranging his thoughts in advance. He had a habit of absenting himself from the Capitol for days at a time, every hour of which he devoted to reading and study, his acquaintances generally supposing him to be engaged in a debauch. After getting thoroughly crammed and armed at every point, he would come into the House, looking exhausted and haggard, giving color to the notion that he had been on a frolic, and watching his opportunity, would pour forth the fruit of his study in a strain of off-hand, striking eloquence that hardly ever failed to astonish his hearers. And the remark was often heard, 'What a brilliant man! What could he not accomplish if he was industrious and regular in his habits!'"

Mr. Preston, for some time Mr. Calhoun's colleague in the Senate, was an accomplished gentleman and a very popular orator. He never spoke without commanding the attention of his hearers, and few men in Congress, had a higher reputation for extemporaneous eloquence. But he never spoke without the most ample and careful preparation. Soon after he retired from Congress, he was chosen President of a college in South Carolina. In an address to the students, he said he knew of no such thing as genius or natural inspiration. Whatever of a reputation he had acquired was by dint of constant, untiring labor. He had trusted to study and hard work solely. He never spoke in Congress or at a popular assemblage without arranging what he had to say, and even premeditating his sentences and the precise collocation of his words. And he assured his hearers that the only road to public distinction lay through the field of study and research.

Mr. Webster was so thoroughly instructed upon all subjects which came up for discussion in Congress, that he was equal to almost any occasion, and rarely needed any special preparation. And yet he was not above the weakness of concealing his studies, and the sources whence he drew his inspiration. No man better understood the weight and value of language than Mr. Webster, and what he said was always marked by precision and perspicuity; but when coping with a formidable antagonist, he omitted no means that promised to aid him in the contest. He was accustomed to speak of the master production of his life, his celebrated reply to Hayne, as a sort of casual effort, made on the spur of the moment, without much previous consideration.

Probably the two men in public life who could most safely trust to their own resources and acquirements, under all circumstances, were Mr. Adams and Mr. Calhoun. The endowments of Mr. Calhoun were of a higher order, and his creative power was superior to that of Mr. Adams; but the " old man eloquent," as he was called, had a memory so tenacious, and his knowledge was so extensive and exact, that he never seemed to need any special preparation. He was the most laborious and methodical man in Congress, and, probably, in the country. He kept a voluminous diary, in which every event, incident, or circumstance of the day was carefully noted down; and this, with his habits of industry, made him a very Doctor in all matters of controversy and argument. It was a knowledge of his equipment and his power as an antagonist that prompted the reply of Mr. Clay, when asked when he proposed to renew the discussion with Mr. Adams on the vexed question of the fisheries of the Mississippi, as connected with the treaty of Ghent. Finding himself getting the worst of the argument, Mr. Clay closed the consideration of the matter, so far as he was concerned, with the remark that he should drop the subject, hoping to renew it at some future period more favorable for calm discussion, when he expected to show that Mr. Adams was altogether in the wrong.

Some time afterward a friend asked him when he proposed to re-open the controversy. " Never !" was his emphatic reply. "A man must be a born fool who voluntarily engages in a controversy with Mr. Adams on a question of fact. I doubt whether he was ever mistaken in his life. And then, if he happens to be in doubt about anything, he has his inevitable diary, in which he has recorded everything that has occurred since the adoption of the Federal Constitution."

CHAPTER III.
JOHN QUINCY ADAMS AS A STATESMAN.

CONTENTS.—His thorough Training in his Profession —His Historical Knowledge — Dealing with Henry A. Wise—Letter to Dutty J. Pierce—His Personal Appearance in Age—What he did when he left the Presidency—A Representative in Congress —Address to his Constituents — Superior to party —Advocates the right of Petition—Holds the House at bay for four days—How he managed the rebellious clerk—His death in the Harness.

He was by profession a lawyer. As such he gloried in his profession. Only five years before his decease, he said, in an address to the bar in Cincinnati, "I have been a member of your Profession more than fifty years. I chose this under the impression, which I first received from my mother, that every one in this country should have a trade. After having completed an education, in which, perhaps, more than any other citizen at that time, I had advantages, and which, of course, brought with it the incumbent duty of manifesting by my life, that these extraordinay advantages had not been worthlessly bestowed, I chose the Profession of the Law."

He was versed in history beyond almost any of his contemporaries, and his opinion upon any controverted point was almost always well founded. It is well known that the authorship of the Letters of Junius has never been settled. Upon this disputed subject, Mr. Adams expressed himself as follows: — "Junius was esentially a sophist. His religion was infidelity; his abstract ethics depraved; his temper bitterly malignant, and his nervous system timid and cowardly. The concealment of his name, at the time he wrote, was the effect of dishonest fear. He magnified mole hills into mountains; inflamed pin-scrahces into deadly wounds, and, at last, abandoned his cause in despair, when he might have pursued it with the most effect. Sir Philip Francis was, undoubtedly, the author of these Letters."

It has already been said that, as a *political* man, Mr. Adams had very strong feelings; and it is not surprising, if, upon some exciting subjects, and towards some of his opponents, he should have said some things which he had better not have said, and manifested some feelings which had better have been concealed.

Andrew Jackson, who was his immediate successor as President of the United States, was never a favorite of Mr. Adams, and when Jackson came to the Presidency, the latter did not disguise his feelings.

Henry A. Wise, the late Governor of Virginia, was another political opponent, never loved by Mr. Adams. They frequently came in collision in the

House of Representatives; and it was generally considered that, the latter usually came off conqueror. Indeed, so frequently was this the case, that a statesman of considerable eminence said, when Mr. Wise was appointed Minister to France, that the "Administration sent him out of the country, as much to get him out of the grasp of Mr. Adams, as for any other purpose." Probably, the man has never lived, who had such power of *sarcasm* as Mr. Adams possessed.

There was more scorn and biting irony conveyed by the twirl of his tongue and the accompanying twirl of his finger, than ever any other man could convey. No person, who has not seen and heard him, can form any just idea of his power in this particular. Heaven seems to have raised him up to fill an important place in advocating the right of petition on the floor of Congress. He was, undoubtedly, in the *right* by so doing, and the whole North and West sustained him in it. Like many other politicians, Mr. A. had vacillated, occasionally, from the standard of the party to which he belonged. This was first manifested in his forsaking the old Federalists, of which John Adams, his father, was to the end of his life a staunch advocate. This was said to be the reason why the father said, when it was announced to him, that his son, John Quincy, had been elected President by the House of Representatives, "That is no pleasure to me." So, about the time the subject of petition came up, Mr. A. had veered somewhat from the Whig party, of which he had formerly been an active member. About, that period, he wrote the famous letter to

Hon. Dutty J. Pierce of Rhode Island, in which he used the graphic expression that, "The Whigs had always been ready to sacrifice any man who had more principle than they had," or words to that effect. This had led many of the Whig party to suspect, or desert him, at that time. But his championship of the right of petition brought him up again in the estimation of all the Northern Whigs.

The appearance of Mr. A. was peculiar. He was below the medium stature, compact and firmly built, with the tears always over flowing from his eyes, on account of the lachrymal ducts being obstructed. To remedy this infirmity, he wore a style for many years, but on account of the irritation produced by it, he laid it aside several years before his death. There has been an anecdote connected with the subject of his tears, as follows: "Mr. Adams and Henry Clay boarded at the same house, and there was a beautiful maid servant there, whom Mr. Clay, jocosely, attempted to kiss. She firmly refused and said to Mr. Clay, "How can I allow you to do such a thing, when I have just refused Mr. Adams *with tears in his eyes?*" Our remarks will be confined to the public career of Mr. A. after he left the Presidential chair, in March 1829. He retired, as he then supposed, forever, from public life. He directed his attention to studying the works of Cicero, translating the Psalms of David, writing Commentaries upon the Scriptures, making astronomical observations, collecting and planting seeds, and recording their growth and development. But he was not permitted to remain long as a private citizen, for, before two months of the Administration of President Jackson had elapsed, a citizen of Washington spoke to him with great severity of the course pursued by the President in reference to his removals from office. Mr. A. ascribed very much of the course pursued by the Executive to Mr. Van Buren, who was then Secretary of State. He considered Mr. Van Buren as the mover of all the wheels of the Administration.

At the same time, he wrote as follows on the subject of slavery: "It is possible that the danger of the Abolition doctrines, when brought home to Southern Statesmen, may teach them the value of the Union, as the only thing that can maintain their system of slavery." His far-seeing eye, then discerned in the distance that the only guarantee of slavery was for the South to stand by the Union, as has since been demonstrated.

Of Mr. Jefferson's expressions and feelings on the subject of slavery, Mr. A. said: "His love of liberty was sincere and ardent. He was above that execrable sophistry of the South Carolina nullifiers, which would make of slavery the corner-stone of the Temple of Liberty. He saw the gross inconsistency between the principles of the Declaration of Independence and the fact of negro slavery, and he could not or would not, prostitute the faculties of his mind to the vindication of that slavery which, from his soul he abhorred."

In 1830, Mr. Adams was nominated in the Newspapers as a candidate for Representative to Congress. When asked if he would consent to be a candidate, he replied, " It must first be seen whether the people of the District will invite me to represent them. I shall not ask their votes. I wish them to act at their pleasure." In the month of November, he was elected their Representative. He took his seat in the House in December, 1831. Upon this occasion, Mr. Clay asked him " How he felt at turning boy again, and going into the House of Representatives, and observed that he would find his situation very laborious." Mr. A. replied, " I well know that, but labor I shall not refuse, so long as my hand, my eyes, and my brain do not desert me."

No sooner did Mr. A. take his seat in the House, than he announced to his constituents that " He should hold himself bound in allegiance to no party, whether sectional or political." Ten years afterwards, he had occasion to explain to his fellow-citizens his policy and feelings at this period. " I thought this independence of party was a duty imposed on me by my peculiar position. I had spent the greater part of my life in the service of the whole nation, and had been honored by their highest trust. My duty of fidelity, of affection, and of gratitude to the whole was not merely inseparable from, but identical with, that, which was due from me to my own Commonwealth. The internal conflict between slavery and freedom had been, and still was, scarcely perceptible in the national councils. The Missouri Compromise had laid it asleep, it was hoped, forever. I entered Congress without one sentiment of discrimination between the interests of the North and the South, and my first act, as a member of the House, was on presenting fifteen petitions from Pennsylvania for the abolition of slavery in the District of Columbia, to declare while moving their reference to the Committee of the District, that I was not prepared to support the measure myself, and that I should not. I was not then a sectional partizan, and I never have been." This is part of his address to his Constituents at a meeting in Braintree, September 17th, 1842, which the writer heard.

Mr. Adams Would not be shackled by party. Perhaps, his father, a strong party man, a true blue Federalist, never forgave J. Q. Adams for leaving that party, yet he would not be shackled by it. During the stormy period of John Adams' administration, J. Q. Adams had been Plenipotentiary abroad, first at the Hague, and then at Berlin. When he returned in 1801, and after he had been elected to the Massachusetts' Senate, he proposed that, part of the Governor's council should be chosen from the party that was a minority in the State. This was a new meaure and strongly opposed by the Federalists, and he gave his first vote to that measure. Here he showed his independence. He was asked, "What were the recognized principles of politics?" He anwered that " there were no *principles* in politics. There were recognized *Precepts*, but they were bad ones." " But," said the inquirer, " Is not this a good one— " To seek the greatest good of the greatest number?" " No," said he, " that is the worst of all, for, it looks specious, while it is ruinous. What would become of the minority in that case ? This is the only principle to seek, the greatest good of all."

The period of Mr. Adams' service, in the United States Senate, was one in which the position and the interests of the country were surrounded by embarrassments and perils of the most threatening character. The party which had supported his father had become divided and defeated. Mr. Jefferson, elevated to the Presidency after a heated and angry contest, was an object of the dislike and suspicion of the Federalists. The conflicts of the belligerent nations in Europe, and the measures of foreign policy they severally adopted, not only affected the interests of the United States, but were added elements to inflame the party contests at home.

In 1804 Bonaparte stepped from the Council-chamber to the throne of the French Empire. All Europe was bending to his giant rule. Great Britain alone, with characteristic and inherent stubborness, had set itself as a rock against his ambitious aspirations and prosecuted with unabated vigor, its determined hostility to all his measures of trade and of conquest. In November, 1809, the British Government issued the celebrated "Orders in Council," forbidding all trade with France and her allies. This measure was met by Napoleon in December, with his Milan "Decree," prohibiting every description of commerce with England or her colonies, Between these checks and counter-checks of European nations, the commerce of the United States was in peril of being swept entirely from the ocean.

During most of this perplexed and trying period Mr. J. Q. Adams retained his seat in the United States Senate. Although sent there by the suffrages of the Federal party, in the Massachussetts Legislature, yet he did not, and would not act simply as a partisan.

This, in fact, was a prominent characteristic in Mr. Adams throughout his entire life, and is the key which explains many of his acts otherwise inexplicable. This noble and patriotic spirit rose above the shackles of party. He loved the interests of his country, the happiness of Man more than the success of a mere party. So far as the party with which he acted advocated measures which he conceived to be wise and healthful, he yielded his hearty and vigorous co-operation. But, whenever it swerved from this line of integrity, his influence was thrown into the opposite scale. This was the rule of his long career.

No persuasions or emoluments, no threats, no intimidations could turn him from it, the breadth of a hair. It was in consequence of this characteristic, that it has so frequently been said of Mr. Adams, that he was not a *reliable* party man. This was to a degree true. He was not reliable for any policy adopted simply to promote party interests and secure party ends. But in regard to all measures, which in his judgment, would advance the welfare of the people, secure the rights of man, and elevate the race, no politican, no statesman the world has produced could be more perfectly relied upon.

Mr. Adams well knew the pernicious influence of parties, and hence, he ignored them, when in his judgment, they would do wrong; and no man could influence him to act or vote against what he believed to be right. In this respect, he was a model man, for party is the abounding curse of our nation. The question, from the election of the President of the United States down to the lowest officer of one of our smallest towns, is, not is this man qualified for this position? but, is he of *our* party? Will he uphold our side of the question? This brings into office men utterly unfit for the places they are thrust into. Hence it is the gravest of all the curses of the nation. Hence come the swindles, embezzlement, stealings, forgeries, and all the henious crimes that blacken our national escutcheon and render us a stench among the nations of the earth. Had we enough of such men as Mr. Adams was in this respect, we should be a very different people from what we now are — from what we have been for the last fifty years.

Then all business would not be done by "rings," as it now is. We have rings for office, rings for gold speculations, rings for coal, rings for every thing, even all the common necessaries of life. Cursed be such "rings," for they are cruel. They are the abomination of heaven, and cause jubilations in hell.

On the 7th of January, 1837, Mr. A. offered to present the petition of one hundred and fifty women for the abolition of slavery in the District of Columbia. Mr. Glascock, of Georgia, objected to its reception. This was the first objection ever made to a petition being received by Congress. Mr. A. said " That the proposition not to receive a petition was directly in the face of the Constitution. He hoped the people of this country would be spared the mortification, the injustice and the wrong that such petitions should not be received. It was, indeed true that all discussion, all freedom of speech, all freedom of the press, had been, within the last twelve months, violently assailed in every form in which the liberties of the people could be attacked. He considered these attacks as outrages on the Constitution of the country and the freedom of the people, as far as they went. But the proposition that the petitions should not be received went still further." His remarks were strong and there was great confusion, but the petition was finally received. This was properly the opening of the flood-gates of wrath, which from that day till the abolition of slavery, operated as a tempest between the North and the South. Mr. Adams had espoused this cause. He was in the right, and he was not the man to relinquish that right in consequence of being browbeaten.

On the 18th of January 1837, the House of Representatives passed a resolution — one hundred and thirty-nine ayes to sixty-nine nays — " That all petitions, relating to slavery, without being printed or referred, shall be laid on the table, and no action shall be had thereon."

On the 6th of February, Mr. Adams stated that he held in his hand a paper, on which, before presenting it, he wished to have the decision of the Speaker. It purported to be a petition from slaves, and he wanted to know if it was consistent with the rules of the House that such a paper should be presented? Mr. Adams then took his seat. The House was greatly excited. The slaveholders expressed their astonishment at such a proposition. One member said, "It was an infraction of the laws of the House, and ought to be severely punished." Another said, "It was a violation of the dignity of the House, and ought to be taken and burnt. Waddy Thompson of South Carolina, offered a resolution, that the Hon. John Quincy Adams has been guilty of gross disrespect to the House, and that he be instantly brought to the bar to receive the severe censure of the Speaker. Charles E. Haynes of Georgia, and Dixon H. Lewis, of Alabama, followed, apparently in great heat, and each offering resolutions, or modifying the one already offered, the purport of which was that Mr. Adams be severely censured or expelled.

Four long days did the House do battle valiantly over this petition from slaves, and during all the time, the old Nestor sat quietly in his seat, not opening his mouth. Well did he know how firmly he had them in his grasp, and that when the time came, he would scatter their resolutions of four days to the winds of heaven in *four minutes.* At length, he rose. That shrill voice, which could penetrate to the greatest distance, rang out, "Mr. Speaker, for what am I to be censured or expelled?" "For offering that infamous petition," rang out a dozen voices. Mr. Speaker, I haven't offered any petition. I only asked the Speaker, if it came within the rules of this House to present a petition from slaves. The petition is in my desk. If I had offered it, it would be in the hands of the Speaker."

Then in a strain of irony and burning sarcasm, he proceeded to tell them how they must modify their resolution of censure. "Nor have I said what the prayer of the petition was. One of the proposed Resolutions says it is for the *abolition of slavery.* The gentleman must amend his resolution ; for, if the House should hear this petition, they would find it very much the reverse of what this resolution calls it ; and if the other gentleman from Alabama wishes to bring me to the bar of the House for censure, he must alter his resolution, for he says it is for attempting to offer a petition for the abolition of slavery ; whereas, the petitioners pray that slavery should *not* be abolished. Thus, Mr. Speaker, the petition prays for just what the authors of these resolutions wish to accomplish." Thus, never were men more completely foiled, and never was the declaration of Solomon more clearly proved, "He that answereth a matter before he heareth it, is a fool."

During this discussion, Mr. Thompson of South Carolina said, "The conduct of Mr. A. was a proper subject for inquiry by the grand jury of the District of Columbia, and that in a like case, he would be proceeded against in South Carolina."

To this language, Mr. A. replied, "If this is true — if a member is there made amenable to the grand jury for words spoken in debate — I thank God I am not a citizen of South Carolina! Such a threat, when brought before the world, would excite nothing but contempt and amusement." Afer a debate of four days — one of the sharpest and most exciting ever held in the House of Representatives — only twenty votes could be found, indirectly and remotely, to censure. So complete and triumphant was Mr. Adams' vindication of his cause.

The paper was, doubtless, sent to him by some slaveholder to see if he would present it, and he turned the whole force of it against them. Never was more shrewdness manifested by any living man. He knew all those four days what he would do.

We will give one more instance of the wonderful power of Mr. Adams. On the 2d of December, 1839, at the opening of the Twenty-sixth Congress, the Clerk began to call the roll, according to the custom. When he came to New Jersey, he stated that five seats of the members of that State were contested, and that, not feeling himself authorized to decide the question, he should pass over those names, and proceed with the call. A violent debate arose. It was declared by one party that, it was a preconcerted plan to exclude these five members from voting in the organization of the House, and by the other that, these members had no right to seats. Three days were spent in the most bitter controversy ; and the close of the scene was described as follows by an eye witness :— "Mr. Adams, from the opening of this confusion and anarchy, had maintained a profound silence. He appeared to be engaged the most of the time in writing. To a common observer, he seemed to be reckless of anything around him. But nothing, not the slighest incident, escaped him.

"The fourth day of the struggle had now commenced. Mr. Hugh A. Garland, the Clerk, was directed to call the roll again. He commenced with Maine, as usual in those days, and was proceeding with Massachusetts. I turned and saw that Mr. Adams was ready to get the floor at the earliest moment possible. His eye was riveted on the Clerk; his hands clasped the front edge of his desk, where he always placed them to assist him in rising. He looked, in the language of Otway, like a 'fowler waiting for his prey.' 'New Jersey!' ejaculated Mr. A. Garland, and Mr. Adams immediately sprang to the floor. 'I rise to interrupt the Clerk,' was his first exclamation. 'Silence! silence!' resounded through the hall. 'Hear him!

him! Hear what he has to say! Hear John Quincy Adams!' was vociferated on all sides.

"In an instant the most profound stillness reigned throughout the hall. You might have heard a leaf of paper fall in any part of it, and every eye was riveted on the venerable Nestor of Massachusetts — the purest of statesmen and the noblest of men! He paused for a moment, and having given Mr. Garland a withering look, he proceeded to address the multitude.

'It was not my intention,' said he, 'to take any part in these extraordinary proceedings. I had hoped this house would succeed in organizing itself; that a Speaker and Clerk would be elected, and that the ordinary business of legislation would be progressed in. This is not the time, or place to discuss the merits of conflicting claimants from New Jersey. That subject belongs to the House of Representstives, which, by the Constitution, is made the ultimate arbiter of the qualifications of its members. But, what a spectacle we here present! We degrade and disgrace our constituents and the country. We do not, and cannot, organize, and why? Because the Clerk of this House—the mere clerk, whom we employ, and whose existence depends upon our will—usurps the *throne*, and sets us, the Representatives, the vicegerents of the whole American people, at defiance, and holds us in contempt. And what—this clerk of yours? Is he to suspend, by his mere negative, the functions of government, and put an end to this Congress? He refuses to call the roll! It is in your power to compel him to call it, if he will not do it voluntarily.' (Here he was interrupted by a member, who said that he was authorized to say that compulsion could not reach the Clerk, who had avowed that he would resign rather than call the State of New Jersey.) 'Well, sir, let him resign,' continued Mr. Adams, 'and we may possibly discover some way by which we can get along without the aid of his all-powerful talent, learning, and genius! If we cannot organize in any other way—if this clerk of yours will not consent to our discharging the trust confided to us by our constituents—then let us imitate the example of the Virginia House of Burgesses, which, when the Colonial Governor, Dinwiddie, ordered it to disperse, refused to obey the imperious and insulting mandate, and, like men,—'

The multitude could not contain or repress their enthusiasm any longer, but saluted the eloquent and indignant speaker, and interrupted him with loud and deafening cheers, which seemed to shake the capitol to its centre. The turmoil, the darkness, the very 'chaos of anarchy,' which had, for three days, pervaded the American Congress, was dispelled by the magic, the talismanic eloquence of a single man, and once more the wheels of government and legislation were put in motion.

Having by his powerful appeal brought the yet unorganized assembly to a perception of its hazardous position, he submitted a motion requiring the acting clerk to call the roll. Mr. Adams was interrupted by a burst of voices demanding 'Who will put the question? How shall the question be put?' The voice of Mr. Adams was heard above the tumult, 'I intend to put the question myself.' That word brought order out of chaos. There was the master-spirit. As soon as the multitude had recovered itself, Mr. Rich and Barnwell Rhett, of South Carolina, leaped upon one of the desks, waved his hand and exclaimed, 'I move that the Hon. John Quincy Adams take the chair of the Speaker of the House, and officiate as the presiding officer till the house be organized by the election of its constitutional officers. As many as are agreed to this will say aye, those'—He had not an opportunity to complete the sentence,—'Those who are not agreed will say no! For one universal deafening, thundering *aye* responded to the nomination. Hereupon it was moved and ordered that Lewis Williams, of North Carolina, and Richard Barnwell Rhett conduct John Quincy Adams to the chair. Upon this, Henry A. Wise said to Mr. A., 'Sir, I regard it as the proudest part of your life; and if, when you shall be gathered to your fathers, I were asked to select the words which, in my judgment, are best calculated to give at once the character of the man, I would inscribe upon your tomb the sentence, '*I will put the question myself!*'"

Mr. Adams died under the roof of the capitol, in the Speaker's room, at 7 o'clock, on Wednesday evening, February 23d, 1848, in the eighty-first year of his age. His mental vigor held out to the last, and he died with his armor on. He composed and gave to Miss Edwards, of Springfield, Massachusetts, the following lines the day before his decease :—

"In days of yore, the poet's pen,
From wing of bird was plundered,
  Perhaps from goose, but now and then
From Joves' own eagle sundered.
  But now metallic pens disclose
Alone the poet's numbers;
  In iron inspiration glows,
Or with the poet slumbers.
  Fair damsel, could my pen impart,
In prose or lofty rhyme,
  The pure emotions of my heart
To speed the flight of time,
  What metal from the womb of earth
Could worth intrinsic bear
  To stamp with corresponding worth
The blessings thou shouldst share ?"

CHAPTER IV.

The Old Unitarian and the Episcopal Churches—Rev. Dr. Cutler—Efforts for a Trinitarian Church—The Council and its Organization—Names of members—"Chief Women" in the Church—Decease of the first member, Mrs. Mary Baxter—A part of the sermon on that occasion.

As already stated, the old Congregational Church in Quincy was Unitarian. Rev. Peter Whitney, a very affable and pleasant old gentleman, had been the Pastor for many years, Of course, his preaching had been characteristic of the denomination to which he belonged. It is not necessary here to enter into the old controversy between the Unitarians and those called Orthodox.

The Episcopal Church had for several years, previous to my going to Quincy, been presided over by the Rev. Benjamin Clark Cutler, afterwards Rev. Dr. Cutler, of Brooklyn, N. Y. He was one of the best men of the age—a true "son of consolation" to all christians. He labored faithfully in the Episcopal Church here for several years, and the good fruits of his labors were visible. After he left, that church had a Mr. Potter for Rector, in whom they were not united, and, as we shall see, some of that church came off and united with the new Congregational church. Had Mr. Cutler remained with them they would always have continued Episcopalians, beyond a doubt. There were, also, some in the town who were not exactly Unitarians, though the mass of the people were. Deacon Seth Spear, at the "neck," so called, never quite harmonized with Mr. Whitney's views of Christ; and, it is said, on meeting Parson Whitney, when the "Old Stone,"—the present Unitarian Church,—was building, Mr. W., said, "Deacon, we shall need a new bell, when the house is done, shan't we?" The Deacon replied, "we shall want a new bell *inside*."

It has never been proved that John Quincy Adams was a Unitarian, and when in Washington, he always attended on Presbyterian preaching. Still, there is no doubt but the mass of the people of Quincy were Unitarians. There were, however, some aside from the Episcopal Church, who were not of that opinion, and one of them will hereafter be named, who used to walk over two miles to Rev. Dr. Storrs' church in Braintree, to hear the gospel, as she believed.

In 1831, some effort was made to get up a Trinitarian meeting in Quincy, and Revs. Drs. Lyman Beecher, William Jenks and Nehemiah Adams, with Dr. John Codman and David Sanford, of Dorchester, preached, as opportunity offered. In process of time, a church was organized, as the following minutes, the original record of their doings show.

"An Ecclesiastical Council was convened in Quincy, at the house of Mr. Benjamin R. Downes at 10 o'clock A. M., on the 16th of August 1832, in consequence of Letters Missive from a Committee of several professing Christians, wishing to be organized into an Evangelical Congregational Church. The churches represented in the Council, were the following:

Green Street Church, Boston Rev. Wm. Jenks, Pastor; Deacon Wm. Hyde, Delegate.

Evangelical Congregational Church, South Boston; Rev. J. H. Fairchild, Pastor; Br. Sam'l Gale, Delegate.

Charlestown, First Church, Rev. Warren Fay, Pastor; Br. Benjamin Brown, Delegate.

Dedham, First Church; Rev. Ebenezer Burgess, Pastor; Deacon Jonathan Richards, Delegate.

Wrentham, First Church; Br. William Harlow, Delegate.

The Council was called to order by the Rev. Wm. Jenks D. D. The Council chose the Rev. Warren

Fay, D. D. Moderator, and the Rev. Ebenezer Burgess, Scribe. After some consultation, the Council adjourned to the Hall, where public worship is now held. The session was opened with prayer by the Moderator. Letters of dismission and recommendation were read from the Pastors of the churches, of which the individuals had been members, who propose to be formed into a distinct church. In addition to these, certificates of regular membership in the christian church. The Council examined these Brethren and Sisters with a view to obtain satisfactory evidence of their personal piety, and in their sincere belief in Christian doctrine. A Confession of Faith and Covenant were then submitted and read as the proposed Platform of the contemplated church, it being understood that the phraseology of the confession may be altered at the discretion of the church, on condition that they retain the essential principles of christian doctrines, which have been handed down from the days of the Reformation, and transmitted to us by the Father's of New England.

The Council adjourned for dinner and assembled in the Hall for public services at 2 o'clock P. M.

The Minutes of the Council were read by the Scribe, who offered an introductory Prayer. The Moderator preached a sermon on Cor. 15, 58. The Rev. Dr. Jenks implored a special blessing on the church to be formed. The Moderator then read the covenant to the Brethren and sisters standing, and gave them a solemn charge, and declared them to be a regularly instituted Congregational Church entitled to all rights and privileges as such.

The members of the Council then united with the church in the celebration of the Lord's Supper. It was a tender and impressive hour, some spectators wept. Rev. Messrs. Fairchild, Fay and Jenks officiated at the table in prayers and addresses. The service was closed with singing the christian doxology to the Father, Son and Holy Ghost.

A true record of the Council.

Attest:

WARREN FAY, Moderator.
EBENEZER BURGESS, Scribe.

NOTE: The names of the Brethren and Sisters, who were present and entered into a mutual covenant as members of the Evangelical Congregational Church in Quincy were the following:

Mr. Nathaniel Pittee, from Village Church, Dorchester.
Mrs. Tamar Pittee, " "
Mr. Nathaniel S. Spear, Union Church of Braintree and Weymouth
Mrs. Lois Spear, " "
Mr. John Burrage, South Church in Braintree.
Mrs. Nancy Burrage, " "
Mr. Cotton Pratt, Episcopal Church in Quincy.
Mr. William Pratt, " "
Mrs. Mary Trask, " "
Miss Mary T. Trask, " "
Mrs. Susan Nightingale, " "
Mrs. Hannah Porter, " "
Mrs. Mary Hardwick, " "
Mrs. Sarah Pratt, Congregational Church in Quincy,
Mrs. Sarah Murdock, " "
Mrs. Mary Baxter, " "

Mrs. Prudence Savil, Congregational Church in Quincy.
Mrs. Lucy Marsh,   "   "
Mrs. Louisa Nightingale,   "   "
Mrs. Esther Spear,   "   "
Mrs. Mehitable Page,   "   "

Attest: E. B.

It is natural to suppose that the organization of such a Church, upon the Congregational platform, was not altogether congenial to the feelings of the old church, as they supposed it implied some want in their church. But they bore it, perhaps, as well as could be expected, especially, as the numbers of the new church were so small, their influence so circumscribed, and their wealth so inconsiderable, that it was not likely they would ever do much.

The Rev. John Codman, sometime after its formation, said to the writer, " it (the church) was the feeblest infant that I ever knew live." The male members were but five, and it could not be said even of them that their influence was great. Indeed, it was not a " good report" that some of them had among " those that were without." It would not seem to be stretching the application of Scripture very far, if this church was ever to do much in Quincy, especially, if we consider the brethren only, and leave out the sisters, (of which more will be said anon) to apply to them the following—" For ye see your calling, Brethren, how that not many wise men after the flesh, not many mighty, not many noble, are called. But God hath chosen the foolish things of the world, to confound the wise; and God hath chosen the weak things of this world, to confound the things which are mighty ; and base things of the world, and things which are despised, and things which are not, hath God chosen, to bring to naught things that are."

There were, however, among the noble women some such as helped Paul in the gospel, among whom wers Mrs. Mary Baxter, Mrs. Lucy Marsh, Mrs. Hannah Porter, Mrs. Sarah Pratt and Mrs. Susan Nightingale, all of whom have now " entered into their rest," except the one last named. The one named first, went first to heaven, and of her we said at the time in the sermon preached at her decease, as follows, (and, had we continued the Pastor and attended the burial of the others here named, we might have said similar things of them. A part of the sermon at the decease of Mrs. Baxter was as follows :—

" This woman was full of good works, and alms deeds which she did."—Acts 9. 36.

The woman spoken of in our text dwelt at Joppa, a seaport town in the tribe of Dan. Joppa is frequently mentioned in Scripture. The materials for Solomon's temple were sent hither, by Hiram, king of Tyre, and from this place, they were easily conveyed by land to Jerusalem. At this port Jonah embarked, when he attempted to flee from the presence of the Lord. Here, Peter had that remarkable vision, which intimated to him the abolition of the Mosaic ceremony and the removal of those distinctions which had for a long time separated the Jews from the Gentiles. But the history of Dorcas, or as she was originally called in the Syriac language, Tabitha, has given peculiar prominence to the town of Joppa.

The memorial of this excellent woman is short, but very instructive. The sacred penman entered into no minute detail of circumstances unnecessary to develop her character, but sketched it at a single stroke and set it in the most brilliant light.

She is at first simply introduced as "a certain disciple." By which we understand, one who professed faith in Christ, and was baptised, and united with his visible church. What her situation, in other respects was, we are not told. It would have been of little consequence for us to know. This invested her with real glory; with an excellency surpassing every external splendor and glittering honor of the world.

"*She was full of good works,,*" a very comprehensive expression. The faith, which constituted her a disciple, was manifested by *works*. "Faith without works is dead, being alone." But the faith of Dorcas was not alone. The faith which constituted her discipleship was not alone. It was operative and produced *good* works. Faith is a belief in the testimony of God; a reposing of confidence in his word. It glorifies its great Author, by an implicit obedience to his authority. The most proper definition of faith is belief in the testimony of Jesus. It recognizes Him, especially, as the Saviour of ruined and undone sinners.

The faith which constituted Dorcas, a disciple, stimulated her to perform the most laborious duties. It worked by *love*. She was a flourishing plant of grace, and was *full* of *good* works. The faith of Dorcas was not of that kind, which *says* to a brother or sister, who is naked or destitute of daily food, "Depart in peace, be ye warmed and filled, though it give them not the things which are necessary for the body.

She was *prompt* in bestowing her charity. She was not all promise, and little or no performance. "She was *full* of good works and alms deeds which she *did*." Yes, she *did* them. She was not a hearer only, but a doer of the word. Ample testimony is borne to this fact by those who stood around her death bed " weeping and showing the various articles of clothing which she made " *while she was with them*." She did with her might, what her hand found to do. She felt, that life was the proper time for action, and let not her opportunities of usefulness pass unimproved.

Her record was not only among those who wept around her corpse, but it was, also, on high. And the righteous Judge, no doubt, laid up for her a crown of righteousness which he has long since placed upon her head.

She was the almoner of her own bounty. She *made* the garments which she bestowed upon the poor. No doubt she often visited the abodes of those on whom she bestowed her beneficence. How often she wept over their sorrows and prayed God to relieve them, we are not informed. But all her acts are registered in an imperishable record, her name enrolled in the Lamb's book of life, and when the Lord Jesus shall appear to judge the world, we shall all know, how much is comprehended in the expression, "This woman was full of good works and alms deeds which she did."

The object for which I have selected this text is to call your attention to the life and character of a member of our church whose remains have recently been committed to the grave. Though, on account of most of her surviving family, being of a different faith from hers, her own Pastor was not called to officiate, or be present at her funeral, yet, still, we feel, that, *so far as she was connected with us*, we have a right, and are in duty bound, to speak of her character and lament our loss.

She was, originally, a member of the Unitarian church in this town. Whether that church had come out openly on Unitarian ground, when she became a member of it, we have not the means of ascertaining. Nor do we know the precise number of years since she there made a profession of religion. But, that she long since became convinced, that she had no religion when she became connected with that church, and also that the great truths of the Bible, through the belief of which God sanctifies the hearts of men, were not there preached, we have known from her own mouth. For a number of years, she worshipped, when she could attend, in a neighboring town. The distance to that place of worship was so considerable, that she could not attend steadily; but when she *could* go, she did. She felt that her soul was fed and nourished with those truths, which she esteemed, as the bread and water of life, and which, she could not hear preached in the church of which she had become a member. In her welfare and trials the Pastor and members of that church felt deeply interested, and as a token of their affection, they have recently made her a life-member of the *Palestine* Missionary Society. In her death, Rev. Dr. Storrs and his church showed they deeply felt their loss as well as ours.

"Whosoever believeth that Jesus is the Christ is born of God." Faith dwelt in the heart of Peter, when he exclaimed, " Lord save me." It dictated the prayer of the thief upon the cross, " Lord, remember me, when thou comest, into thy kingdom." It inspired the prayer of him who said, " Speak the word only, and my servant shall be healed." It is pleasing to God, and necessary to salvation. Enoch walked with God, and had this testimony, that he pleased God; but without faith it is impossible to please him. " A man is justified by faith," consequently, faith is inseperable from salvation.

After attending worship there for a term of years, finding that the truths which she believed the Bible contained, were faithfully preached in the Episcopal Church in this town, she made that, her place of worship. Though never a believer in the Episcopalian form of church government; yet, rather than worship under Unitarian preaching, or be exposed to the inconvenience of travelling three miles to a neighboring town, she tolerated the forms and ceremonies of that church. There under the faithful exhibition of truth, by the Rev. Dr. Cutler, she believed, she profited and grew in grace.

But it was not until the organization of our church,

that she removed her church relation from the one of which she originally became a member. When this church was organized, four years ago last August, she was received as one of its members. Thus she was one of the first members of our church. Since that time, she has statedly worshiped with us: and while her health permitted, she was a constant and punctual attendant in this sanctuary. She was rarely absent from the praying circle, or the conference-room. The testimony of those who best knew her, and with whom she often associated, is, that she was truly " a mother in Israel." Her piety, like that of Dorcas, was not dormant. It was an active piety. The faith of her discipleship, was a faith that worked; and worked by *love*. She was *ready* to every good work. She felt for temporal calamity and distress, and when in her power, relieved them. But, especially, did she feel for the spiritual wretchedness, degradation and misery of sinners, both at home and abroad. Like Mary, " she did what she could" to have the gospel preached here, and to the remotest parts of the earth. Of her domestic concerns we are neither able, nor would it become us to say much. Yet, we have often heard, that (however diverse the sentiments or views of her companion and most of her children, might have been from hers, in religion,) they still bear ample testimony to her domestic economy, prudence, discretion, and affection. She was a mother at home, as well as in Israel.

She felt most tenderly for the spiritual welfare of

her companions and children. Often has she asked for the prayers of her Pastor and the church, in their behalf. After her health began to be impaired; to the inquiry, whether she felt willing to depart, with tears, she replied, " how *can* I die, and leave my husband and so many of my children impenitent? It seems as though, if I could see them brought into the kingdom, I should rejoice to go."

During the last years of her life, she had several paralytic shocks which affected, not only the powers of her body, but also, somewhat, impaired her mind.

It was visible to all, that she was failing. She ever manifested a deep interest in the welfare of this church. Brethren and sisters, you have met with a great loss. I do not say an irreparable one, for God can raise up others to fill her place, and we hope and trust, He will do it. Still, the loss is great. Once did she say to me, relative to this church, after you had a sanctuary and Pastor.—" I have been so faithless and God so good, that I feel overwhelmed with a sense of my own unbelief, and of his unbounded grace. I never expected to live to see a Congregational church, and a sanctuary, and a minister in this town, where the doctrines of the Bible were faithfully preached, and firmly believed. But, in view of what God has done, I feel as though, I could say like aged Simeon, with the infant Saviour in his arms, " Lord, now lettest thou, thy servant depart in peace, for mine eyes have seen thy salvation." I always believed that God would have a church here, but I did not expect it *so soon*." It will not be known, till the day of final account, how much her prayers hastened these events. That they did not remain unanswered; that she had access to the mercy-seat; and that God avenges, speedily, his own elect who cry day and night unto him, we verily believe. But her prayers are to ascend no more for the church. The weapon of prayer, which in her hand so prevailed with God, and brought down his blessing upon us, is changed into a never-ceasing song of praise.

You, ye beloved sisters, of this church, will feel in a special manner the breach now made in your precious number. No longer, will her presence cheer you in the sanctuary; no longer will you hear her voice in the social prayer meeting; no longer in your maternal association will she encourage you in your domestic duties, or instruct and pray for your children. *Sisters in Jesus*, you feel your loss, now; you cannot but feel it, and you will feel it in time to come. *Ye children* who often sat and received the words of instruction from her lips, you, also, are deprived of inestimable privileges by her removal. The impenitent in this place, how little soever they may believe it, are deprived of one who felt most deeply, and labored most abundantly, and prayed most fervently, for their conversion. The whole church sustains a loss, for a devoted christian " has fallen in Israel."

And is she *dead?* Ah, she *sleeps* in Jesus. She has gone from us; but she has gone home. She no longer buffets the storms of this dead and sinful world. She fought a good fight, and finished her course, and *kept* the faith, " the faith once delivered unto the saints," and we have no doubt, has received a crown of righteousness, a diadem of unfading glory in yonder blessed world, from the Lord, the righteous Judge. Our loss is her gain. Yes, her unspeakable gain. And shall we mourn? Yes, we have a right to mourn—and we do mourn: But not as those without hope.

Bretheren and sisters, the Lord liveth—the Lord reigns, and let us rejoice. A *breach* has been made in our little church, and it is the first of the kind. The Lord has been good to us, and his tender mercies have been over us. Our lives have been precious in his sight. The shafts of death have flown thick around us, but we have been spared. In recounting the dealings of God towards us since the organization of this church, we have often thought of the wonderful preservation bestowed upon us, that, no member of the church for so long a time should be called to taste of death. And, often, has the inquiry arose in our mind, who shall be called for first. Who shall be the first soul, that from this church shall enter the church triumphant? Had it been some of us who still survive, there might have been some doubts of our being prepared. But *can* there be a doubt in the case of her, whose loss we are called to mourn? Was she not as well prepared as any of us? Is it too much to say, we trust, she was better prepared? Who among us would be more worthy, like the blessed few in Sardis, to walk with the Redeemer in white, than she? Was " she not *full* of good works and alms deed which she did?'

We mourn, bretheren and sisters, but, nevertheless,

we rejoice and will rejoice, that the Redeemer liveth. His church on earth changes, but He is the same, yesterday, to-day, and forever." We hear a voice from Him, saying, " Blessed are the dead, which die in the Lord, from henceforth, yea, saith the Spirit, they do rest from their labors and their works do follow them."

CHAPTER V.

CONTENTS.

Rev. Daniel D. Smith—Rev. Elias Smith—Father of Daniel—A wonderful man—A Scourge of all the Learned Professions—A member of some half dozen Religious Denominations.

It was natural, perhaps, that the old society should not feel very cordial to the new enterprise; and so it happened. The town-hall, in which they first worshipped, under Rev. Mr. Field, who supplied a while, was suddenly closed against them. Then, they worshiped over a store where feathers were sold, and were dignified by the name of the " Feather Society." Then, they met over the Post Office, till their first house was completed. Rev. Stephen S. Smith was the preacher; and being somewhat zealous, rasped the outside people a little, by saying " the old parish worshiped a man," because a Tablet was erected in their house to the memory of John Adams. Nor, did he spare the Episcopalians, for, on a Christmas exhibition, when the green boughs were waving, he said, "see the rags of popery."

The 20th of August, 1834, the first house was dedicated, and the same day, I was installed, as the first Pastor of the church. Every thing was pleasant, and went smoothly as a marriage-bell within and without, Rev. Mr. Whitney, and Rev. Mr. Lunt, his colleague, being pleasant companions; and, probably, all would have continued so, had not Rev. Daniel D. Smith been Pastor of the Universalist church. Here it is necessary to diverge a little from our direct story, to sketch the descent of this Mr. Smith, for, we fully believe in the hereditary transmission of both natural, moral and mental qualities. In great men, the greatness descends to their children, as much in mind, as in body. John Quincy Adams, whom we have pretty fully sketched, was the re-creation of his staunch old father, John Adams, and Mary Smith, his mother; and the younger Edwards, but the reproduction of the elder, of the same name. So, to show the art and cunning and mischief-making spirit of Daniel D. Smith, we must sketch the character of his father, the famous Elias Smith Though this may occupy some space, yet we assure our readers the time spent in reading it will not be lost, as he was one of the most stirring, famous and excentric characters of the past generation. Indeed, a physiological question of great moment is herein involved, to wit, how far the children of very peculiar and excentric men, are responsible for their habits or traits of character; or in other words, whether Daniel D. Smith was responsible for the mischief he intended to do, when the character of the said Elias, his father, is taken into the account. He did not really do any harm; but the intent, nevertheless, remained. The wrath of man God makes to praise Him, and restrains the rest, as anciently, " Moab was his wash pot."

I consider the following sketch of Rev. Elias Smith in connection with his two sons Daniel and Matthew Hale Smith, both of whom were my colleagues in Quincy, as the best illustration of the hereditary transmission of mental qualities that has ever come within my personal knowledge, and therefore, I feel perfectly justified in inserting it, though it occupies considerable space.

HISTORICAL SKETCH OF THE LIFE OF THE LATE ELIAS SMITH,

In a memoir of his life, written by himself, the Preface to which is dated, March 5th, 1816, Portsmouth, N. H. he says, "I was born, June 17th, 1769, within two years of the birth of J. Q. Adams, in the town of Lyme, County of New London, State of Connecticut. My father's name was *Stephen Smith*. My mother's name, before she was married, was *Irene Ransom*. My father's family were originally from England; my mother's I have been told, were from Wales." " My father was a *Baptist* by profession, till one year before he died." " My father's mother gave me the name *Elias*. This name never pleased me."

He says, he remembers when he was less than three years old. " My father then removed into a new house. I remember the event from this circumstance; a little girl, then five years old, with whom

I was at play, wanted a case-knife, which I called mine. I refused to give it to her. Soon after my refusal, she, with a stick, dug a hole in the ground. I asked her what she dug the hole for? She said, to plant my knife, adding, that 'if I planted it, the knife would come up, and be more.' I had seen beans grow, and expected knives would, in the same way. But I lost my knife.

This was very young to remember anything. The writer remembers an event which took place when he was *four* years' old

The next thing which *Elias* says he remembered was when he tried to catch a Whip-Poor-Will, which one evening came near his father's house; upon which, he makes some very sensible reflections, upon trying to catch pleasures.

He says, "when I was four year's old, I was sent to school, of which, I now remember nothing, save that I was once chastised for being unwilling to go to school. After he was ten years old, he attended school three winters, and he had no more schooling, except thirty days to learn "Dilworths' Grammar," ten days to learn Arithmetic, and eight evenings to learn music.

When he was five years old, the Revolutionary war between England and America commenced. He says, "I was six years old, the day the battle of Bunker Hill was fought." "I heard the name of *Tories* and *Regulars*; and though I knew not the meaning of the words; yet, had then a rooted aversion to them, which has continued ever since, (forty one years, to the time when he wrote.)

When eight years old, he says, he was "sprinkled," his mother then being a "Congregationalist," and his father, though a Baptist, not opposing it. He resisted as he did every thing that was orderly, and attempted to run out of the church, but was pursued by his uncle and brought back. "Notwithstanding all my exertions, I was brought in front of the basin, and was so confined, hands and feet, that I was obliged to receive what they called ' the seal of the covenant.' I felt such malice against the minister, and my uncle, that had my strength been equal to my desire, we should all have been like Sampson and the Philistines, with the house about our ears."

In 1782, in his 13th year, he says, "I had my last schooling, excepting forty days, and eight evenings, in the State of Vermont. My knowledge of letters was such as to be able to read the Bible some, though I did not know the meaning of a comma, semicolon, colon, period, note of interrogation, admiration, or any other marks used in reading. These things were not then taught in country schools. I had then never heard of a book called ' Dictionary.' "

May we not well say, what a change has taken place in ninety-one years, now 1873 ?

"In 1782, my father sold out his property in Lyme, came and purchased one hundred acres of land in Woodstock, Vermont. The journey of removal of a hundred and eighty miles, we performed in 13 days.

How striking the improvement in the mode of travelling since this period, as this journey could now be performed in a day!

The description Elias gives of the woods and the log house is amusing indeed.

1784, he says, "was the first time I saw a *Dictionary*. The minister used the word *canticles*. Two men who had been to meeting, conversed about the meaning of the word; one of them took Entick's Dictionary, and soon found the word and its meaning. It appeared strange to me that the word used by the minister should be in that little book." It may seem strange to some that a person fourteen or fifteen years old, should be so ignorant of a book now in common use. "About all the books, I had ever known to that time, were the Primmer, Dilworth's Spelling book, Watts Psalms, and Hymns, and the New Testament and Bible. "When I was fifteen years old, I first saw a Geography. It was called Guthrie's Grammar."

"In 1785, when in my sixteenth year, my uncle, (Elisha Ransom, a Baptist minister,) taught a school, two miles from our house, and I was permitted to go one month. My uncle said to me, "you must learn grammar." "He gave me a lesson from Dilworth's—on my return home, I informed my father of the study I had entered upon. He was not at all pleased with it, and told me Arithmetic was much more useful. My uncle, however, overpersuaded my father, and I studied grammar one month."

The writer can tell a story to match this. When he was fourteen years old, he began to study Websters' grammar, at a public school, in one of the most enlightened towns in Bristol County, in Massachusetts; and he was the only one in the school who studied it, and was laughed at by all the other scholars for doing it.

As they had no candles, Elias studied by fire-light, lying on the floor, till he nearly ruined his eyes. In the year 1785, when he was writing, he says, "I experienced religion." He was then, not quite sixteen years old.

He says, "when I was eighteen years old, I borrowed of my uncle Entick's Dictionary, and carried it in my pocket, wherever I went, for one year, that, whenever a new word was mentioned, I might know the meaning— a good idea for any young man to adopt.

About this period, he describes the school house in which he taught three months in Vermont. "All the covering upon the frame was hemlock boards, feather-edged, and nailed on. There were no clapboards on the outside, nor plastering or ceiling upon the inside. The chamber floor consisted of loose boards, laid down, being neither jointed nor nailed. The lower floor was the same, and there was not one window in the room. All the light, excepting what came through between the boards, was as follows—there were two or three holes cut through the boards of the side, and end of the house. These were filled up with a newspaper, Spooner's Vermont Journal, which was oiled to let the light through, and fixed into thin strips of wood, and made fast.

"These were all the windows we had; sometimes the boys would by accident, make a large hole through them with their elbows. Often, when I first came into the room I could discern but little. In this cold, dark, inconvenient place, I spent three months instructing others according to the best of my ability."

Some of us can remember school-houses that would

not carry off the palm, when compared with this, of Elias Smith's.

About this time, for want of light, or some other reason, or all combined, his eyes became very bad; and he applied a " particular kind of eye-water." He has not informed us what it was, if he knew. He " used it several times a day, as the only remedy." Probably it was the beetle leaf, as most quack eye-waters are.

He had sometime previous, borrowed a pair of green spectacles, and, now, to add to his affliction, these were called for. What could he do? The eye-water, with all its virtues, could not enable him to read, without the *green glasses*, and none of these were to be had where he resided. But, he heard they were to be sold in Windsor, ten miles off.

To Windsor he must go. But the school must not stop. So, he says, " I engaged a horse, took one bushel of wheat in a bag, and, after midnight, and very cold, started for Windsor. The snow was deep, the path poor, the road very hilly, and the weather cold. Sometimes I rode, and sometimes walked. Just as the daylight appeared, I arrived at the store where it was said, *green glasses* were kept. I knocked at the door of the store several times; at last, a man in the chamber, half awake, cried out, " who is there?" I replied, " a friend." He spoke out again, " What do you want this time of night?' I told him, " a pair of spectacles." " We have none," said he. This at once, sunk my raised expectation. I then asked him, if he had any *green spectacles?*. "Yes, said he, but it is too cold to get up now." I told him my necessity, and how far I had come in the night, and that he must let me have them. He was quite mad, at my urgency; but finally, came down with a candle, showed me the glasses, and told me the price, which was four shillings. I asked him if he would take some wheat for them? "Yes," said he, and quite mad about it. "What do you give per bushel?" "Five shillings," said he. All my desire, for that time was granted. I took the bag off the horse, and brought it in, good measure, which he accepted. I bid him farewell, and he in return, said, he hoped, if I ever wanted any more, I would stay for them till daylight."

In his nineteenth year, he returned to Lyme in Connecticut. On a Saturday afternoon, he, with some friends whom he found on the way, and who gave him a ride, arrived at Springfield, Mass. He says, "Sunday afternoon, I went to meeting, and heard a man preach called Dr. Howard

"As I had been brought up in the woods, every thing in such a great town as Springfield attracted my attention, particularly, things under the name of religion. The first thing that drew my attention was the meeting-house, which was adorned beyond what I had ever seen in the log meeting-houses in Vermont. The next thing I noticed was the dress of the young men, who were in costly array, compared to my clothing. The third object which set me to staring, was the minister, who made such an appearance as I had never before seen. In the first place, he had a long black outside garment on, with a broad belt of the same round his waist. The sleeves, I then thought, were as wide as the meal-bags used in Vermont. It then seemed strange to me that he should wear such great sleeves, unless his arms were so stiff that he could not wear such as were near the size of his arms. Next, he had something fastened under his chin, which then appeared to me like what the children in Connecticut used to wear, when they were cutting their teeth, called a bibb. Why he wore it, was unknown to me. In addition to this, he had on his head, what Dr. Baldwin, an old Baptist minister of Boston used to call a *folio-wig*. This was very large, white, and powdered, or, as I then thought, covered over with flour. From all this pompous appearance, I supposed much dignity and good matter was contained in the head the wig contained."

About this period, he taught a school in East Hartford. When he came to teach the catechism, as was then the custom on every Saturday, he found two children from an Episcopal family, with their catechism. "This, says he," was a new thing to me, as at that time I did not know there was another on earth, save that composed by so many Divines at Westminster. In reading it over, I came to the following questions and answers. Question, "What is your name?" Answer, N. J. "Who gave you that name?" Answer, "My godfather and godmother, in my baptism, in which I was made a member of Christ, a child of God, and an heir of the kingdom of heaven." "After looking at all this, I told the children, I could not teach that to them, for, it was false, and, I could not knowingly, teach falsehoods. I went through with the Presbyterian catechism, but the poor, little Episcopalian children were obliged to set and hear, without any part in that which was as bad as their own catechism in many things."

When the children returned home, they told their father what the teacher said about their catechism. The Episcopal man was highly offended; but after an interview with the teacher, in which he maintained the falsity of the catechism, the matter was adjusted by the following compromise—The teacher was to ask the questions, and when the children answered, he was to tell them the answers were false.

In 1789, he was immersed by Elder William Grow, in Queechy river, near the house of Ichabod Churchill.

Soon after his baptism, he began to think about preaching. He read, he says, the Bible chiefly. " Osterwald Christian Theology," and, a short system of Divinity, written by Norton, " Edward's History of Redemption, Boston's Four Fold State, and Flavel's Sermons."

He went to Elder Grow, the man who baptized him, to get him to teach him to preach. He says, " The Elder received me kindly, and gave me permission to read his books. He had one book called "Skeletons of Sermons," that is, bones without meat. They were properly, " blank Sermons." Elder Grow handed me the book, and said, " there is the book they gave me, when men undertook to make a minister of me." I read and examined it, till I said, as David did, of Saul's armor, " I cannot go with these." Cruden's Concordance gave me the most information of any book he had

The Baptist ministers at that time were poor, and made a mean appearance in the world, to what many now do. To have dressed one of them in black then, with a band and surplice, and called him Rev. or D. D. would have affrighted him, especially, had he, in addition to this, received a salary.

The first association of Baptist minsters he ever attended was at Adams, at the house of Elder Peter Wardon, a worthy preacher. Among the ministers present were the following, Elder John Gano, from Kentucky, his son, Stephen Gano, who now (1816) lives in Providence, R. T. Elder John Waldo, Elder Henry Green, Elder Isaac Smith, &c.

"On the 19th of July, 1790, when I was twenty-one years, one month, and four days old," says Elias, appointed a meeting, at the house of Deacon Lawrence, who lived in Woodstock. This appointment made some talk, as many concluded it was impossible for me to preach, because, they said, I had never said much in my whole life; and, they concluded it was not likely I should say much then." " I finally went. Stood by a low case of drawers and read this for my text, " John X: 39, Search the Scriptures.

I remained in about one position, through the whole time of speaking. My arms remained on the drawers, my feet in one place, and, I do now know that for once, my eyes were on the assembly." I told the brethren they must improve, in the afternoon, as I had no more to say, and meant to stop from that time. Through the week, I felt ashamed, vexed, mortified, and, at times, sorry, that I had so exposed my ignorance. Still, at their urgent request, I appointed another meeting next first day, and this time, came almost the whole city together to hear what the stripling had to say."

Thus, like Whitefield, from his first appearance in public, he carried the *hoi poi*, the multitude, with him. Soon after this, he says, " I committed the whole New Testament to memory, from Romans to Revelation," and 25 years after, he says, " it remained with me to this day.

Elder Leland told him, he must be indoctrinated, and recommended " Osterwald's Theology." This book he also committed to memory, and then told Mr. Leland, " it gave him the same knowledge of the Scriptures, that the moon does of the sun."

In his 22d year, crossing the Merrimac river at Concord, he says, " A clergyman, from Pembroke, by the name of Zacheus Colby, came across the river, to the side where I was waiting. As he came out of the boat, he looked earnestly at me, and said, " Sir, I thought whether you were not a clergyman; I beg, leave to ask?" My only reply was, no."

" A clegyman, at that time, was almost as great an abomination to a *Baptist Minister*, as a Shepherd was to the Egyptians in the days of Joseph. At that time I was marvellously shy of clergymen, because, the old Baptist ministers had told me some unfavorable things about them. They told me that, when I saw a man dressed in *black*, called *reverend*, reading his notes; having a salary, taking property from others by force and despising such as travelled and preached &c. that such were the *devil's ministers*, and ought to be avoided.

This I believed. and shunned them, and when I lived

(25 years longer), to see the Baptist ministers making the same appearance, wearing the same titles, using notes, and taking a salary, that was forced from the people, the instructions they had given me caused me to leave them, and keep separate, as I had from the *clergy* before them."

(The writer's first recollections of a Baptist clergyman, accords with the above. The discourse was about hirelings, wolves in sheep's clothing, smoked paper, and all applied to Presbyterians, all they called Congregationalists.)

"In the month of July," 1792, he says, " Dr. Shepherd and the Brentwood Church, N. H., (he was then 23 years of age) appointed for me to be ordained the third Wednesday in August, and wrote letters to the Baptist Churches in Northwood, Medbury, Haverhill and the two Baptist Churches in Boston, requesting them to send their Elders, and chosen brethren to assist in ordaining their Brother, Elias Smith. As they wished the Elders and churches to know who they were to ordain, it was agreed for me to carry the letters to Boston and Haverhill."

His account of this, his first visit to Boston, is sufficiently amusing. He came in sight of the City in Charlestown, on Commencement day at Cambridge, and supposed the whole City to be in such confusion that he did not dare to enter it that night. He was delighted with Doctors Baldwin and Stillman. He preached each evening while he remained in Boston to the admiration of all who heard him.

The third Wednesday in August, 1792, he was

ordained, and Dr. Baldwin preached the sermon.

The evening after the ordination, Rev. Mr. Shepherd told Elias a story like the following—" An Indian, having a river to cross, thought to save the trouble of paddling by setting up a bush in the bow of his boat. When about two thirds across the river, the wind blew so hard that it upset his canoe, and he was obliged to swim ashore, while his canoe floated down the stream. Several people on the land saw the difficulty he was in, and when he landed, asked him how it happened that he had to swim ashore, instead of coming in his canoe ? " O said he, me carry too much bush." Now, said the Doctor, you are a young man, and just set out in the world, and will do well enough, if you do not carry too much bush."

Elias in his life, makes some good remarks upon this story, but they seem to have been designed for others, for, it was too much bush that upset his own canoe. He was not born to be led, or crushed.

He married Mary Burleigh, first daughter of Josiah Burleigh, of New Market, N. H. Jan, 7th, 1793. He was then twenty-three years, six months, and twenty-one days old. His wife was nineteen years, seven months, and thirteen days old, when they were married. She died of typhus fever, Feb. twenty-seventh, 1814, after they had been married twenty-one years.

He says, " We lived in harmony through the whole time, and she was a faithful friend to me, the children, my interest, reputation, and the cause of religion."

His eldest child was born, September 18th, 1794, in

Salem, Mass, and received the name of Unsula; she was named after a daughter of Governor Griswald of Lyme, Connecticut.

He says, " from the first of my apppearing in public I had been in the habit of dressing plain, though I sometimes dressed in black. As my residence was near Boston, and being frequently there, the two Boston ministers often made mention of my plain dress, and, particularly, Mr. Baldwin, who was a very fashionable man. He one day said, " you are not yet fifty years old, intimating that at such an age, my dress might be suitable. In this, I soon begun to conform, and went on, they with me till we all left that simplicity, which at first was seen among the Baptists. I was soon dressed in fashionable black, a large three cornered hat, and black silk gloves, to wear in the meeting-house, in *dog days.*

In 1789, then being a little over 29 years of age, he says, he was installed over the Baptist Church, in Woburn. This new fangled ceremony, he says was performed, as the Boston ministers said it would do' and, as he could not be a state minister, and get the fees for marrying people without it. Our popery was performed in the congregational meeting house, and it was a high day within. We made something of a splendid appearance, as it respected the ignorant. We had two Doctors of Divinity, one or two A. M's. and we all wore bands. When we came out of the Council-Chamber and walked in procession to the meeting house, we looked as much like the Cardinals coming out of the Conclave after electing a Pope, as our practice was like them. When we returned to the council chamber, we were more merry than the rule given to Christ's ministers would allow us to be.

Dr. Smith said to me after installation, "I advise you to wear a band on Lord's days." This was a piece of foppery I always hated, and, when I walked with it on, I then thought I acted with it as a pig does when he is first yoked, almost strike it with his knees, for fear he should hit it. I should not have worn it that day, but Dr. Stillman, who was as fond of foppery as a little girl is of fine baby rags, brought one, and put it on me."

About this time, that is, during my residence at Woburn, George Washington died. A day was appointed to take some public notice of the event. Rev. Dr. Jedediah Morse, of Charlestown, the old geographer, and I may add, the father of our present telegraphic Morse, was chosen to deliver the discourse. He came with his surplice and band, and his old notes, which he had read in Charlestown, and the prayer on a piece of paper which he had said over. As I was to make the last prayer and Daniel Oliver the first, he shamed me by his long made prayer, thinking it might help me to pray on the occasion; but, like Saul's armor, it was too long for me and I could not go with it." Elias fixes up Dr. Morse's discourse in anything but praise. About this time, 1801, he became a Republican, and about the same time, began to doubt about the doctrine of the Trinity.

About this period, he determined to preach no more. But his youngest brother, who was a Universalist minister, vsited him and preached in the Baptist meeting house in Salisbury. Elias confounded him in the evening—became converted to his faith the next day, and preached two sermons in favor of the doctrine, the next Sabbath--renounced the doctrines in fifteen days, with Calvinism and Deism, and became a free man, Jan. 30th, 1816. He says, "some were pleased, some were mad, and christians grieved at his renouncing Universalism.

While at Woburn, he had become engaged in mercantile business. But peace between England and France took place, and he lost all his property by the fall of his imported goods. He was now pretty sure that entering into mercantile business was wrong, so he got out of it as soon as he could.

In 1802, having renounced Calvinism, Universalism and Merchandising, he became convinced that the only proper name for all the followers of Christ was that of Christians, and called himself by that name. In thirteen years, that is, in 1815, he says, "I did not think to see so many preachers and brethren with the name and law of Christ only, as I now see. There are about fifty preachers in the New England States, and in the State of New York. Our brethren in Virginia, North and South Carolina, Georgia, and the Western country, are striving for the faith of the gospel. The commandments and doctrines of men are perishing in the using." During this time he labored incessantly, preaching, writing and publishing, scathing the regular clergy of all denominations, making proselytes wherever he went, and collecting larger congregations that any other man ever did in this country, except Whitefield.

In Feb. 1814, he lost his wife in Philadelphia, and was left with five children in poverty. In the latter part of the same year, he married Rachel Thurber, daughter of Samuel Thurber, Esq., of Providence, R. I. She was a rich man's daughter, but he says, she brought only her own earnings with her to recomend her. She died lately in the city of Lynn, Mass. In 1805, he says, this year I commenced the publication of a work entitled, "The Christian's Magazine, Reviewer, and Religious Intelligencer; containing subjects, historical, doctrinal, experimental, practical and poetical."

This was published once in three months for two years. Reviewing so many of the popular sermons of the day greatly enraged the clergy and their subjects. The first book which he wrote was entitled, "The Clergyman's Looking-glass, or ancient and modern things contrasted." Here is a specimen, comparing the Apostles and the clergy.

Apostles—"And how shall they preach, except they be sent?"

Clergy—"And how shall they preach, except they be sent to the college?"

Apostles—"For I neither received it of man, neither was I taught it, but by the revelation of Jesus Christ."

Clergy—"For I received it of man, and was taught it by man, and not the revelation of Jesus Christ."

Apostles—"But we have this treasure in earthen vessels, etc."

Clergy. "But we have this treasury in our notes, etc."

In 1805, he says, I issued proposals for 22 sermons on the Prophecies yet to be fulfilled, which were afterwards published.

In September, the 15th day, 1808, he published the first number of "The Herald of Gospel Liberty," at Portsmouth, N. H., which was the first religious paper in this country, and perhaps in the world." It had then 274 subscribers, and in seven years, they increased to 1500.

In August, 1812, his "New Testament Dictionary," was published, containing the meaning of 1108 words. In this he compared the regular Baptist, and Congregational ministers to "The Locusts," named in the Revelation, "having stings in their tails."

"In the month of June 1809," he says, "I am now forty years old. The principal people in Bristol county, Mass., requested me to deliver a discourse on Taunton Green, the 4th of July. This request I complied with, and delivered a sermon from "Psalm cvii. 43. Whoso is wise and will observe these things, even they shall understand the loving kindness of the Lord."

The discourse was, like its author, unique. I have read it more than once. It was thoroughly Republican, and closed with good advice in the following brilliant and eloquent sentence. "I leave these things for your consideration; wisely observe them, prize your privileges—love your country—make a right use of your liberty, obey the gospel—believe in the Saviour—trust in God—live as pilgrims—look out for death, hope for the resurrection and eternal glory."

"He added to the printed copy two short Poems, one on Tom Paine's "Age of Reason;" the other entitled "Priestcraft Exposed, in the mitation of Watt's Indian Philosopher. The following is from the former

"Then let us once take up the Bible,
See what is truth, and what is libel,
If it supports church monarchy,
Or buoys an Aristocracy,
With all those things which do attend e'm
And Church, and State together blend e'm,
And holds religion in that light,
The "Age of Reason" sure is right,
But if it proves Republican,
The "Age of Reason" cannot stand.

The following verse is from "Priestcraft Exposed;"

The stupid power that formed the mind,
One priest to every town designed,
And fixed his Station there;
This be a priest for this, he said;
Then forth he sent the priests he made,
To seek a parish here.
But parting hence, commencement day,
Mistook their business by the way,
And went to pleading law;
Ah, cruel fate, and crossing chance,
Our modern priests can sing and dance;
Such times who ever saw."

Hitherto, I have spoken of him from his own life or autobiography, and from the statements of others, The remainder will be from personal observation; commencing in 1816, when I was a child; but when memory was tenacious and when such an excentric man put it upon the full stretch.

"In the first number of the Herald, notice was given

that on the 7th day of the month, 1808, Peter Young, of York, was to be ordained. This meeting I attended, and spake from these words, "Behold, I send you forth as sheep in the midst of wolves; be ye therefore wise as serpents and harmless as doves." When I came to contrast man and ministers, with the ministers of Christ, as wolves in the midst of sheep, instead of sheep in the midst of wolves, and show that they were as wise as doves, and harmless as serpents it made a cracking among the wooden fences."

I believe this was the first ordination sermon he ever preached, The same week, he says, he was glad to escape from a mob in Hampton, through the backdoor. People came to meeting with their guns, &c.

Elders John Rand and Frederic Plummer, he says, stood by him. Of this Plummer and Smith, a young man who lived in our neighborhood used to sing a song, in his rudeness, one verse of which ended as follows.—

"Glory, honor, Smith and Plummer
Preached out doors all last Summer."

He published "the Christian's Pocket Companion and Daily Assistant." Three Sermons on Election—History of Anti-Christ—other volumes of sermons—Pamphlets on various subjects, and, as he says, he here was not idle.

The first time I saw Elias Smith, he was forty-six years old, of noble and commanding form, and dressed in brown, or, what was then called snuff colored clothes. It was on this wise—In my native town, there was but one denomination, and that Congregational; or of the standing order. There was a man of some wealth, who had left the parish, because he would not pay the ministerial tax. His oxen had been taken, and impounded for this tax.

Smith came to Berkley, and was excluded from the Congregational meeting house. On this account, he was very bitter. Elias was in the neighborhood. He had made converts in Taunton, and in Freetown. His preachers and exhorters had come to Berkley. But Smith himself had not preached there. Captain Burt, the man referred to, was determined to have him. Time came, when our minister was to hold a Lecture at the next house to our disaffected man, whose name was Edmund Burt. Burt was not in the habit of attending weekly lectures, nor, of visiting his neighbor, where this one was held. But as the Parish minister, Rev. Thomas Andros, was about to commence the exercises, Burt and Smith entered and, were attentive listeners. When the service was closed, Burt introduced Smith to Andros, and invited the latter to go with them, (Smith and himself), to his house to tea. Andros, however declined, and went home.

That evening, Smith preached in Burt's house, which, though large, was thronged. I was present. It is before me now, as it was that night. I see a noble looking man, corpulent, but not unwieldly so, arise, read a hymn from a hymn book, published by "Elias Smith, and Abner Jones." Then sing it, and pray, and then, announce his text "But if our gospel be hid, it is hid to them that are lost, in whom the God of this world hath blinded the minds of them that believe not lest the light of the glorious gospel of Christ who is the image of God should shine unto them." Our gospel, "said he," is hid to the hireling ministers and their vassals—but it is hid to them that are lost, &c. He talked two hours and a half, and then apologized that the time would not allow him to say all that he desired to. During this speech, the audience laughed, or cried, just as Elias chose to have them. They were entirely at his command. When he compared Congregational preachers, and their churches to an old pewter spoon, sometimes made bright, but soon becoming tarnished again, all must laugh.

The next day, the Congregational meeting house was solicited for Smith to preach in. This was refused. But the matter was arranged as follows—Mr. Burt had a large Brig on the stocks, nearly ready to be launched. The staging, some ten feet, high answered for a pulpit, and there, by Taunton river, by the side of the Brig, Smith preached. The people came pouring in from every direction, as they did under the Miller excitement, into Boston, in 1843, till it was judged there were 6000 present. His text was Isaiah XXXIII. 21, 22. "For there the glorious Lord shall be unto us a place of broad rivers and streams, wherein shall go no galley with oars, neither shall gallant ship pass thereby. Then is the prey of a great spoil divided and the lame shall take the prey."

He first described the river Amazon; and, from that down to the river before us, in which vessels had that day gone both ways. But, in the place named in the text, "there should go no galley with oars." Upon "the prey and dividing of the spoil, he said, "many have said to me, Mr. Smith, you are lame."

Why? "Because you have not received a College education:" Well, bless the Lord, said he, the lame shall take the prey.

In the afternoon, Elder Hicks, of Dartmouth, preached, "Look straight at me," said he, as he commenced.—"It is old black Hicks, come right out of Dartmouth woods."

I was then a boy, mounted far above these speakers, where I could survey the vast multitude of more than 5000. In that great assembly, Smith made all laugh, and strong men cry, just as he pleased. Soon after, several Congregational ministers preached against him and his doctrine and published their sermons. The Rev. Thomas Andros of Berkley, and the Rev. Dr. Porter, of Ballston, N. Y., were among the number. In his Gospel Herald, the first religious newspaper ever published in this country, he said, of these sermons, "It had long been the question, why don't you answer Smith? Oh, he is beneath our notice, had been the reply. But, one thing is now pretty evident—Smith has either come up some, or they have come down some, for, now, they can not only preach against him, but publish whole sermons."

Soon after this, he was again converted to Universalism. This time, it was not by his brother, but by reading the following verse, "For we are, also, his offspring." If we are the offspring of God," said he "it follows that we must all be saved."

Then, he returned again to the Christians; and, at one of their Quarterly meetings, in my native town, when this erring brother was received back upon confession, I was present. Never shall I forget the appearance of that assembly. It was in a grove, and "the Elders and brethren" formed a kind of hollow square, with Elias in the centre. There he sat, in humility, with a large silk bandanna handkerchief tied around his head. By and by, he commenced to acknowledge his errors, and to confess how greatly he had fallen, by a second time embracing Universalism. The brethren freely forgave him. He then arose, thanked them for their restoring favor, and then exhorted them "to buckle on the harness and go up with him to possess the land."

But, he again became a Universalist, and the last public meeting which I ever heard of his attending was one of Abner Kneeland's, in this City. It was generally supposed that he became frightened at Kneeland's impiety, and, from that time forward, withdrew from all public assemblies.

He had been for thirty years a scourge to the regular ministry and to the Churches. But, it is very certain that he did some good. Like Napolean, a great friend of whom he was, Smith overturned some things which needed to be overturned, and spurred into action many sleeping ministers and people. For such a work no man could have been better adapted. His personal appearance was in his favor. His eloquence was natural, his power of sarcasm, and aptness at poetic effusions remarkable.

He had now done with ministers and churches. But his mission was by no means accomplished. Henceforward he was destined to scourge the Doctors.

About this time Samuel Thompson discovered the wonderful property of Lobelia inflata, or Indian tobacco. Thompson and Smith went into the enterprise together. Thompson could not write. Smith could. Thompson could mix Lobelia, Cayenne and Baberry and Hemlock bark, and make emetics and composition; Smith could proclaim by his pen their virtues.

But this new system of medical practice must be christened, and it began to be called Thompsonism, or, Thompsonianism. Smith could be second to no one, and no where. He had made the book, and he claimed the discovery. The consequence was, Smith and Thompson separated, never to come together again until as now in death.

For sometime, Smith, as he was everywhere known, was the more famous, and took precedence of his colleague; but, the *hoi poy* seemed determined to give the name of the new system to Thompson.

Smith performed some remarkable cures in Bristol county. Capt. Stephen Hathway, of Dighton, was supposed to be far advanced in Consumption. Smith was sent for and gave him sixteen cupfuls of lobelia. He recovered, and lived twenty years after, and died at the ripe age of about ninety years. Smith charged a fee of $50 for his service. Capt. Enoch Tobey, of Berkley, who had just returned from a foreign voyage, was also sick, had Smith, but died. In Taunton, he performed several cures, and one young lady died under the operation of the lobelia. This raised a storm about his ears, and a mob collected to lynch him. But, he escaped out of their hands, and was conveyed to Boston, it was said, through the aid of the Masonic fraternity. No sooner had he safely arrived in this city, than he published the following : " The regular doctors kill fifty where they cure one. I cured fifty in Bristol county, and one died, and the people were about to tar and feather me."

Soon after this he published the following poetic effusion, which, I know not can be found anywhere at present but in the head of the writer, where it has remained for more than forty years:

> "The nests of College birds are three,
> Law, Physic, and Divinity;
> And while these three remain combined,
> They'l keep the world oppressed and blind.
> On laborer's money Lawyers feast,
> Also, the Doctor and the Priest.
> The Priest pretends to save the soul,
> Doctors to make the body whole,
> For money Lawyers make their plea;
> We'll save it, and dismiss the three.
> This is the way the craft has gained;
> When sick, we for the doctor send.
> He says, there is no chance to live,
> Unless, I deadly poison give.
> When this is done, the sick grows worse,
> This takes the money from his purse.
> He says, I've great regard for you,
> But money is the most in view.
> And when they find that you must die,
> Call in the Priest, the Doctors cry.
> The Priest will come, and with him pray,
> And clear the Doctor every way.
> They always say, he has done well,
> No man of skill could him excel,
> His time was come, the Lord had sent,
> No doctor could his death prevent.
> But *natural* Doctors have no chance,
> No Diploma can they advance.
> No Quack can have a right to kill
> Unless he's past the College mill,
> Should he the butcher then excel,
> The tender say, it's very well,
> We know that bleeding causes death.
> We bleed a beast to stop his breath.

The same is used to save man's life,
To ease his pain, they take the knife.
Much as these moderns take man's blood,
So much his life goes in the flood.
If any life should yet remain,
They then, the lancet use again.
Mercury, Arsenic, opium, too,
Physic, blisters, lance, adieu,
And, all who use them, we deny,
Excepting when we wish to die.
Craft tells the Doctor, make your bill,
And let the Lawyer write the will,
And, then to execute the same,
The Lawyer takes it in his name.
Soon as the man is dead and gone,
The *Will* is read; the work goes on.
The Doctor brings a shocking charge,
The Lawyer says, it's none too large,
Because we three have well agreed,
To charge the people as we need.
We claim the power and full control
Over the body, will and soul.
Adieu; we've spoiled the tree
Of Hartford Tory monarchy,
Did twenty lawyers there agree
To form this great conspiracy.
The clergy met at their own place,
To bind us, freemen in disgrace.
The Doctor, with the same intent,
Petitioned to the Government,
To make a law to stop the plan
Of equal rights in every man.
What could the Doctor's object be,
Except, a general massacre.

Thus, as in early and middle life, he had scourged all the regular clergy, so now, in his latter years, he scourged all the regular Doctors. It should be remembered that the famous Hartford Convention of Federalists had taken place a few years before this, which was detested by all the Republicans of that day, and, also, that there was a law in Massachusetts, prohibiting any man from collecting fees for medical practice, unless he were a member of the State Medical Society, or had a diploma from Harvard Medical College; also, that every body was taxed for the parish minister's support. These facts, give peculiar point to the foregoing poetry, the pith of which would not be seen by the present younger generation without knowing them.

I remember Smith when his office was in Hanover Street, and called on him when it was in High Street, at the corner of High Street Place.

He had then in his office some half dozen miserable looking creatures, who were putting up medicine in different parts of the room, which was a large one. Directing his speech to me, he said, " you see these persons all about here. I've taken them all from the graveyard, that is, the Doctors would have soon had them there, if 1 had not saved them." Seeing what miserable plight they were in, ragged and haggard, I replied, I should judge by their appearance that you had not yet removed them far from the churchyard. At this, the old man, (who always loved a joke,) laughed heartily.

Referring to his having belonged to so many different denominations, Smith used to say, it " had always been his custom, when he found something better than what he possessed, to leave the poorer and take the better. His brethren called these changes, but he called them changes only from glory to glory."

As a specimen of his views of the Doctors, I may also, recite the following verses—

Physicians of the highest rank,
(To pay their fees, we need a bank,)
Combine all wisdom, art and skill,
Science and sense. in calomel.
Howe'er their patients may complain,
Of head, or heart, or nerve, or vein,
Of fever high, or parch, or swell,
The remedy is calomel.
When Mr. A. or B. is sick,
"Go fetch the Doctor, and be quick"—
The Doctor comes, with much good will,
But ne'er forgets his calomel.
He takes his patient by the hand,
And compliments him as a friend;
He sits a while, his pulse to feel,
And then takes out his calomel.
He then turns to the patient's wife,
"Have you clean paper, spoon, and knife?
I think your husband might do well
To take a dose of calomel."
He then deals out the precious grains—
This ma'am, I'm sure will ease his pains;
Once in three hours, at sound of bell,
Give him a dose of colomel.
He leaves his patient in her care,
And bids good bye, with graceful air;—
In hopes bad humors to expel,
She freely gives the calomel.
The man grows worse, quite fast indeed,
"Go, call for counsel—ride with speed,"—
The counsel comes, like post with mail,
Doubling the dose of calomel.
The man in death begins to groan—
The fatal job for him is done;
His soul is winged for heaven or hell,—
A sacrifice to calomel.
Physicians of my former choice,
Receive my counsel and advice;
Be not offended, though I tell,
The dire effects of calomel.
And when I must resign my breath,

Pray let me die a natural death,
And bid you all a long farewell,
Without one dose of calomel.

CHAPTER VI.

CONTENTS.—Hereditary Descent—Daniel D. Smith's Subtlety—George W. Beal, and Josiah Brigham—The town meeting—The results—John Quincy Adams in a Petty Parish Quarrel—Lucius Manlius Sargent and Dr. Cutler—Kind treatment by John Quincy Adams—Matthew Hale Smith and Temperance in Quincy.

I believe in the hereditary transmission of character from parents to children, and I refer any unbeliever to the cases of Daniel D. and M. Hale Smith, sons of Elias, as proof of this doctrine. Daniel commenced a Baptist minister, then became Universalist, and then, a Christian, and the last I heard of him, he was a Doctor of Medicine. Indeed, in those days, I did not know one Universalist minister who was not also a Thomsonian Doctor, thus following in the wake of the famous Elias.

Matthew Hale commenced a Baptist, then became Universalist, then Congregational, then a Lawyer. Then, it was said he attempted to become an Episcopal clergyman, but not succeeding, still remained a Lawyer, and is now a Baptist minister in the city of New York.

Can any one say, they did not legitimately inherit this changeableness, from their father Elias, who belonged to almost all the religious denominations of his day, one at a time? The last time I ever saw Elias Smith, I asked him why his two sons were so changeable? " Don't you know," said he? " No," I replied. " Why, they are Smithy," said he, " that's what's the matter."

Having thus given the genealogy of my Univeralist Colleague, Daniel D. Smith, in the life of his father, Elias, my next business is to set before my readers, Daniel's effort to bring me into notice. So, one bright morning, I was honored with a call from two gentlemen, who proved to be George W. Beal and Captain Josiah Brigham, most worthy gentlemen of the town of Quincy, and members of the good old Unitarian Society. They had in their hands a slip, cut from the newspaper called the Trumpet, edited by my jolly friend, Thomas Whittemore. Now any body, who ever knew Thomas, knew also, very well, that he loved a good joke. This slip contained the statement, without the name of any writer or any town, which I will give briefly. They had found it in the " Home Missionary," a monthly periodical published in New York, and, having detached it from thence, where it was nameless, had printed it, and said, it was my writing. These two worthy gentlemen wanted to know, if I had been slandering the good town of Quincy! To which interogatory, I replied, I had not—that I had been treated very kindly by said town, as I had been by invitation to a fourth of July celebration, and had other privileges, and, that I had ever spoken well of the town.

Whereupon, friend Beal, waxing a little warm, said, " we don't care what else you have said about the town, if you wrote this." I replied, " I was not in the habit of writing for the Trumpet, and had never been a correspondent of it." Upon this they left me. After a little reflection, I called at Captain Brigham's store for further conversation, and, with a view of any explanation that might be made. I found the Captain pretty considerably excited. He said, " it was no use to talk, for they were going to have a town-meeting about it." At this sensible remark, I said, very well, Captain ; if the town of Quincy wants to have a town meeting to see if this description suits them, they can have it; and, if the garment fits them, they can wear it ;" and, with this remark, I left, to let matters move on, calculating that the heavens might not fall, if the leading spirits of Quincy called a town meeting, for report said, they had voted at such a meeting once, that no one should preach at the Poor-House, save the minister of the town, and, as he was a very quiet, venerable and pacific old gentleman, it was not likely that he would trouble them with very many sermons. This was on the occasion of Rev. Dr. Cutler, of the Episcopal Church, one of the best men of the age, having preached to the inmates at the " Poor-House."

The Honorable Lucius Manlius Sargent, one of the most talented men of the age, the writer of the famous " Temperance Tales," had just then become a member of Dr. Cutler's Church ; and, in the warmth of his first love, did not like to have his minister prohibited from preaching " the gospel to the poor" of Quincy ; so, he attended a meeting of the town, and said, " the law of God and the law of my country, allow my minister to "preach the gospel to the poor," and he shall go there and preach it, and if need be, I will go with him, bringing down his fist, which much resembled a sledge hammer." I do not vouch for the truth of this story, but I was told it by those who ought to have known. Dr. Cutler was allowed to preach to the poor when he pleased after this rencounter.

In the Diary of John Quincy Adams, under date of July 12, 1839, we have the following (Mr. Adams taking it for granted that Cornell wrote the article, which was not proven) : —

"The Rev. William M. Cornell, some time minister of the Orthodox Church, called this morning, and said that he had been compelled by the state of his health to give up his profession as a minister of the gospel, and had opened a school to prepare boys for college; and in making references for character it might be useful to him to give my name, as other gentlemen of the town had authorized him to do.

"I said that as regard to his peculiar qualifications as a teacher I had not the pleasure of being sufficiently acquainted with him to speak of my own knowledge; but that *to the respectability of his character, and his integrity,* so far as he was known to me, he might rely upon my disposition to render him any service in my power; and, if called upon, I would cheerfully bear testimony in his favor.

"Just four years ago, Mr. Cornell, in the heat of youthful zeal for Orthodoxy, wrote certain strictures upon the moral and religious character of the inhabitants of this town, which were published, and raised their resentment vehemently against him. Town meetings were held, and a large committee was raised, of which I was chairman, to vindicate the character of the town. We had a correspondence with Mr. Cornell, and reported resolutions declaring his aspersions false and groundless, which were adopted and published; and there it ended. Mr. Cornell's burning zeal was cooled, and his conduct has ever since been prudent and exemplary."

A meeting was called, which, however, was but thinly attended, and the moderator sent me a courteous letter, which I answered in the same courteous manner, and the meeting adjourned for one week. The town-clerk said, it was marvellous that they should have adjourned that meeting for a whole week. "Why, the man will be a thousand miles off before that time." They expected he would take to his heels, and run away.

The Hon. John Quincy Adams was moderator of the meeting, and the Hon. Thomas Greenleaf wrote the first letter. After receiving my answer, John Quincy Adams, wrote me a very pleasant letter, speaking of certain published reports vouched with the authority of my name, which had done serious injury to the good town of Quincy, and hoping to find in me a disposition to repair the injury done! I replied to this letter, that, "I had seen no published reports vouched with the authority of my name." This was true. The trumpet had said, they were mine; but as I did not write for "the Trumpet," nor vouch for the truth of what it published, and as the "Home Missionary" had nowhere said, that report was mine, of course no published report had appeared, vouched with the authority of my name.

This ended the correspondence. The town met, at least, a few of them, made out and published their report, in which they said that the statement, as related to the town of Quincy, was false and slanderous.

But they nowhere said that report was mine. They said, it was reported to be mine, and said to be mine, but did not say it was mine. The committee were composed of the most honorable gentlemen of the town, and of the highest respectability, thus exhibiting what a little religious zeal can do.

Our little Church was crowded with strangers for two or three Sabbaths, no doubt expecting to hear something about the great affair; but, as no reference was had to it, we were soon left to our usual congregation. The whole matter died of starvation, though my beloved colleague, Daniel D. true to his pedigree, as my readers have already seen, endeavored to keep up the excitement by praying for several Sabbaths, that "the affair might die, the culprit be forgiven, and the people cease to talk about it."

It did us no harm; but, as Pat said of his gun, when the recoil knocked him over, so this gun kicked at the wrong end, for the two denominations, who had been mutually engaged in getting up the sport, soon began to taunt each the other, by saying, "you did it." My colleague, Daniel D. soon left, and I staid.

Now, let it be remembered that we said, in our sketch, in reference to the statement that, "John Quincy Adams never forgave; we could tell a better story of him." Here it is: He evidently felt that, he had been inadvertantly hurried into this "little petty Parish quarrel," as Hon. Tristam Burgess, (the old bald-headed man of Rhode Island was called in Congress,) called this town meeting. Never after did I lecture to the Lyceum, but Mr. Adams came, even in a snow-storm, to hear me. Nay more, when about to open my school, of which I shall speak hereafter, I waited upon Mr. Adams, and informed him of my purpose, and told him, "I should like to refer to him." He said, "so far as direct qualifications to teach are concerned, I am not able to say, but, so far as uprightness and integrity of character are concerned, I shall be pleased to bear witness to your competency." More still, I had two young men fitting for the Military Academy, at West Point. Mr. Adams came to my school, examined them in Mathematics; and, also, a class in the Greek Reader, and introduced one of them, as a member from his District, into the cadetship.

As said above, the committee were of the most respectable citizens of the town, and not one of them, who had children young enough to attend school, but afterwards sent them to me. Noah Curtis, one of the committee, a father of the town, whose word was as good as his bond, not only sent his youngest daughter to my school, but said, when I was about to move to Boston, "just as we get acquainted with you, and begin to like you, you are going to leave us. I am sorry for it."

They chose me Moderator of the town meeting, and, in 1842, elected me chairman of the School Committee of the town, which indicated a great change towards one who had slandered the good town of Quincy." Master Seaver, who taught school in Quincy, almost from the time that the memory of the oldest inhabitant ran not to the contrary, was not friendly to me, when I was chosen on the committee but his daughter was examined by us, and her school commended, as it justly deserved, and from that time, Master Seaver was a personal friend. Never man left a town with better wishes of the whole class of those who had thought I spoke disparagingly of them, than I did, when I left Quincy. They had verily thought, my sole object was to build up a parish, by pulling down theirs; but, when I went to teaching, they were among my best friends.

Perhaps, it may be truly said, the town of Quincy was not as far back as that time, the most temperate one in the Commonwealth. They had then, no Henry H. Faxon to purchase Hotels for Temperance Boarding houses, and to offer large rewards to Societies who would procure the best Lecturers on temperance ; a least, Mr. Faxon was then young; and not on the stage of active life.

There were some, as said in that wicked report, in some parts of the town, who did not attend public worship. I may here relate a little incident. Elisha Marsh, one of the most candid and conscientious men living, a Unitarian himself, was always a good friend of mine. When the town meeting, very much like one of old, when certain persons "cried out, great is Diana,"— was over, Mr. Marsh said, " I am very sorry about this matter; I have ever had a good opinion of you, and my wife attends your Church." I said, Mr. Marsh, what is there in that report that is not true, of some parts of this town, and of some parts of every town ? Oh, said he, there is not any of it true. Well, let us read, " many families attend no place of religious worship." There, said he, that isn't true. The people go to Church in this town." Very well, this doesn't say but that they do. Mr. Marsh, said I, you know most of the people, and how many families can you count between your house and where I live, that do not go to Church ? He thought a minute, and then added, " I think, there are five or six ! Well, said I, if, on a single street, within less than a fourth of a mile, there are five or six families, may there not be said to be "many" in all parts of this town Then, I read another sentence, " in some parts of this town the Sabbath is devoted to labor, amusement and intoxication." How is this? said I. Do you know none who labor on the Lord's day? 'Oh yes, several.' Do you know any who get intoxicated on that day? yes, but the people of Quincy don't understand it in that way—they say, it refers to the whole town. But, how can it refer to the whole town, when it expressly says, in some parts of it? "Well, said he, "it is true enough, as it reads, but, they do not so understand it."

That was, undoubtedly, the case. They didn't understand it as it read, for, they thought their religion was aimed at, and, then, even good men can't always see straight. Cowper says,

> "Religion should extinguish strife,
> And make a calm of human life;
> But friends that chance to differ
> On points that God has left at large,
> How fiercely will they meet and charge?
> No combatants are stiffer."

Even good men labored under a mistaken idea about a missionary being sent to Quincy, a town that had raised up more Presidents and other great men than all the others in the State. As the Irishwoman said, when her antagonist called her a "Kilkenny Cat," "it was an indacent reflection upon her birth-place, as ye must know." So, at first thought, the idea of a missionary in Quincy was considered as a reflection upon somebody; and Father Taylor, the Seaman's preacher, when he preached the Dedication Sermon of the Methodist Church at the Point, (of whom more anon) well said, " No, don't call it a missionary station."

It was not taken into the account that different denominations send Missionaries, to even our largest cities and most enlightened places, where their own parishes are new, or small, as Presbyterians, of Philadelphia, now aid in supporting Presbyterians with home Missionary funds; in Boston, and Congregationalists now aid in supporting Congregational Missionaries in Philadelphia. But, this is no reflection upon the general intelligence, morality or religion of these two cities. These cases are taking place in all our States. But, as Mr. Marsh said, they don't so understand it, and few can understand what they don't want to.

MATTHEW HALE SMITH.

He was my second Universalist Colleague in Quincy. When Daniel D. left, he introduced his brother, Matthew H. He was more polished, more like his father, and a better speaker than Daniel, and had less of the serpent and more of the dove, in him. Notwithstanding the people of Quincy were, as we have seen, so very temperate, M. Hale Smith was driven away from Quincy for a good deed. So far as I recollect, we had but one member of the Temperance Society from the Universalist denomination; so you can see, there has since been a great change, for now, the Universalists are among the foremost in the cause of temperance. We had a temperance society, and it was somewhat active. Jonathan Marsh, a brother of Elisha, above named, was our President. We had monthly meetings at which we had a lecture, either by some Clergymen or laymen.

M. Hale Smith made me a friendly call one day, and among other topics of conversation, said, ' I wonder the Temperance Society have never asked me to give them a lecture."

I replied, would you do it, if they should? Certainly, said he, I am a temperance man, and have often lectured upon that subject."

Well, said I, I think they would like to have you do it, and I will speak to the President about it.

Very soon, I met Mr. Marsh in the street and he said whom shall we get to give our next temperance lecture? I replied, Rev. Mr. Smith. Mr. Marsh looked curious, and said, "do you think he would do it?" I said, I think he would. How would his parish like it, said Mr. M? I don't know, was my answer. Well, I will try him, said the President. Would you give notice of it to your people? said he. Yes, I replied. Would you attend? Certainly, said I.

The next Saturday, the President called on Mr. Smith and asked him to lecture. He said, " he would, the next evening in his church, the Universalist. I am to exchange with Mr. Cobb, of Malden, but I shall be at home and will lecture in the evening."

The arrangement having been made, notice was given accordingly, and in the evening, we all repaired to the Universalist Church. It was full of people, but there were no lights in it. It was said, the sexton had received orders from the Committee to open the house, but not to light it. Soon Mr. Smith came in, lights were also brought in, and he commenced his lecture. He said, "a man ought to take as much spirit as the good of his constitution required, physically, mentally and morally." This seemed to meet with the approval of some of his parishioners, for, though their heads were down before, they now raised them, seemingly, as a token of approbation.

But, soon, Smith, turned a short corner and said, "I shall now show you that the good of man, neither physically, mentally, nor morally, requires that he should take one drop." He then argued well to support this proposition. He said, "it is taken to keep out cold, to keep out heat, to give men more physical strength, and to answer the purpose of medicine. It does none of these for the body; and so, he went on with the mind, and the other objects for which spirit is used, and closed by saying, "it thus clearly appears that, spirit always does harm instead of good, and no man needs one drop of it."

Though this was liked by Mr. Tirrell, the one member of Smith's society who belonged to the temperance society, yet, it was a round turn, (as sailors say) about the necks of some of them who really loved " a little of the crater." Still, it might have all passed away, had not Smith, feeling a little chagrined, because the house was not lighted, gone to the chairman of the committee, while the steam was yet up, and asked, why was the house not lighted?

This was a little too much; to have to take such a dose of total abstinence all at once, and from his own minister, was the straw that broke the back. He could have borne it from one of the hideous Orthodox ministers, or, possibly, from a Unitarian; but, to come from his own chosen clergyman, it could not be brooked.—So, he broke out upon Smith, "you rascal! we didn't get you here to beat our brains out. You are a club which the Orthodox and the Unitarians are using to kill us with, and, you shall never preach in that house again;" and he never did.

M. Hale Smith was popular in Quincy, and when thus

abruptly driven away, some were mad; some rejoiced; and some said, long after, "if it had not been for that wretched temperance business, we should have had him now; and, perhaps, they would. But Smith never preached Universalism again. This Temperance Lecture proved to be the winding sheet of his Universalism.

CHAPTER VII.

CONTENTS —My School in Quincy—Rev. John Gregory—His Temperance and Trouble—The Little Church— Its various Pastors—A reign of peace.

Some years after this storm had blown by, and I had left my parish in Quincy, on account of chronic weakness of the vocal chords, that prevented my speaking in public, I opened a family boarding school in Quincy. It was, probably, the most prosperous school that town had even seen. I began with two little, boarding boys, from abroad, and did not expect a single pupil from Quincy. But, in less than one year, my schoo numbered more than forty pupils, reaching from St. John's, N. B., to Mobile, Mo.

I had already had much experience in teaching, and there was a grand opening for a school, such as I commenced.

The secret of its success was, I stole the hearts of the children, and, as they ruled the parents, of course, they had to send them, *nolens. volens.* I believed in physical culture, as an accompaniment of mental discipline, and had a lot appropriated to playing ball, in which I always delighted, and where I played with my pupils. This lot was in sight of a considerable part of the village, and where the lads from the shoe-manufactories could see the boys at this sport; the result of which was, that few of them could be kept from the school. One man, who, while I was Pastor of that little, obnoxious church, was, to say the least, not over friendly to me, came in one day and said, " I don't know what is the matter with my boys, but they dun me every day to let them come to your school, and to have peace, I must send them." Another said, "you charge so much for tuition, so much for books, and it comes to so much that I don't know as I can send my son." I replied, yes, I charge so much, and I can't take your son for any less sum. Besides, my school is full, and I had rather not take him at all." " But," said he, " I must send him."

They came from families of every denomination, among whom were the children of Noah Curtis, Samuel Curtis, Nathaniel White, Daniel French, Ibrahim Bartlett, Souther, General Taylor, and many more than I can name.

The discipline of the school was strict, and no difficulty was found in maintaining it, though I had pupils who had been excluded from the Boston Schools for insubordination, and from the Farm School, on the

Island in Boston harbor. All the pupils were made happy, for, in addition to playing ball, we swam in summer, and skated in winter. A happier school no man ever had, and I made and saved more money in a single year, than I had done by preaching all my life; and, had I continued the school, should have become a rich man; and, I should have so done, had not the health of my wife prevented.

I could relate many incidents connected with this school which afford pleasant recollections to this day, now thirty-five years since. I will give one or two. I had a young man from St. John's, who was under the protection of the Bishop of the Episcopal Church, and who was competing for a scholarship there, with several others. He said, "I do not expect to succeed, for they have but a poor opinion there of the Yankee teachers. But, in the next letter, he wrote, after returning home, he said, "I have got the appointment, and they now have a better opinion of Yankee teachers."

Mine was a mixed school, and we had none of the loss of health, so gravely depicted in Dr. Clarke's recent book. Not a girl, nor a boy, as I remember, was taken sick while at the school. We had now and then, a little incident, showing human nature. I remember one like the following. My school was in a building separate from the house, and over the school-rooms were lodgings for some of the pupils, and with them, lodged, also, my Assistant in teaching. I always visited these apartments before retiring for the night, acting upon the principle that a General must always know the state of his army, and a shepherd his flock. On making this visit one evening, I missed two of the pupils, each of which was named Charles. I inquired of my Assistant, if he had given them permission to be absent? He said, he had not. I locked the outside door, put the key in my pocket, and went into the house. About bed time, I heard the two boys talking around the house, but paid no attention to it. As I took my light to retire, they, aware of the signal, and thinking it their last chance for lodgings that night, knocked at my door. I opened the window, and asked, who is there? We's here, said one of the Charles's. Who's we, said I. Charles and I, said he. Ain't you a bed? said I. We can't get in, said he. I gave them the key and the next morning, called one of them to account for their absence. He said, my Assistant teacher gave them permission to go. I replied, he says, he did not. You ask Charles, meaning, the other Charles, said he. Upon inquiring of the Assistant teacher again, as to his having given them leave of absence, he said, ' when they had spelled, these two boys remained after the others had retired, and one of them said, ' may we go?'" To which he answered, yes. Here was a ruse. They meant, as they said, may we go where we please. He meant, they might go, or be dismissed from school.

Well, said I, where did you go? We went to Adam Curtis' house. How came you to go there without my permission? The girls asked us to come, and the old folks were gone away, said they.

Now, here was a dilemma. The girls wanted them

to come, the boys wanted to go, and had contrived the ruse, to tell me that the Assistant allowed them to go. Under all the mitigating circumstances, I could not find it very easy to inflict punishment in this case. This was the only incident of girls and boys mingling unduly, *i. e.* without full permission, during the whole school, and, it did not appear that any serious difficulty followed this meeting. The principle holds as good in schools as elsewhere—the more you prohibit boys and girls from mingling together, the more they will strive to do it: and hence there have been more freaks of love and more elopements from separate schools—ten to one—than from those where they are educated together. It is time this monkish notion should be abandoned.

Rev. John Gregory

was my next Universalist Colleague in Quincy, after M. Hale Smith. There was a little talk—"the tongue is an unruly member"—when he first came to town about his then having two wives. Some, who felt for the credit of the town—we have seen it to be a credit-loving town, you know. There are some such in every town, as there were in Quincy—said, "it did't look well to have a minister in town, who had two wives, both living:" and, as this talk became " pretty considerably" wide, the Universalist Society held a meeting, at which they passed some Resolutions in favor of their Pastor, in one of which they said, " We have examined into all the circumstances connected with Rev. John Gregory's first marriage (but they hadn't as you will see) and believe that he has broken no law, human or

Divine." These Resolutions were duly signed by a large number, all I believe, of the Society, and handed to Mr. Gregory as a solace for the fangs of "backbiters:" and such, in the end they proved, not to him, but, to those who signed them.

Mr. Gregory was a very agreeable gentleman, and I ever had a very pleasant acquaintance with him. We were associated in several benevolent enterprises and served on the School Committee together. He was frank and open, and had none of the serpent about him. He was a good painter and painted my doors, and marbled my fire places, in the house, which I built in Quincy. When he had done, he asked me how I liked his work? I told him, I liked it very well—he was a first rate painter, and I thought he was a better painter, than preacher, and advised him to give up the pulpit, and "stick" to the brush. He smiled, and said, "I was about right:" and afterwards, took my advice,

Mr. Gregory was a strong temperance man. Temperance was a great question in Quincy in those days—and soon, some of his parish were out upon him for this. It seemed as though this temperance question was almost as unwelcome to the Universalists of Quincy, at that day, as future punishment; indeed, it was quite difficult to decide which they liked the best. How different it was then, from what it is now, when all the Universalists, (in Quincy, I suppose, as well as everywhere else), are total abstainers from all spirit. The world does move, and we move with it, and so do the Quincyites. The temperance people talked of nominating Rev. John Gregory for Representative. The leading men of his parish said, if they did, they would have him arrested for bigamy. He was run for Representative, was elected, and was arrested for bigamy. The leading men of his parish, who signed the Resolution—" We have examined all the circumstances of John Gregory's first marriage," &c., as given above; were the complainants against him for bigamy.

Mr. Gregory published the names of these men in the Quincy Patriot, in parallel columns—" We have examined all the circumstances &c., and the complaint against said Gregory for bigamy, the same persons being the complainants.

To be sure, it made things look a little mixed up; but, you know, they will be so sometimes, in this wicked world. As the old woman said, " blessed be nothing," so, the only safe way, sometimes is, to say nothing, and, above all, write nothing. Many a politician has lost an election by saying too much, or writing too many letters.

So, these men, anxious to show that Mr. Gregory had violated no law, &c., ought to have stopped there, and not complained of him for bigamy; because, you know, it don't look well to say the first, and then complain of him for the last.

But, as a good Providence takes care of her favorites, so, Mr. Gregory escaped from the hands of his persecutors, as " smoothly as Paul did when he was let down in the " basket by a window."

Mr. Gregory was to be tried at Dedham, that being

the county town of Norfolk County. Thither his opponents hied, and thither the minister had to go.

To make assurance doubly sure, and to subtantiate a fact which Mr. Gregory would never have denied, his accusers sent Thomas Adams, then Deputy, afterwards, High Sheriff of Norfolk County, to Albany, New York, to find the man who married John Gregory to his first wife, and to bring him to Dedham. This was done. The question was asked him, are you a Clergyman? He answered, no. Are you a Justice of the Peace? He said, I am not. Well, what are you then? I am a Commissioner. Are Commissioners authorized to solemnize marriages by the laws of New York? I don't know as to that. All I know is, I married John Gregory.

Now, as none were authorized to solemnize marriages in the State of New York, but Clergymen and Justices of the Peace, the Judge said, it appears that John Gregory was never legally married to the woman called his first wife, and, consequently, has never had but one wife.

Thus, he slipped through the fingers of his persecutors without their having found even a fin, or a scale by which they could hold him, he having, according to the vote of the parish, "broken no law, either human or divine." How apples did swim in this world, even in Quincy! Now, what a change, as to temperance in that town, as well as everywhere else! Why, I was told the other day, that all the people there were converted to total abstinence! that Mr. Faxon had bought the only Tavern in the town; and, now, there was no place where a traveller could get a meal of victuals or a drink. What a pity that Quincy, which used to stand so high on the roll of accommodation upon these matters, should have fallen so low !! Times do change, and we change with them. Do we not ?

The Little Church in Quincy.

From the smallest beginning this Church has gradually increased. As has already been stated, the men or some of them, at least, who commenced this enterprise, were not men of " wealth and standing." From the fact that Nathaniel Pittee, a poor and ignorant man, was one of the founders of it, the polite aristocrats called it " Old Pittee's Society." Also, because Cotton Pratt was another of its original members, the *elite* called it " Cotton Pratt's Society." Various epithets of honor were given to it by outsiders, which were calculated to keep strangers away ; such, for instance, as the following : " You go to that meeting !" Why, the people there are not respectable ! ! Nobody goes there who is thought any thing of !!! Oh ! I wouldn't go there ! ! !

One young woman came to teach the public school in a District, remote from the Centre. She arrived at her boarding-house on Saturday evening. Sabbath morning, her polite host, who was, also, the Agent of the District, said, " where will you go to Church." She inquired, what Churches are there ? He said, " there are a Unitarian, a Universalist and an Episcopalian." She said, " are these all ? I have not been in the habit of attending any of them." He said, " there is one other; but I don't know much about it. I believe, some call them Orthodox." "That is the Church I have been in the habit of attending at home," said she. Said he, I own a pew in the Unitarian, and also, one in the Universalist Church. I will carry you to either of them." I do not choose to go to either of them" was her reply." "I am sorry you are so odd," said he, "but, I will carry you as far I go that way, and you can walk the rest."

So, he carried her as far as he went that way, and she walked the rest.

This young woman was a jewel. She acted from principle; but few who came to Quincy were as firm as she. On the contrary, many came into town, who, at home, were members of Orthodox Congregational Churches, who were unable to stand the pressure from *liberal* Christianity, and were whelmed in the vortex of awful liberality.

It afforded a grand field to study human nature, and to see the corrupting influence of inuendo and slander. Never was a better opportunity to see the influence of wealth, and aristocracy, upon poor humanity, than was here presented. But, amidst being "counted the off-scouring of all things," amidst reproach and obloquy, the little Church grew, and through the good women, formerly named, increased, the Tobiahs, Sanballists and Gasmu's to the contrary notwithstanding.

My Illustrious Successors.

The little Church, after my resignation, like many other small churches in the country, was sometime before they could select a new Pastor. During this period, many of the first young men from Andover, preached to them, among whom were Charles Abbott, the youngest brother of the famous and talented Abbott family; Mr. Smith, now Professor in Andover Seminary, Mr. Haven, since President of a College at the West. Many others followed. I would not say, they were very hard to please; but Robert Hall said, " the disposition to judge of a minister's qualifications was generally in an inverse ratio to their ability;" and, the celebrated Commentator, Albert Barnes, used to say, " I preached in a little country parish, and they held a meeting to see if they would give me a call, but, as they paid $400, salary, they concluded I was not quite up to their standard, and so, I did not succeed in getting a call."

After many trials, they called Rev. William Allen, who was ordained, and installed Pastor, Jan. 28th, 1841. Mr. Allen was dismissed, at his own request, Aug. 28th, 1849. After going through the ordeal of candidating again for some time, they called Rev. Nelson Clark, who was installed, Jan. 2d, 1850. He was dismissed in 1859. Mr. Clark was a kind, lamblike looking man; but they had trouble with him; and for a time, were divided into two bands, one part worshipping in the Church, and the other in the townHall. This was unfortunate; but, they finally came together again, after Council upon Council, and, upon Mr. Clark's leaving, and one of their Deacons being Deacon no longer. Rev. J. H Thayer and Rev. Oliver Brown, then labored several years without being installed; and in 1867, Rev. Edward P. Thwing was installed, as Pastor.

During his ministry, about sixty were added to the Church. His health failing, under the pressure of parochial duties, he was dismissed, at his own request, and subsequently accepted a Professorship in one of our oldest Seminaries. Rev James E. Hall was installed, April 16th, 1868, and dismissed in 1872. During his pastorate, a new, beautiful Church was erected near the centre of business. The present minister Rev. Ed. Norton, is employed as stated supply. Thus, when God, in his Providence, has removed one Pastor, He has sent them another, and all the Pastors they have ever had are now living, and all who have preached there any length of time, save Rev. S. S. Smith. They are sufficient to make a very decent Association, at least, for numbers.

Now, the tempest has passed by, "in this highly respectable town." So far as any want of brotherly love is concerned, the halcyon day of peace has come; indeed, "the Spring has returned, the time of singing of birds has come, and the voice of the turtle is heard" through all that land, from Germantown to the quarry, and from Penn's Hill to Neponset. There is none to hurt, nor destroy, through that highly privileged country. The lion and the lamb have laid down together—peace and plenty prevail, and all is as it should be, except that subject of temperance—always a bone of contention in this town, and still, not carried to absolute perfection, even though Mr. Faxon has loosed the strings of his full purse, for this good cause.

CHAPTER VIII.

CONTENTS.—Rev. Edward T. Taylor—Dedication of the Methodist Church in Quincy—Father Taylor's Temperance Addresses—His Dedication Sermon—His laying us all on the shelf—His Prayer for the bigots of Albany, N. Y.—Getting the Rail Road—J. Q. Adam's Funeral—The Turn Pike—Deacon Newcomb and John Tappan—Quincy Then and Now—The Doctors of Quincy then—Wollaston Heights.

The first time I ever saw "Father Taylor," as he was called, he told me the following, as to his conversion.

"I was walking along Tremont Street, and the bell of Park Street Church was tolling. I put in; and going to the door, I saw the port was full. I up helm, unfurled topsail, and made for the gallery; entered safely, doffed cap or pennant, and scud under bare poles to the corner pew. There I hove to, and came to anchor. The old man, Dr. Griffin, was just naming his text, which was. "But he lied unto him." As he went on, and stated item after item,—how the devil lied to men, and how his imps led them into sin,—I said, a hearty ' Amen'; for I knew all about it. I had seen and felt the whole of it.

Pretty soon, he unfurled the mainsail, raised the topsail, run up the pennants to free breeze, and I tell you, the old ship, Gospel, never sailed more prosperously. The salt spray flew in every direction; but, more especially did it run down my cheeks. I was melted. Every one in the house wept. Satan had to strike sail; his guns were dismounted or spiked; his various light crafts, by " which he led sinners captive," were all beached; and the Captain of the Lord's host rode forth " conquering and to conquer." I was young then. I said, Why can't I preach so? " I'll try it "

Our object is simply to give a few personal reminiscences of this remarkable man, leaving the general history of his life to those who were more particularly engaged with him in ecclesiastical standing. Indeed, most of the religious papers, and some of the secular ones, have already given a more general and particular account of him than we are able to do.

It is now more than thirty years, since we became acquainted with " Father Taylor," as he was then, and has ever been called. He was a man of nervous temperament, and hence, not always, feeling the same. Indeed, he was very much given to ups and downs. We have heard him, when his flights of eloquence exceeded almost any public speaker, we had ever listened to, and, perhaps, the next time, he would fall below himself. This is characteristic of great men. We remember hearing Dr. Lyman Beecher, when no man could seemingly have exceeded him; and, then, in the next effort, he would be " weak, like another man."

We remember Bishop Simpson, during the war, in an address in the Academy of Music, in Philadelphia, when that capacious edifice was filled to its utmost capacity. His eloquence seemed almost superhuman; and George H. Stuart, the President of the Christian Commission, exclaimed at the close, " God bless Bishop

Simpson." Soon, some of our New England friends were visiting us, and we took them to hear the Bishop Suffice it to say, he did not come up to the former address.

Rev. Mr. T. was invited to give us an address on temperance, at Quincy. It was one of the grandest performances to which we ever listened, and everybody was so charmed and delighted that we asked him to come and lecture again. He did so; but it was not equal to the first. This was no disparagement to his ability. On the contrary, it placed him among those who have been the most eloquent of the sons of men.

Our good brother, Wise, now Rev. Dr. Wise, of New York, was stationed in Quincy, and when their new church was to be dedicated, he invited "Father Taylor" to preach the sermon. All the clergymen of the town were invited to attend, and all had some part assigned them in the services. We were all present, in full force—Father Whitney and his colleague, Mr. Lunt, the Episcopal clergyman, ourself, a Calvinist, the Baptist minister, then on the Quincy side, at Neponset, the Universalist, and the Restorationist, from the Railway Village.

Father Taylor commenced his sermon, and felt it to be his duty to take us all to task for our various errors and peculiar notions. Commencing with "Father Whitney," as was meet, he being the oldest minister, present, and addressing himself to brother Wise, he said, "My brother, preach the depravity, the natural wickedness of man. Some make him very good by nature, and think there is no devil in him. But, there is. Dress him up ever so much—make him never so learned, adorn him in all the robes of politeness, and all the refinement of the most polished society, of the most ornamented age of the world, and you cannot make him good. Oh! no, you have only to pull off the winding sheet, and there he is, poor, weak, sinful, human nature still." Thus much for "Father Whitney" and his colleague.

When he started on a new denomination, he directed his address to Brother Wise, by saying, " My brother. Here, he took the Universalist; he was of the then modern school of Mr. Ballou, as he believed in no future judgment.

"My brother," said he, "preach the judgment, a future judgment. For my part, I never could see why any man should be afraid or ashamed to preach it." There sat the Universalist minister in the pulpit, within his reach. But he did not spare him.

It was now our turn. " My brother, preach free agency. Don't be a fatalist. Some ministers preach fatalism—tie men's hands behind their backs, and then, tell them to work,—tie their feet together, and then tell them to walk. Don't preach that—don't make the Almighty decree everything, from all eternity, and then, call on man to break the decree. Preach man's free will. Who ever heard of any will, but a free will?" As we supposed, this was meant for us, we laid it to heart, and, though we did not admit this to be a true exhibit of any Calvinism, it was " Father Taylor's" view of it.

Here he took the Episcopal minister, "My brother, keep your pulpit doors open. Some ministers shut them against every minister except one of their own stripe. Don't do that. If I could have my will, there never should be a pulpit door in the land. There are no doors to my pulpit, and so, none can be shut."

Next, he took the Baptist. "My brother, preach baptism. It is an ordinance of God. Baptize the converted; but don t make baptism all the gospel. Don't make water, everything. There are other elements in the world besides water; and there are other things in the gospel besides baptism; though some ministers never see anything but baptism. Don't make dipping all your gospel."

Then came the Restorationist. "My brother, preach future punishment. "The wicked shall be turned into hell, and all the nations that forget God!! Leave them there, my brother, and let any minister get them out who can. But don't *you* try it."

Having thus laid us all on the beach, stranded high and dry, he took another tack—showed his Catholicity, and spread his wide mantle of charity over us all, and said, "This is one of the most blessed seasons I ever enjoyed. Indeed, I have never seen but one like it, and that was when my own church was dedicated. Then, we had all the stripes in the Union; and, bless the Lord! we've got them all now."

Brother Wise published a full account of the dedication services in the *Quincy Patriot*, and another minister wrote us from Connecticut, inquiring about what kind of a "sheet" that was, that "gathered of every kind." An Episcopal paper came out with an article denying that one of their clergy was ever found taking part with birds of such diverse feathers.

This account, which we vouch for as true, should silence the stories floating about that, " Father Taylor," had no rigidity in his creed, but was a mere wit!" He was rigid enough in that wonderful sermon to cut and slash us all—to spare none but his brother Methodist; and then, he was charitable enough to throw his long arms around us all, and give us a real Methodist hug, a genuine John Wesley "love feast," and assure us that, " during his whole ministry, he had never had but one such glorious time before."

We think he proved two things, to wit, that he believed that all of us had some faults, (except Brother Wise), and he had independence enough to tell us plainly what they were; and, also, that he had charity to cover this " multitude of sins."

Perhaps the most critical situation in which " Father Taylor" was ever placed was the following. Soon after the Unitarians commenced holding their morning prayer-meetings, Anniversary week, the writer attended one of them. Among other things presented to the meeting was a report from one of their missionaries. He had been to Albany, New York. He said, " The people of Albany were the most bigoted of any he ever visited, and the clergy were more so than the people. They would not allow him to preach in any of their churches, and he found it extremely difficult to get even a hall. After attempting to labor there for several weeks without success, he gave up the field." Some one proposed that they should offer prayer for the " bigots" of Albany. This was agreed to, and they called upon " Father Taylor" to lead in prayer. This was a trying position; as his own denomination, the Methodists, were included among the " Albany bigots." He managed the case however, with his usual skill and adroitness; including them all in the same category, praying with great zeal and energy for his brethren, the Methodist bigots, as well as for the others. Some men would have found it difficult to manage such a case, but he managed it as skillfully as he ever did to get " Jack" into the pulpit. When all the seats in the pews were occupied and another sailor entered the door, even if he were in the midst of his sermon he would say, " Jack, come up here." Jack would move very slowly toward the pulpit, and would usually stop at the lower stair; and " Father Taylor" would say, " Jack, come up here I say." Jack would usully stop again half way up the stairs, when he would say, " Come in here, Jack; you've as good a right here as anybody;" and finally, he would get Jack seated in the pulpit. His prayer was so unique that he made all the ministers and churches of Albany, appear very deficient in Christian charity.

When efforts were made to get the " Old Colony Rail Road" through the town it met with decided opposition. The town, as already has been seen, was somewhat famous for holding " town meetings," upon subjects of great importance. Well, one was called about this road-business. Hon. Josiah Quincy was present and made a speech in favor of the road. But, the citizens could not see it. They brought forward numerous objections;

such as, it would injure the town—a question upon which, some were always tender. But, another was, it would injure Mr. Gillett. He had done great things for Quincy. He had horses and stages; indeed, all his property was in these materials. He had driven a stage from Quincy to Boston, eighteen years; and, now, his business was to be ruined.

Mr. Quincy answered this objection by stating that, Mr. Gillett could, doubtless, have a position in connexion with the road, &c.

Another objection was, it would injure all those who had horses; indeed, there would be no further use for horses.

Then, it would cut up their land—always a sad thought to any Quincyite, who ever had land. On this point, the old settlers were as conscientious as "Naboth" was about his "vineyard." Certain old families owned large tracts of land; and, as they would not sell a foot of it, it greatly damaged the growth of the town. The famous Adams family were prominent in this matter. John Adams had entailed a quantity of his land, and it could not be sold. This was the case with the site where the "Adams Academy," now stands. This land might be leased, but could not be sold.

Old President Adams, being a Federalist of the first water, had the same ideas of owning land that the English lords had, and, could he have done it, he would, probably, have entailed his large landed estate till the day of doom.

When John Quincy Adams died, the people supposed that much of the land that he owned, would come into the market. But, in this, they were mistaken, for, he had walked, in this respect, (though not in some others) in the steps of his illustrious father. So, when a town meeting was called—these meetings were much in vogue—to see if the town of Quincy would pay the charges of removing the body from Washington, where John Quincy Adams died, to Quincy, that his remains might be placed by the side of his father's in the "Old Stone Church," the town voted they would not pay them. This parsimonous spirit, or rather, this standing in the way of town-improvements, was, doubtless the reason, why John Quincy Adams, while commanding the votes of his Congressional District, never, or very rarely, if ever, carried his native town; and even to this day, as a gentleman has just told me from Quincy, "the Adams family, if anything, has been a detriment to the town." We do not vouch for this for, we know the present J. Q. Adams has been several times chosen to represent the town in the "General Court."

We remember another town meeting—which, to be sure, had more sense in it than some others—to get the toll lowered on the old Neponset Turnpike. The writer was chosen one of this Committee, and that of Quincy was joined by a similar Committee from Weymouth and Braintree. The owners of the Turnpike employed, Hon. Samuel D. Parker, then Attorney for Suffolk County, as their lawyer. To match them, we engaged Hon. Robert Rantoul, Jr. We had a great fight, and suffice it to say, we gained our point and the toll was reduced.

Deacon Jonathan Newcomb was not exactly a Quincy man, as he lived in the edge of Braintree. Nevertheless, he had much to do with Quincy. He was a benevolent man and gave away a large amount of property; and those who did not like him, said (enemies will talk) " the widow's two mites would outweigh all that he gave," yet, we believe he was a good man and did much good. He said to some one, that asked him, how he got so much to give away ? " The Lord blesses me, and the work of my hands always brings me more than I expected. I have not taken a job that has not prospered."

He had given considerable to erect the little Church in Quincy, and called once upon John Tappan to ask him to aid the same work. Mr. T., was engaged for a few moments, and asked the Deacon to sit down till he was at liberty. Mr. T., was unacquainted with the Deacon, who was an inveterate tobacco-chewer, which Mr. Tappan hated as much as he hated rum. The Deacon had spit all over Mr. Tappan's stove the few minutes he had sat there. At length, Mr. T., was at liberty, and the Deacon made known his request; to which Mr. T., replied, " I have but one rule,—I never give to any object, when the person who presents the request is an intemperate man." The Deacon's face turned red, and with much spirit, he replied, " I am not an intemperate man ?" " You are not" said Mr. Tappan ? " No, I am not," retorted the Deacon. " Look at my stove," said Mr. T., " See it all covered over with tobacco-juice."

Mr. Tappan told me this story himself, and added " the Deacon never chewed any more tobacco."

Quincy in 1834, and Quincy now, were somewhat different. Then, the population was, comparatively small, now it is nearly large enough for a City. Then, it was quite famous as a drinking, dancing, high flying town. Now, it has greatly improved, as respects temperance, and in the character of its amusements. Then, it was not in advance of other towns, either in education or refinement. Now, it stands among its neighboring towns, in the first rank for education, business and refinement. Then, it bore somewhat the character of those given in history, of the early settlers of Morton's companions, of the " merry Mount" Colony. Now, they are a very different class.

The Doctors in Quincy, when I was there, were Woodward and Stetson, chiefly. Some others came and went, as " birds of passage," as is specially the case in Boston, for, it is well known that young Docters are not very apt to " stick."

Dr. Woodward was Senior of the two named, and the first time we called a phyiscian, he was the man. We joked him a little about being a bachelor. He said, "when I marry, I shall do it for money only." Well, " then" some one said, " marry one of Lemuel Bracket's daughters." He replied, " but, I want the money in hand. Le'm Bracket is more likely to live thirty years than I am." He did live thirty years from that time, but died before Dr. Woodward did.

At that visit, the writer took occasion to recommend to Dr. W., the life of John Mason Good, a prominent

English physician, which had then been just published. " I will now recommend to you," said Dr. W., "a book just published on Theology, by another prominent English physician, named Smith." I have it, said I, and took it from the shelf and handed it to him. I afterwards learned that, he stated at several places, that " he believed that Cornell kept better posted than most ministers, for, I recommended to him a book on Universalism, then new, and I found, he had it in his library." He, evidently, seemed to think that Trinitarian ministers read only what corresponded with their creed.

About three weeks before Dr. W., was taken sick, I was called out to Quincy to consult with him on a case at Germantown. He carried me down in his chaise, and when we returned, I took dinner with him at his residence. He then said, " I have been in Quincy more than forty years, and have made more visits the past winter, (it was then March) than in any preceding one. My health is perfect." But, in a few weeks, he was dead.

At that interview, I said, what Doctors have you in Quincy, now ? He replied, " Dr. Stetson, you know, is here, and there are two or three others. I got a young Docter here by the name of Ogden. But he has not answered my expectaions ; he is away now, and I don't know whether he will return or not." Little did I then think that this same young Doctor would, in a few weeks, attend Dr. Woodward in his last sickness ; and, still less, from the casual statement that, " he had not answered his expectations," did I suppose, he would become heir to a considerable portion of his estate. Thus, strange things happen sometimes. Dr. Stetson is still living and once carried me well through a fever, and last year represented the town in the Legislature.

WOLLASTON HEIGHTS.

This is a new part of Quincy, that is, as to its settlement. The old hills were there, of course; but very few people inhabited them. Some three years ago, a company, mostly from Boston, bought a large territory of land, and commenced operations. Some one hundred houses, of good style, have already been erected there, and a Hotel, Post Office and a large School-house, a Baptist Church, and all, is in a very prosperous condition. It is, indeed, wonderful, to witness the improvements that have here been made. It is a beautiful spot, and there is scarcely another location in the vicinity of Boston from which so grand a view of both the country and the ocean can be had.

A grand street, called Newport Avenue, has been laid out by the Commissioners, nearly fifty feet wide, straight, smooth, and of easy grade, and to extend from the old John Adams House, the whole length of the Wollaston Heights territory, to Boston.

The gentlemen connected with this enterprize are of the first character, and have, what is always necessary in such a work, a good share of money. These honest, but shrewd men, engaged in this settlement, publish the following :—" Ten reasons for selecting " Wollaston Heights," as a Home.

"First. Land suitable for building purposes is cheaper than at any other place an equal distance from Boston.

Second. The quality of the dwellings now built is better than in any village in the Commonwealth, and the restrictions placed upon all will keep them so.

Third. The place can never be marred by cheap structures or objectionable population, the blot on many an otherwise fair spot.

Fourth. The character of the inhabitants is high in respect to morals and social and intellectual qualities which render any place desirable as a residence.

Fifth. The prospect both of land and sea is unsurpassed in any place around Boston.

Sixth. The domain borders on the Railroad nearly a mile and a half, consequently, no part is very far away; three-fourths of the dwellings must be within seven minutes of the station.

Seventh. Trains run very often and at convenient hours for the accommodation of the people, there being sixteen each way.

Eighth. The Adams Academy, Prof. Dimock, Principal, has just been opened, and is designed to be one of the best in the country; it is about three quarters of a mile from Wollaston, and is free to the resident children of the town.

Ninth. It is only about six miles from Boston, and has the advantage of so many trains, both Sabbath and week-days, that one can easily attend lectures and religious services in Boston, day and evening, with more convenience and less time than in many parts of Boston.

Tenth. The Old Colony Rail Road Company, gives a FREE PASS FOR THREE YEARS to, and from, Boston, to every one who buys or builds a house and becomes a resident there."

CHAPTER IX.

CONTENTS.—The Lyceum in Quincy—Lectures, J. Q. Adams, his Themes—Peter Parley —Debates—New Science of Phrenology—Its wonderful popularity— My Lecture, Exposing its Falacies—Prediction fulfilled—The Records of the Defunct Phrenological Society, of Boston, in one of the Pigeon Holes of the N. E. H. Genealogical Society.

The lyceum was no small affair, as it was the only place where all classes used to congregate. Here, all Quincyites, from an Ex-President of the United States, more than one ex-President of Harvard College and an equal number of ex-Mayors, of Boston,—such as John Quincy Adams, Josiah Quincy, Sen. and Jr. —men of great eminence,—with vast numbers of lesser stars, all did congregate in the Quincy lyceum. Indeed, with the various literary and professional men of the town and others, who had originated here, we formed quite a small army of domestic lecturers. President J. Q. Adams gave the opening lecture several years in succession. I remember his Lecture upon "Aristocracy," which, by defining and comparing the Greek word, he made out to be "the best of any, and of every thing."

Another of his lectures was on "faith, hope and charity," showing how *Charity* was the greatest of the three.

I had the honor, one year, to be chairman of the lecture-Committee, which carried with it, the work of procuring lecturers,—no small job. In this capacity, I engaged, Hon. S. G. Goodrich; then better known, especially, by children, "as Peter Parley." They all knew "Peter Parley," as he appeared in the books, as an old man, with a cane in his hand, and a broad brimmed hat on his head. So, when it had been announced that "Peter Parley" was to lecture, the children were there, all on tip-toe, to see and hear the said "Peter." When I introduced him, a murmur of disapprobation ran through the whole line of juveniles, —"that's not Peter Parley. He wears a great big hat, and is an old man, with a cane." So, they were disappointed in seeing a man, for "Peter Parley," who looked like other men, as the boy said of Washington, "he's only a man."

The lyceum was a great place for debating and arguing questions. I doubt, if Quincy, with all its vast improvements since those days, is even now, in advance of what it was then, in discussing subjects, calculated to "teach the young idea how to shoot."

On one occasion, the question for discussion was, the "morality of Liquor-selling,"—(for, as I have often said, liquor, in some shape, was very apt, in those days, to come in somewhere.) You see, things are different now, since " the only Hotel has been turned into a Scholar's Boarding house, and nobody can get a meal of victuals, or a dram in the town"! (It wasn't so doleful then ;)—which called out a full house. Capt. Brigham, who had formerly made much money by the sale of these popular drinks, had just relinquished the business; and, in order to reap the full benefit of such a sacrifice, made a speech, in which he spoke freely of the evils of selling, &c.—that it was not right to take a man's money without rendering an equivalent—that liquor was of no value, and that it was bad business, and wicked, to take people's money for it—and he had given up the business. This was all very well. But some one; probably, some wagish fellow, here raised an inquiry like this—"Suppose a man has become rich in such an iniquitous business, as has now been described, what is *his* duty, as to making restitution ? In a word, ought not a man, who has become rich by selling rum—if this is such a dishonest business, to disgorge this ill-gotten gain ? This had a look towards a *practical* use; and some thought, such a course of refunding would afford evidence of sincere conversion ! as Zacheus on such an occassion, said, " Lord, the half of my goods, I give to the poor, (a good start) and, if I have taken anything by false accusation, I restore him four fold," out of the other half. I never learned that the Captain made any restitution.

We had not only great men among us in Quincy, in

those days, but others came there to teach us. Among these, were Animal Magnetizers, and the propagators of new Sciences, for, indeed, we Quincyites, were somewhat like the old Athenians, "spending the time in nothing else, but either to tell, or to hear some new thing." Of course, we differed from those " too superstitious" old fellows, as, smong them, the telling came first, which might imply, that they invented some things which they had not heard. This, of course, could never have been the case in Quincy.

PHRENOLOGY, the then "new" science, had taken us by storm. The people were all agog upon this subject. We had lectures of all stamps, by Rev., Doctors, Professors of Colleges, of teaching, and almost all other classes. Rev. Daniel D. Smith, (of whom the reader has already heard), Rev. John Pierpont, of Boston, a man of more than ordinary talent, and a multitude of others, too wise and too talented to be here named, had come to enlighten us upon this new and wonderful discovery, some giving but a single lecture, and others, full courses.

When the tide was at full flood, and all seemed carried away with the new and astounding discoveries, it came the turn of the writer to lecture before the lyceum. Phrenology towered aloft, like " Goliah of Gath." It looked like a foolish attempt for a mere stripling to encounter this giant. But, I ventured to sling "a smooth stone" at him' and to predict what has long since taken place. A Phrenological Society had been formed in Boston, and men of the greatest names and proudest honors, were officers and members of it.

I predicted that, in twenty years, the whole pretended science would be classed in the same category with Mesmerism, Perkins, Tractors, the Weapon Ointment, &c. Suffice it to say, that the Society died, and several years since, the last Secretary of that defunct body, brought into our " Histori'c Genealogical Society," their books, which he requested might be preserved in its Archives , and there they have been for years, and still are, in one of the " Pigeon Holes," of the Society, a monument of the folly and absurdity of what hallucinations great men sometimes fall into.

The following is the Lecture, delivered to the Lyceum in Quincy, April 16th, 1838—thirty-six years ago, this present month of April, 1874.

Phrenology Exposed.

In a Lecture, which, I sometime since, had the honor to deliver before your highly respectable body, an attempt was made to expose some of the impositions practiced upon the community in former times, and at the present day. Particularly, it was designed to scare away the Humbug, *Animal Magnetism*, which had been for sometime buzzing about the land. Whether any thing was effected in that Lecture, or not, it is certain, some birds of a kindred feather still remain; the plumage and texture of whose wings, it may not be amiss to examine. Whether it will be possible to pluck a feather from them, or to clip them, in any degree, must be left entirely to your candor and good sense to determine.

Whether we live in the iron, or golden age, little is

hazarded in saying, that we live in an age of wonders. There are astonishing Phenomena in the moral, intelectual, and religious worlds. Everybody wishes to be somebody, and almost everybody aspires to be more than he really is. Every man, who can use a pen, though " he never had a dozen thoughts in all his life, and never changed their course," must make a book. Philosophers swarm " thick as the locusts, on the land of Nile ; and, though, in the days of Solomon, there was "nothing new under the sun ;" new theories of curious texture and surprising mechanism are now fast developing themselves. Every generation is growing wiser than its predecessor ; and all that the world has known, in former ages, is now cast into the shade. Aristotilean and Pythagorean systems of philosophy, with their numerous descendants are consigned to oblivion, and a new progeny has sprung up in their stead, who are astonishing the world by their mighty achievements. The cobwebs of modern spiders are woven thickly across our path, under the names of panaceas of health, morals, politics, religion, and developments of new sciences.

The one of these cobwebs, which, we shall attempt to brush aside, this evening, is the so called " Science of Phrenology."

I design first to give a brief history of the founders of the science ; second, to explain it ; third, show its fallacy.

1. The history of the Founders of the phrenological science. These were Drs. Gall and Spurzheim. But before speaking, particularly, of them, a word must

be said, respecting some of their predecessors. Aristottle, the Grecian philosopher, more than three hundred years before the christian era, drew up, for substance, a system of craniology, or phrenology. His map of the head, however, was very different from those of modern phrenologists. He made a *small* head the standard of perfection, and indicative of a superior intellect. He made the *forepart* of the head, the abode of *common sense*, the *middle* part the residence of the *imagination, judgment* and *reflection*, and the *backpart*, the home, or seat of the *memory*. This scheme was followed by many writers in the "middle ages."

Since his day, there have been many other schemes, and each has had its separate followers. Bernard Gordon had one, Peter Moula-na-na, another, Michael Servetus, another, and there were many others, too numerous to be named. But among them all, that of the celebrated Swedenborg approached the nearest to the one now current.

The science of craniology, in modern times, originated with Dr. Gall, who was born in Wirtemburg, in Germany, 1758. It was more fully developed by Dr. Spurzheim, born at Treves, 1776, and educated at Vienna, under Dr. Gall. Gall laid the corner-stone of phrenology. It was edged and squared by Dr. Spurzheim, and more subsequently still, received its proper latitudinal and longitudinal position and finer polishings from Dr Combe, of Edinbourgh.

Gall delivered his first course of lectures on phrenology, at Vienna, where he resided, 1796. He continued them for five successive years, when the Austrian Government prohibited him from lecturing further, on account of the immoral and irreligious tendency of his doctrines. Persecution, however, operated as it generally does, and increased the anxiety of people to hear, and he still continued his operations.

Soon, he associated with him Spurzheim, his favorite pupil. In 1805, they journeyed together through Germany, Prussia, and Switzerland, to France. They visited most of the principal towns and taught their doctrines. Their stay at each place was short; not long enough, says Gall, to form practical pupils, and he advised not to repeat the experiments, as it was not easy to do so.

Gall and Spurzheim travelled and labored together until 1813, when they separated, and each conducted his investigations alone.

Gall made Paris his home, where he acquired great celebrity, accumulated a large fortune, and died in 1828, at the age of 71.

Spurzheim travelled through several kingdoms on the continent; visited England, Scotland and Ireland; took up his abode at Paris in 1817, and in 1832, visited America. He landed at New York, and came directly to Boston, where he was received with great courtesy and respect, and commenced lecturing and examining heads, with a promise of much success. But his career was short. He died of a fever within three months from the time of his arrival in the city, and was interred at Mount Auburn, with every mark of respect; where a beautiful monument has been erected to his memory by the citizens of Boston.

He was, indeed, a wonderful man,—full of novelties, and not a little tinctured with infidelity. His schemes were discarded, as crude and visionary, even, by the neologising philosophers of his own country. But, as though crossing the Atlantic, could regenerate folly, and baptize infidelity in the waters of the sanctuary, the exiled philosopher was received among us, not only with hospitality, but also, with unbounded admiration. American philosophers, and divines, even, have not only opened their hearts to give him a cordial welcome, but have, also, yielded up their understandings to his control. We are willing that this land, ever ready to succor the exiled from the old world, should form an asylum for the unfortunate Doctor. We are willing his dust should find a quiet resting place in this land of the Pilgrims. We are willing his industry (for industrious undoubtedly he was) should be duly applauded. But, we are not willing to bend our own necks awry, because Alexander's, the Great, was naturally so; nor, to raise one shoulder far above the other, because, "Amon's great son" had this natural defect, nor, to render ourselves cross-eyed, because Pope could not see without squinting. Nor, are we willing to swallow Dr. Spurzheim, bone and muscle, with all his crudities, simply, because he was industrious, and started many novelties. If we mistake not, we have heard quite too much of the "great philosopher." We believe, many wise and good men have listened too much, and held out too much encouragement to the itinerating retailers of his mental quackery. His too volumes are characterised by low vanity and prejudice against religion. His conclusions are anything, but the result of calm calculation and analogical deduction. He more resembles the alchymist, than the philosopher. He is always seeking for mind externally. He ransacks all the various chambers of the skull, shakes about the brains, and gives their dimensions,

Such, is a brief history of Gall and Spurzheim, the illustrious founders of modern phrenology, and, we predict, their whole scheme will be buried in oblivion in a few years.

11. I am to explain the Science.

PHRENOLOGY IS THE SCIENCE OF MIND.

Phrenology teaches that the brain is the organ of all our instincts, propensities, sentiments, aptitudes, intellectual faculties, and moral qualities. That each of these, has a portion of the brain, specifically, appropriated to it, and, that the developments of the several organs, or parts of the brain, are manifested by protuberances on the cranium or skull; and by examining these protuberances, or bumps, an adept in the science can ascertain and describe the disposition and intellectual and moral character of the person.

Or, it teaches, that the brain is the material organ of the mind—that, in proportion to the volume of the brain, (other things being equal) will be the power of the mental discoveries—that the exercise of the mind increases the development of the brain—that the form of its various parts, and their adaptation to each other, determine the character of the mind,—that each of the sub-organs of the brain is the appropriate seat of a propensity, sentiment, or faculty—that a specific cerebral organ is necessary to the existence of each original propensity; and, that each specific mental operation must be performed by means of its appropriate organ,—that the brain is composed of three, four or five organs, or pairs of organs, all commencing at the top of the spinal marrow, and radiating to the surface of the brain—that they commence at a point, and like so many inverted cones, become more and more voluminous, as they approach the cranium, or skull, until they are bounded by its walls—that the strength of each particular faculty is in proportion to the size of the organ, or cone, in which it resides.— The size of these organs is estimated by their length and breadth; and, consequently, each prominence of the skull indicates the size, or degree of development of that organ of the brain, which is placed immediately under it, and, of course, the power of the mental faculty, sentiment, or passion, in which it resides,— that, to exercise any particular faculty of the mind will promote the size or development of the appropriate organ of that faculty.

Such are the principles of phrenological science, so called, as stated by the founders.

An eminent writer on this subject, says:—" By a knowledge of phrenology and craniology, the experenced phrenologist is enabled to judge of the natural amount, and general character of the intellects of individuals, by an inspection of their heads." For this purpose, the cranium has been mapped out into thirty-four or thirty-five distinct territories, which are supposed to correspond with the bases of the different organs of the brain, in position, form, and size. When any one of these is so prominent as to tower above the neighboring parts of the skull, the organ, which is distinctly under such size, or swell, is said to be full, and the faculty proportionately strong and vigorous.

These thirty-four or thirty-five organs have been made to constitute three distinct families,—one for the animal propensities, whose domain is in the back of the head—one for the moral sentiments, whose home is the upper story of the head, and the third, for the mental faculties, whose abode is the forepart of the head, or the forehead.

III. We are to show the fallacy of this pretended science.

One would have supposed, in the outset, that a scheme, which arrogates to itself the title of the science of the mind, would have laid its foundations in consistency with the established laws of mental and moral philosophy. But, instead of this, the whole fabric is professedly built upon the anatomy of an organ; and that organ, the most frail, and delicate, of the whole body; for such is the brain, and yet, this wild scheme would feign make us believe, that the growth and development of this organ, not only mould the bone of the head in infancy, but also, that the cultivation of different faculties, so increases different parts of the brain, as to produce a prominence, or bump, upon the external surface of the skull, by which the form and shape of the bony casement is so changed, that the phrenologist can detect and describe the moral and intellectual character of the individual, by seeing, and feeling, and measuring the head.

Now, if this scheme does not look wild and visionary, at the outset, we know not what would look so.

But, as it is based upon the anatomy of material parts, we shall not examine it, simply by looks.

If it can be shown that the anatomy of the brain, its structure and organization and that of the skull, and other parts concerned, do not harmonize with, but are directly opposed to, this scheme, the supposed science must fall. That such is the fact will now be attempted to be shown.

1. The structure and organization of the brain itself present a physical impossibility to the whole scheme.

Phrenologists tell us there are three grand divisions, or tenements in the brain, each the residence of a separate family of organs. But what says the brain itself? (A brain was exhibited). Here is one, and but one, grand, horizontal division. There are no walls to prevent these houses of the animal propensities, moral sentiments and intellectual faculties from all mingling together. There is not so much of a division line, as the three families had, who all resided in one room, that of a chalk-mark on the floor. The brain itself, then, defeats their scheme, and converts their three grand houses into two. If they had told us, there were two separate families, the one, residing in the upper story of the brain, and the other in the lower, they would have had some foundation for such a general division; but, now, they have none, for their divisions.

Being thus easily relieved of one of their grand divisions, or, having thus destroyed their three palaces, or superior houses, we will now knock at the doors and attempt to look into their smaller domicils, (if, indeed, they, are to be found.)

Phrenologists tell us, there are thirty-four or thirty-five, of these cells, or organs, all commencing at the top of the spinal marrow, somewhat resembling, though not perfectly, an inverted cone, pyramid, or cider-tap, having the base outward. These are all separate apartments, and the abode of separate propensities, &c.— But what says the brain? (brain shown) Here, instead of thirty-five separate cells, or organs, or pairs of organs, we find multiplied and beautiful convolutions, plainly discernable, through its whole structure. They are all interwoven together.

Now, this completely overthrows the possibility of the existence of such separate cells or organs; for, each of these convolutions would, not only cross from one organ into another, of different, and even opposite, functions; but, also, be divided itself, by the imaginary line, which separates one organ, or cell, from another; consequently, parts of the same convoluion of the brain, must, not only, perform these various, and essentially different offices; but, must be active in one portion, and inactive in another; and, as each organ is described, to be of inverted conical form, the apex or point being at the spinal marrow, or inferior portion of the cerebrum, and radiating to the surface next the skull, it is manifest, that every organ must be formed wholly irrespective of these convolutions; the lines, which divide the one from the other; passing latitudinally, longitudinally, and diagonally, through their successive layers. What then becomes of these phrenological cells or organs? The convolutions of the brain have commingled them in one general mass— have thrown their supposed walls into one general heap of ruins.

There is also an essential difference in the convolutions of the brain in the two hemispheres. Now, phrenologists locate each of the organs pertaining to the same propensity, or faculty, in the same relative position in each hemisphere. If such organs existed in each side of the brain, it is strange, that they shonld be entirely unlike in their organization; especially, when they perform the same office. And, yet, the variations of the opposite organs show such a dissimilarity.

Furthermore, no part of the brain, when dissected, discovers any os those compartments, or organs, the supposed existence of which is the foundation of phrenological science. No such divisions have ever been discovered. No phrenologist, not even the illustrious founders of the false science, have ever ventured to assert, that any such discovery has been made upon dissection.

That there are no such tenements in the brain, and that the intellect does not depend upon these supposed organs, is proved to be true, by the statements of many eminent Anatomists. They tell us that large portions of the brain have been destroyed, and in so many different parts of the head, as to sweep away nearly all the supposed phrenological organs ; and yet, not a single case has occurred, of such partial destruction of mind, as must have been the result, if the doctrine of separate organs were true.

It has, furthermore, been demonstrted, that the elevations and depressions upon the brain, in no case, have corresponded with the *bumps* upon the outward surface of the cranium.

Here, then, we might leave the subject, with the incontrovertible fact, that, the structure of the brain itself destroys the science. We must not, however' leave it here, for, as it is a new and flippant science, it must be finished at once, so that the record of its once having lived, shall be found only in the catacombs of a bygone age.

2. The *skull* or *cranium*, presents as inseparable an objection to the science of phrenology, as the configuration, or structure of the brain : For, if the supposed phrenological organs really existed in the brain, it would be impossible to ascertain the volume of that organ by measurement or observation.

The phrenologist tells us, " We are able to judge of the natural amount and general character of individuals from an inspection of their heads."

A fundamental principle of the science is, that the intellect is in proportion to the volume of the brain, and this amount of the brain is to be ascertained by a measurement of the head. For this purpose, two instruments have been invented by Phrenologists, which, I have neither time, nor will it be necessary to describe, as I trust, to demonstrate, that there are natural impossibilities to ascertaining any thing, that can be depended upon, by such a measurement, however perfect, may be the instruments. In the first place, the integuments of the head present an insuperable objection to such a measurement. The human brain is entirely covered within the skull, by three distinct coats, or membranes, which separately interpose between the brain itself and the interior of the skull.

(COATS SHOWN.)

This shows the *three* coats, or membranes, with which the brain is enveloped—the dura-mater—the tunica arachnoid, and the pia-mater. The first is thick, dense, and opaque, the other two, very thin and transparent.

The integuments of the head are much thicker at the meridian of life, than in infancy, or old age. They vary much in persons of the same age, sex and condition, and of these variations, we cannot possibly judge in a living person. We must first kill the man before we can discover the size of the head; but, until, these are known, we cannot tell the amount of brain.

In the next place, the different thicknesses of the skull, in different individuals, presents as insuperable an objection to ascertaining the amount of brain, by measuring, as the integuments of the head. Two skulls of persons of the same age and character have been found to differ from one-eighth of an inch, to nearly an inch in thickness. There is frequently a difference of one-half.

(SUCH SKULLS SHOWN.)

Now, what could a phrenologist tell by the delicacy of his touch, and the piercing of his eye, and both, aided by his craniometer, as to the thickness of these skulls, or the amount of brain in each? Would he have guessed, the one of the stout sailor to have been only half as thick, as that of the beautiful female? Who, then, can tell, by a measurement of the head, any thing about the amount of brain? It is, manifestly, impossible. It is a cob-web to be brushed away.

Three skilful Anatomists made the following experiments.—They took five heads of the same external dimensions; and upon reducing the brain in each to fluid ounces, they found more than twice the amount of brain in two of the heads that there was in the other three. They repeated their experiments upon a great variety of crania, and found from one-fourth to one-half the amount of difference between different skulls.

We ask, again, how then, is it possible to ascertain

the amount af brain, by a measurement of the head, when, there is such a difference in the amount of the brains in the heads of the same external dimensions. Certainly no phrenologist can tell, by an inspection of the head, the thickness of the integuments, or, of the skull; but, until he knows these, he cannot know the amount of brain in different heads.

Let us now look at the bumps, or, the supposed basis of the phrenological organs, and also inquire what can be known by measuring; or attempting to measure them.

We have spoken of the different thickness of the skulls of different individuals. We now remark, that a great diversity exists in the thickness of different parts of the same skull. This may be seen, by this skull.

(SKULL SHOWN.)

Different parts of the same skull, then, being of different thickness, no person can possibly tell whether a protuberance on the exterior of the head, is produced by a development of the internal organ, according to the principles of phrenology, or, by an increased thickness of the skull at that place.

And, furthermore, as though nature had determined to contradict every shadow of evidence in proof of such a pretended science, numerous dissections have shown, that the bump on the external surface, presented a convexity, instead of a concavity within; a bump of bone projecting inward corresponding to the external bump. Now, if these facts,—facts attested by numerous and skilful Anatomists, do not completely overthrow all just claims to phrenological science, then, is it in vain to attempt to defeat any pretentions by an array of facts.

One remark more, respecting the skull, as connected with the bumps. It is composed of two tables, or layers of bone, separated by a third layer, and, often, by cavities of greater or less extent, which it is impossible to determine during life. It must, indeed, be an active brain, which can press so hard, as to protrude, and throw out a bump, through such a substance, of from one-eighth, to nearly an inch, in thickness.

If these organs all existed, in perfect symmetry, and (which has been shown to be impossible) as phrenologists conjecture, common sense teaches, that nothing could be certainly known of them by the bumps on the skull, as it is not possible, that they should be made by the brain, and, (as we have already seen), that the protuberances of the brain have never been found to correspond with those on the skull.

We must first *scalp* the individual, after the manner of the Indian, before we could tell any thing of the size or location of such organs. What a useful science to a man while he lives!

We will now glance at some of the *data*, by which, Phrenologists make up their judgment, respecting the characters of individuals, from a measurement of the bumps, or protuberances, on the skull. Judging from these data, we should think there were some chances against arriving at a correct judgment. They tell us, the person, who is to be the judge, by which, is meant, the Phrenologist himself, must have good form, size and locality; and, then, he must understand the doctrine; and this, he cannot do, unless he have all the thirty-five organs in good power, for, every one, phrenologists, or not, admits, that a good faculty is necessary, rightly, to apprehended the same in another. Now, we are told by a distinguished phrenologist, that Gall had neither form nor locality; and, as these are essential to the science, how far, are we to suppose, his inspection of heads, led him to form a correct opinion of the character of the individuals inspected? And, how many can be supposed to have all the thirty-five organs in perfection?

And then, the volume of every particular organ, in order to ascertain its particular power, must be accurately measured. Unless the measure be accurate, the power of the organ cannot be known. Now, setting aside the impossibility of a measurement from the skull and integuments of the head, (of which we have before spoken,) let us inquire, as to the probability of arriving at a correct measurement of these oragns. Every organ, it will be recollected is inverted, having its base outward. And, as a very trifling error in measuring the base of a cone, makes a great difference in the solid contents, as there is no line of boundary defined, or visible, on the outside, it will be readily perceived that an accuratcc masurcment is not easily obtained.

And then, again, we are told, that, one organ may be so largely developed as to encroach on the province of its neighbor; and, as we cannot tell how often this happens, it seems difficult to tell how much lee-way to allow for such encroachments.

And then, again, we are told that there may be a large *frontal sinus,* or vacant space, between the inner and outer bone of the forehead; and, as it is difficult to get between these bones to measure this space, we hardly know how much allowance to make for the difference.

And then, " the firmness of texture" in the brain must be accurately judged of; when we know it can be only guessed at—and then, the temperament must be rightly estimated—And, then again, they tell us, the powers may have been directed to vice, instead of virtue, by external circumstances, and in such cases, the whole character, intellectual and moral, may be mistaken. And, as we have no means of ascertaining how often this happens, it seems, this single item must destroy the whole scheme. Was there ever a greater tissue of absurdities on which great men have come to lecture us!

And, then again, certain combinations of propensities and sentiments may be more favorable to the activity of some particular organs; and some organs may be naturally more active, than others, without regard to size.

Now, as these, and multitudes of other similar considerations are in attendance upon the correct measurement of the phrenological organs, and, consequently, to arriving at a correct opinion respecting the intellectual and moral character of individuals, it would seem as though any one but a Phrenologist would despair of coming to a correct judgment of any one man.

A certain writer, upon reading Combe on phrenology, took care to minute down the difficulties of coming to an exact measurement of the phrenological organs; and, consequently, to a correct judgment of the character of individuals from an inspection of their heads. He sums up his investigations in the following words: "What an invaluable discovery must it be, that enables a practical and professed phrenologist to give a true character of the head once in 2,700,000 times! And what a noble basis on which to rear moral science, education, and the awful interests of religion! one chance in 2,700,000 times! We know very well that they do judge cases more successfully than this would indicate; but, it is by observing eyes, countenance, tone, air, &c., &c., and not by virtue of the science."

Probably, the calculations of this writer are not far from being correct, as they are based upon the difficulties which Combe, himself, an eminent phrenologist, suggests, as lying in the way of making an exact measurement; and, consequently, of arriving at a correct judgment from an inspection of the head.

It is a phrenological principle (other things being equal) that the larger the head, the greater the amount of brain,—and, consequently, the more intellect.

"If, says Combe, we take two heads, in sound

health, of similar age, in each of which several organs are similar in their proportions, but the one of which is large, and the other small, and if the preponderance of power of manifestation is not in favor of the first, then phrenology must be abandoned as destitute of foundation."

Having shown that no just estimate of the amount of the brain can be ascertained from the size of the head, as some heads of the same dimensions have twice the amount of brain in them that others have, let us now inquire how far facts demonstrate the truth of the above proposition.

If, by the volume of brain is meant its absolute size, then, it would follow, of course, that men of small stature must invariably possess inferior intellects to those of larger size, (a theory which we little folks, like myself, are not always ready to admit). And, we do not see why it would not also follow, that the whale, and elephant and ox, and many other animals, as they have larger heads, and consequently, more brain than man, should not be his superiors in intellect. Here, our phrenologists have, also, to contend with facts.

It is the testimony of one who has enjoyed extensive opportunities for dissecting the brains of literary and intellectual men of high rank, and of comparing them with the brains of men in humble life, that, while, he had often found a large brain connected with superior mental endowments, the reverse had been found true in an equal number of cases. Such, he states as the result of his many years experience.

And this is the statement of no less a man than Dr. J. C. Warren, of Boston. One individual, he says, highly renowned for the variety and extent of his native talent, was found upon dissection, to have an uncommonly small brain.

But perhaps it will be said, phrenologists in the above proposition, do not speak of the brain in its *absolute*, but its *relative* size. With what, then, we ask, is it to be compared? With the size of the face, or neck, or spinal marrow, or cerebral nerves, or, with the whole body? Phrenologists have not been very plain on this point. Some things seem to indicate, however, that, the power of the mind is proportionate to the volume of the brain, as compared with the whole body. It is intimated, that as we descend the scale of mental existence, through the various tribes of animals, the brain will be found to be diminished in size. But, here, again, facts are on the opposite side. The investigations of several eminent naturalists prove the reverse, often, to be true. Haller, Wishing, Blumenback and Cuvier, with many other anatomists tell us the contrary. Baron de Cuvier represents the brain in man to be in proportion to the whole body, as one to thirty. While, in one species of the monkey, it is as one to twenty-two, in another species as one to twenty-five, in another, as one to twenty-four, and in another, as one to twenty-eight. So that upon this principle, these species of the monkey would be more intellectual than man. The same would be true of various species of birds.

Hence, if, by the volume of the brain he meant its *absolute* size, upon the phrenological principle, of which we are now speaking, the elephant and whale and many other animals would be more intellectual than man. But if its relative size in comparison with the whole body be meant, then, several species of the monkey and of birds would be more intellectual than man. Either horn of this dilemma is calculated to gore the lord of this lower creation. We have been accustomed to consider man somewhat superior in intellectual endowments to elephants and whales and oxen, or to monkeys or birds, but it seems, according to the new science, we must have been mistaken.

We do not deny that there is a difference in the natural capacities of men. This is demonstrated by every day's experience. But we want proof that this difference depends on the amount of brain —We want proof that men's minds are developed in their progress through life in proportion to the increased size of the head. Now, the proof of these suppositions being true, they cannot agree with such facts as we find the anatomy of the parts in question present to the contrary. This proof we cannot have, while we see as many men renowned for their intellectual power, with small heads as with large ones. Neither analogy nor facts sustain the proposition that the mere volume of the brain is the criterion of the intellectual powers.

Aristotle made a small head the standard of perfection. And it is believed, if the Founders of modern phrenological science had taken the same ground, viz., the reverse of what they have taken, they would have found as much proof of their position, and as many followers as they now have.

Persons have been known to lose a considerable part of the brain, and still find their mental powers increase. But according to phrenological principles, this would be impossible.

A case of this kind was communicated to the Medical Society of Ghent. That of a young man, rather inferior, or by no means surpassing ordinary young men in intelligence. He lost, by the shot of a pistol, two tea-cups full of brain. He lived two years after the loss with his intellect very much improved. There are many cases of a similar character on record. Now, these do not give much countenance to the idea, that, the power of the intellect depends on the amount of the brain ; and, they militate much against the the theory of the phrenological houses or organs.

I have chosen to show how completely this pretended science may be overthrown by anatomical facts, rather, than by metaphysical arguments, because, if there are physical impossibilities in the anatomy of the parts concerned, every one must see, and admit the absurdity of the scheme.

CHAPTER X.

CONTENTS.—The cause of Temperance 1836—John Quincy Adams Address on Temperance—Rev. E. Taylor's—The Address of the Writer on Temperance.

Some hints have already been given in former chapters of the State of temperance in Quincy; in the period here referred to, as have been instanced in driving away Rev. M. H. Smith, for giving a good Temperance Lecture, and in getting Rev. John Gregory indicted for bigamy, because the temperance people elected him to represent the town in the " Great and General Court." These indicate some action in this matter. Other items might be named, showing that the good cause now and then, met with a head flaw. To tell the plain unvarnished truth, there were some places in this most respectable town where a poor famishing traveller, could, by paying well for it, get a dram; and, it was said, probably, by some evil minded persons, that a man or two had been seen, occasionlly, to stagger from strong drink; and, I do remember myself to have seen a person, whom I would have presumed had drank too much, had he been anywhere else but in Quincy. But, as he was on Quincy soil, of course, I must have been mistaken.

Then, too, John Quincy Adams gave an excellent Temperance Address in our little Church, which was attended by Rev. John Pierpont and Deacon Grant, of Boston. Mr. Adams, in this Address, admitted that wine might be taken in moderation, from which Mr. Pierpont dissented. We were all very much interested in the argument that followed this address between these two champions, Mr. Adams and Pierpont. Mr. P's last dart was, " my venerable Friend, you will admit that the vine cannot stand alone, but must have something to lean upon." At this, Mr. Adams and some others of us laughed.

Then, we had a Lecture on Temperance from Rev. Edward T. Taylor, the Seaman's Preacher, of Boston, and it was a grand one. Mr. Taylor was in his element, his nerves were well strung, his tongue loosed, and he thrilled the audience. We invited him to come again, and he did, but he " had become weak, like another man," and was really, to use his own expression on another occasion, " clear down to the lee scupper." This time, he spoiled all the good he did in his first Address.

Then came the following, which I give as a specimen of the temperance movement thirty-eight years ago this present month :—

AN ADDRESS DELIVERED BEFORE THE TEMPERANCE ASSOCIATION OF QUINCY, MASS., JULY 4, 1837. BY REV. W. M. CORNELL, PASTOR OF A CHURCH IN QUINCY.

On this day, 1776, the British colonies in America declared themselves free and independent States.

It will be my object on the present occasion to draw a comparison between the declaration of American independence and the achievement of that event, and the declaration of independence and liberation from the thraldom of intemperance in America.

1. The colonies were oppressed.

In their declaration of independence, they say, "The history of the present king of Great Britain, is a history of repeated injuries and usurpations, all having in direct object the establishment of an absolute tyranny over these States. To prove this, let facts be submitted to a candid world. He has refused his assent to laws the most wholesome and necessary to the public good. He has forbidden his governors to pass laws of immediate and pressing importance, unless suspended in their operation till his assent should be obtained; and when so suspended, he has utterly neglected to attend to them.

"He has refused to pass laws for the accommodation of large districts of people, unless those people would relinquish the right of representation in the legislature —a right inestimable to them, and formidable to tyrants only. He has called together legislative bodies, at places unusual, uncomfortable, and distant from the depository of their public records, for the sole purpose of fatiguing them into compliance with his measures. He has dissolved representative houses repeatedly, for opposing with manly firmness, his invasions on the rights of the people. He has endeavored to prevent the population of these States. He has made judges dependant on his will alone. He has erected a multitude of new offices, and sent *hither* swarms of officers to harass our people and eat out their substance. He has kept among us standing armies in time of peace, without the consent of our legislatures."

The signers of the declaration go on to say, that "he has instituted mock trials—cut off their trade with other parts of the world—imposed taxes without their consent—deprived them of the privilege of trial by jury," &c.

Thus the colonies were oppressed.

The nation was oppressed by intemperance. From Maine to Georgia, and the Atlantic to the "far west," this oppression reigned. I now go back to the time when temperance societies first existed in our country. I have said, a wide spread oppression reigned from intemperance. Do you ask for the proof? We will call up the witnesses and see if they will not testify as plainly as the signers of the declaration of American independence testified to their oppressions. And, as *Interest* always stands pre-eminent in the mind of man, the first witness we shall call is *Expense*. To Expense I would say, Do you know the cost of intemperance in the United States? Answer. It has been computed by the best judges, that for intoxicating liquors, there are expended annually in this country, more than forty millions of dollars. And the expense of pauperism occasioned by the use of these liquors, is more than *twelve* millions of dollars; making in all over fifty millions annually. Such is the testimony of *Expense*, a witness not slow to be heard in all ordinary cases.

The next witness to be called is *Peace*.

You are called upon to testify what you know, Mr. Peace, of the evils of intemperance upon the community. "I know that I am often disturbed by intemperance I know intemperance to be the author of four fifths of all the riots, fightings, domestic trials, separations between husbands and wives, disobedience of children to parents, lawsuits, arsons, robberies and murders in the land. I am fully convinced that three fourths of the crimes against society, and which disturb my quiet, are occasioned by intemperance. And if I am called upon to testify from the records of criminal courts, I can show these statements to be facts by the most unimpeachable witnesses."

Such is the testimony of *Peace*.

The next witness is *Health*. And what says Health? You will please testify. Is alcohol, in any of its combinations, ever beneficial to you?

No. Never. Its effects are most disastrous to me. It promotes neither the growth, nor vigor, nor beauty of any of the bodily organs. The stomach—the great mill, or reservoir on which I depend for existence, will not digest it. It is resisted by every one of the bodily organs, until it is thrown out of the system, without making either bone, muscle, sinew, flesh, blood, or even a finger nail. On the contrary, every part of the animal man suffers from its use. Stimulating drinks produce a thickening of the inner coats of the stomach, and a constant effusion of cold phlegm, of which every inveterate drinker complains. The *liver* is either enlarged or inflamed, Says one of the best anatomists in our land, " take any two individuals who are alike in all other respects, except that one drinks freely every day, though not to intoxication, and the other abstains entirely from the stimulus, and the former will present to the eye of an anatomist, a liver differing from that of the other in color or size, that will be sufficiently indicative of unhealthy action." The effect of ardent spirit is to destroy the appetite, and derange the healthy action of all the digestive functions. The blood is turned darker and loses its vitality. The brain becomes hardened, and, in some cases, its cavities have been found filled with diluted alcohol, which has readily blazed upon the application of a lighted candle. The *skin* becomes red and inflamed. The *muscles* weak and trembling. The voice sepulchral and tremulous, as though the tongue were partially affected by palsy. Jaundice, gout, rheumatism, dropsy, palsy, epilepsy, apoplexy, and dyspepsia in all its multitudinous forms, arise from the use of ardent spirit. Such is the testimony of Health. No man can tell the number of cases where health has been absolutely destroyed, and death ensued in consequence of the use of alcoholic drinks. It has been a *dire oppression*, reigning to a greater or less extent through every portion of our highly favored country.

The last witness which we shall call, (though many

more might be called,) is *Intellect*. And what says Intellect? Have you ever derived any benefit from alcohol?

No. Never. Alcohol produces a pernicious effect upon all the powers of the mind. All the intellectual faculties, which raise man above the brute and render him lord of this world, are intimately associated with the brain. They grow with its growth, strengthen with its strength, and decline with its decay. Every temporay excitement of the brain, arouses the operations of the mind in a corresponding degree; and when this is done, the excitement soon produces fatigue. Alcohol has often been taken to excite the powers of the mind, and, unquestionably, has often done it for a time. But then, its effect has ultimately been injurious. I know not that any of my audience read the poetry of Lord Byron, and probably the less of it you read the better. His Childe Harold was written when the author practised total abstinence from spirituous liquors; and his Don Juan, when he jaded his muse with gin. The former is amusing, chaste, stirring, and beautiful; the latter presents a good commentary on the demoralizing influence of such stimulus. It breathes a debasing and polluting atmosphere.

In past ages, the study, the pulpit, and the hall of legislation, have borne rueful testimony to the direful effects of alcoholic drinks upon the intellect of man; for alcohol has pervaded every rank and class of society. Like the oppression of the British lion upon the colonies, it has oppressed all ranks and classes of society. No place has been too elevated, no profession too sacred, for the touch of this harpey to pollute. Go to our insane hospitals. *Three-fourths* of their wretched inmates, in one way or another, have been brought to *insanity* by ardent spirit. Could all the sufferings of man be brought before you, no doubt you would find far the greater proportion of them has arisen from the use of alcoholic liquors. Thus the testimony of Intellect is, that alcohol is an oppressor.

Now in the mouth of these four witnesses, Expense, Peace, Health, and Intellect, I ask, is not the fact estabished, that our land was sorely oppressed by intemperance? It was indeed a frightful oppression. If any doubt it, let them make the supposition, that a foreign nation should demand of us, and take from us, fifty millions of dollars annually; should subject us to laws that destroyed the peace of our country, neighborhoods, and families, to the same extent that alcohol has; should maim and destroy the health of so many of our citizens, and derange and render insane as many minds, and ask, if this would not be oppression? It would be such oppression as would not be tolerated.

Do you ask where this oppression reigned? I answer, every where. In this town, in every town, in every village and every city throughout this vast country. It was alcohol, in some of its combinations, that was filling the channels of death to overflowing.

It is believed that this was the giant sin, the master evil of the day; that all the other evils and curses of the land—all the judgments and scourges that ever visited this devoted world of sin and death, were small in comparison with this. Intemperance is the sin of sins, the scorpion of scorpions, that can single-handed outdo them all. Well may it be called legion, for its evils are many. It has the fierceness of a wounded tiger—is uncontrollable as a famished wolf—and, as it has stalked through our land, its path has been marked with human gore. It has spared no age, sex, character, or condition—manifested no relentings—mocked at the cries of the helpless—snatched from the child the last morsel of bread, and thrown him houseless and pennyless into the street.

Who will dare say that the nation was not oppressed.

2. The patriots of these colonies bore the oppression of their "father land" for a long time. "In every stage of these oppressions," say they, "we have petitioned for redress in the most humble terms. Our repeated petitions have been answered by repeated injury. We have warned them from time to time," &c. Good men bore the oppression of intemperance for a long time. They saw and felt the evil and remonstrated against it, but in vain. They knew not the remedy. Ministers preached, legislatures enacted laws, and *all drank on.*

3. The colonies found there was no way of emancipating themselves from oppression, but by liberating themselves entirely from the oppressor. They would not use their commodities.

The friends of temperance saw no way of liberating

themselves from the oppression of intemperance, but by an entire renunciation or non-intercourse with the oppressor. Abstinence, total, and forever, they found to be the only remedy. Actuated by the same spirit of resistance to all oppression, which prompted the heroes of the revolution to steep in the great pot of Boston harbor, three hundred and forty-two chests of tea at one mess, some of them closed at once their distilleries, and poured the contents of their rum hogsheads upon the ground. As the colonies would not submit to taxation, or recognize the right of the principle in the least, or pay even threepence on a pound of tea, so the champions of temperance, respecting alcohol, adopted as their invariable motto, " touch not, taste not, handle not." This was found, wherever used, to operate like the club of Hercules in slaying the monster.

4. The colonies when they saw how they might become freemen, *combined* their strength, and thus escaped the paw of the British lion.

They not only said, that the colonies *were*, and of right ought *to be, free* and *independent* States, but that *we*, not individually, but *we collectively*, to the sustaining and the accomplishing this object, pledge *our* lives, *our* fortunes, and *our* sacred honor. Suppose the colonies had labored and fought as *individuals* only, what would have been their strength? It would have been but weakness. Divided, they would have fallen before the oppressor. The friends of temperance found they must combine their strength, or they could never be liberated from the oppression of intemperance. While each labored separate and alone, they showed what the colonies would have been, had they labored and fought in the same manner. A band of patriots indeed, but for want of union, divided, mutilated, and broken assunder. Or, they resembled a company collected to raise a house, each one lifting indeed with all his might, but on different pieces of timber and at different times. The building would never go up. But let their strength be *combined*, and *all* lift at once, and the house is raised—the work is done.

So, when the friends of temperance began to combine their strength, labors, and counsels, by organizing temperance societies, the enemy felt the shock. Those engaged in the manufacture, and vending, and drinking of alcoholic liquors, felt that something would be done. Some of them, indeed, like a majority of the British parliament, took a decided stand against the temperance cause. *Lord Norths* were found, who accounted them enemies to the general government and welfare; but, even from the ranks of those who were supposed to be opposed to the reform, here and there, was heard the sweet, melodious, silver-toned voice, and seen the firm, inflexible, and patriotic principle of of a Chatham.

It is to be attributed wholly to the combined efforts of the colonies, that the independence of these United States was achieved. We believe it is wholly to the combined efforts of the pioneers of temperance, that the reformation has been placed where it now stands-

5. The patriots of the revolution signed the decla. ration of independence. They did not say, we can be independent enough without signing a paper, or giving a pledge. *John Hancock*, whom this town had the honor, and till the flag of liberty ceases to wave o'er the ocean, and the banner of freedom sinks into the western Pacific, shall have the praise of rearing— *John Hancock* signed his name in large letters, in the centre of the declaration of American indepenence. He was followed by an host of others whose names are now dear to every patriot's bosom, and from whose ashes, through unborn generations, will arise a fragrance grateful as that of the Phenix. They gave a pledge—"our lives, our fortunes, and our sacred honor." The champions of temperance signed the declaration of independence from the oppression of intemperance. They did not say, we can be temperate without signing a paper. They were not afraid of signing away their liberty. They did not say, we will give no pledge for the promotion of this object. Unhesitatingly, they put their names in black and white, and came out openly in defence of the cause they had espoused. Some, indeed, who pretended to be friends to the cause, stood back and seemed doubtful "whereunto the thing would grow." Some, indeed, seemed disposed to wait until they saw whether "Israel or Amalek would prevail." Here and there a *Tory* might be seen skulking about the outworks of the reforming process, and croaking the fears of

those who dread innovation, and who seem to wish that all things remain as they were, from the creation till the millennium. Here and there, a *petulant one* cried out, Why need you meddle with the concerns of others? Fear sometimes saw lions and the sons of Anak in the way. The cry of traitors and enemies to the government, was sometimes heard from those whose craft was endangered. They saw, in the organization of societies composed of *all* classes, ranks, and conditions in the community, fearful signs of *sectarianism*. They trembled, lest by and by, the reformation should go farther and bring them down to a state of starvation.

And here and there, a *Benedict Arnold*, alarmed by his fears, and intimidated by the threats of the enemy, and warped by his selfishness, and mortified by his disappointed ambition, turned traitor, and left the ranks of temperance and became a brigadier-general among the troops in the mother country of anti-temperance. But, as in the American revolution, the Lord raised up such men as were needed to carry forward the work; as in the very season when he was needed, he formed, and in the very station where his presence was necessary, he placed a Washington, a Hancock, an Adams: so, in the cause of temperance, at the very time, and in the very place where they were needed, he placed a Beecher, a Hewitt, a Frost, an Edwards, a Sargent, a Hunt, and an host of others, whose hand, and heart, and life, and fortune, and sacred honor, were pledged to carry forward the work of reform.

6. The patriots of the revolution accomplished their object. They emancipated themselves entirely from the oppression of Great Britain.

The friends of temperance have accomplished more than their sanguine feelings dared hope. They have already seen more than two millions of persons in the United States cease to use ardent spirit, and several hundred thousand of them cease to use any intoxicating liquors. They have already seen more than three thousand distilleries stop. They now witnes but three of these pest-houses in the whole State of New Hampshire. They have already seen more than eight thousand merchants cease to traffic in this poison; more than ten thousand drunkards cease to use intoxicating liquor. It has been estimated by the most competent judges that in the single State of New York, more than three millions of dollars were saved the last year by the temperance reform. They have already seen ardent spirit, and to a considerable extent, all intoxicating liquors, banished from funerals and weddings; from tables and the social board; from public trainings and town meetings; from the navy; from hundreds and thousands of farms. They have already seen whole countries where the poison is not sold; and they have already seen many who profess to use it moderately, hide their jug or their bottle in a basket, or under their cloak, or pretend that it contained molasses, or something else, when it had in it nought but the accursed beverage. Why is this?

Though I have not now time to take up the subject

of *licenses* to sell spirit, yet as many complain that they are deprived of a right, when they are prohibited from selling it, I would just ask, might they not as justly complain, because they are prohibited from selling slaves, or counterfeit money, or halters, and pistols, and arsenic, when they knew that those to whom they sold them, would make them the instruments of wretchedness to their families, and of *murder to themselves?*

7. This nation was the first that ever formed a republican government, and proved themselves able by their intelligence and morals to sustain it.

Our nation was the first that found the road to liberty and independence from the intoxicating cup. As the president of the first congress had his birth in our town, so the temperance society had its birth in our own native State. It is not an exotic, like alcohol, against which it has proclaimed war. It did not spring from an Arabian desert, or, amid Mohammedan imposture, but is a free citizen of our happy New England, and from the soil of the good old Bay State. And hitherto, the friends of temperance, like the descendants of the patriots of the Revolution, have not only maintained the rights and privileges guaranteed to them by the constitution of their fathers, but have improved upon those rights and privileges. The cause has been constantly and steadily progressing.

8. The declaration of American independence, and the consequent revolution, were events unparalleled in

history, and gave us a name and honor through the world.

The declaration was received by the people with transports of joy. Feeble colonies without an army, navy, established government, revenue, munitions of war or fortifications, stepped forth against veteran armies and achieved their liberty. Great Britain, their oppressor, acknowledged their independence, and the other nations of the earth followed her example.

The temperance reformation is an event unparalleled in the history of the world, and has given us praise and honor among the nations of the earth. When Dr. Hewitt, one of the American champions of temperance, visited England and France, and lectured on the subject, it was acknowledged by those nations, that light had come from the West, contrary to the course of nature; as it had always, both literally and morally, proceeded from East to West. When Drs. Reed and Matheson visited the American churches as a delegation from the Congregational Union of England and Wales, they spoke with wonder at the astonishing progress of the temperance reformation in this country. When Drs. Codman, Humphrey and Spring, visited England, there was no subject which so interested a British audience, and drew from them such applause, as their representations of the progress of temperance in America. As the American revolution gave a shock to all the powers of Europe, so the temperance movements in this country have been felt round the globe. Requests have been sent to America for light on this subject, and for temperance publications from England, France, Ireland, Scotland, Sweden, Russia, Asia, New Holland, and the islands of the Pacific.

Truly, the temperance reformation, like the emancipation of the American colonies, has been a bright star, hitherto rising higher and higher, and exciting the wonder and astonishment of more than half the globe.

9. If our civil liberty is not abused, and God, for our national sins, does not permit us to dig our own grave and lie down in it to rise no more, our independence will prove a blessing to generations yet unborn. Where is there a nation on the face of the globe, possessed of a country and a constitution like ours? Compare our civil institutions, our literary and religious privileges, with those of other nations, and they throw far into the shade the most highly favored portions of the eastern world. But these privileges are but the legacy of our pious forefathers. They were full-blooded republicans. They would bear no tyranny neither in Church nor State; and as long as our nation lives, the singers of the declaration of American independence will be venerated as patriots of no ordinary stamp. As long as our nation exists, their chivalrous deeds and their acknowledgments of their dependence upon God, will be admired and venerated by their descendants. As long as the American eagle spreads her wings, "Our lips shall tell them to our sons, and they again to theirs."

If the friends of temperance prove faithful, and the

cause progresses, as we believe it will, unborn generations will reap a glorious harvest by our emancipation from intemperance.

The amount of good accomplished — the money and time — the peace and health — the reputation and honor — the number of lives saved from a drunkard's grave — the number of females saved from being doubly widowed, and children orphaned — the blessing reaped from staying that tide of moral desolation, which, like an overflowing scourge, was sweeping over our land and fast laying waste the fairest portion of the world — will not and cannot be told, till that great day for which all other days were made, shall disclose them.

This mighty river, which seemed at first but a little rill; which sprung up in the hearts of a few sons of New England, and which has been already augmented by hundreds and thousands of tributary streams, and which is now making glad every portion of our land as it rolls on its smooth and equal course, will bear down on its gentle current to the latest posterity, liberty, civil and religious; science, human and divine; peace, national and domestic; reputation, honor, plenty, health and happiness. I anticipate the period, when this nation, the asylum of the Pilgrims, the cradle of liberty and glory of all lands, shall be totally emancipated from the accursed beverage of intoxicating liquors. When the pulpit, the bar, the hall of legislation, the shop of the merchant and mechanic, and the field of the husbandman; when every room in every house in the land, from the cellar to the garret, and every vessel on the water, from the cabin of the gallant ship that doubles Cape Horn, to the forecastle of the sloop that transports yonder granite from our beautiful canal, shall be kept pure from this scourge of our nation — this moral miasma — this deadly upas, which for years swept to a drunkard's grave thirty thousand human beings; among whom were many of the fairest forms and brightest intellects, around whose lips the smile of beauty ever played, or from whose eyes the lightning of thought ever flashed, or from whose tongues the thunder of eloquence flowed. Then shall New England be, as it once was, distinguished above all lands for moral and religious principle; then shall " our daughters be as corner-stones, polished after the similitude of a palace, beautiful as Tirzah and comely as Jerusalem." Then shall our sons consecrate the best of their days to the service of God and their country. Then shall they in the pulpit be like Apollos; in the church, like Aaron and Hur to Moses; in the forum, like Tully and Demosthenes; on the battle field, (if battle field there be), like Washington and Lafayette; and in the vineyard or at the plough, like Abdolonymus, the Roman, or Elisha, the son of Shaphat.

Our ancestors signed the declaration of American independence. We rejoice that they did it.

In conclusion, my respected hearers, I have only to ask, Will you sign the declaration of American independence from all intoxicating liquor? Let this be done, and we shall be free indeed. As you wish to be free from the oppressor, I press you to sign the declaration. Suppose all felt on this subject as one of the soldiers of the revolution did, when the constitution of a temperance society was presented to him. As he was about to sign it, some kind friends attempted to dissuade him from it, by telling him that he would injure himself; that he was aged and infirm, and had need of the stimulus, and that he would soon die without it. The veteran of Seventy-six replied, "It is true I am aged and infirm, and I have long used a little spirit, supposing that I needed it. But when my country was in danger from foreign oppression, I was sick; yet I arose from my bed, shouldered my musket, and marched to the aid of my friends to rescue my country from oppression. My country is now in danger; a mightier oppressor than Great Britain has his grasp upon her; and the temperance society is the only remedy. *I'll sign the pledge, I'll sign it.*"

If every lover of humanity, and every friend of his country, felt like him, we should indeed be a *saved* people; saved from a far greater oppression than could be laid upon us by any nation on earth. I ask, then, Who of you will sign this declaration? Or rather, who of you will *not* sign it? But the temperance reform in its *moral* tendency, far outshines the effects of any thing performed by the patriots of seventy-six. One man liberated from a moral thraldom, is a vast conquest. "He that ruleth his spirit is better than he that taketh a city." But in a religious point of view, the temperance reformation has done wonders. It has often prepared the way of the Lord, like John the Baptist. It has been the harbinger of many a revival of religion. It has raised hundreds and thousands from the lowest state of degradation, and introduced them to the sanctuary, and thence to the kingdom of heaven. Let us go on then, my friends, in this blessed enterprise.

CHAPTER XI.

CONTENTS.—The Neighboring Ministers of Quincy in 1834. Rev. John Codman, D. D., Rev. Richard S. Storrs, D. D., Rev. Jonas Perkins, Rev. David Sanford, Rev. Dr. Gile, Rev. John Phillipps, Rev. Ebenezer Burgess, D. D., Rev. Wm. M. Rogers.

Rev. John Codman was born in Boston, August 3d, 1782, of an honorable ancestry, and baptized in Brattle Street church, by Rev. Dr. Cooper. Rev. Dr. Storrs in the Sermon preached at his funeral said, "His parents educated their children faithfully in the principles of Scriptural morality, and strict regard to the institutions of revealed religion." He was ordained and installed Pastor of the 2d church in Dorchester, Dec. 1808. He died Dec. 1847. When he graduated at Harvard, in the first giving out of the parts, his name was omitted. This was so dissatisfactory to his class that they chose him to deliver a Poem at their departure, which he did, and this kindly act of his class-mates induced the faculty to reconsider their act, and they gave him a part in the commencement programme. In this exercise, young Codman manifested no small share of poetic genius. President Willard had then just recovered from illness, and the allusion in the following lines of the poem drew tears from his eyes.—

> " Pause! ye who aim the sacred desk to fill,
> Look, e're you strive to climb the holy hill
> Supremely blest, if with magnetic charm,
> You lead the giddy multitude from harm,
> Stop not to pluck the flowerets by the way,
> That bloom for seizure, but when plucked, decay;
> Receive and give to thousands of the fruit,
> And water with your tears Religion's root.
> Those who have claimed their blest abodes on high,
> To form new planets, risen to the sky,
> *Belnap* and *Clarke*, as sacred Stars, shall guide
> To show how Jesus lived, and how he died;
> But, when a saint, almost expiring, strove
> To join the kindred spirits gone alone.
> Thanks to Almighty power, which from the dead,
> Raised to new life the Reverend Clergy's head,—
> Kind Father of our literary days!
> Permit thy children to express their praise
> To Him, who stretched his ready hand to save
> The guide to truth from a too early grave.
> Indulgent Heaven, with nicest motives fraught
> Our greatest good, by contrast, oft' hath taught,—
> So, from the sky, sickness commissioned came
> To blast the hopes of literature and fame;
> Round our horizon clouds of sorrow hung,

> Prayer filled each heart and trembled on each tongue,
> Till earth unveiled her rainbow to the sight,
> Dispell'd the clouds, and bade the sun delight."

He bade his class-mates farewell, in the following language, beautifully prophetic of his social qualities in after life.

> "Harvard! thy walls now lesson from my view,
> Friends of my youth, Class-mates, a long adieu.
> Old time hath brought our journey to a close,
> Who heeds no feeling, and no friendship knows!
> Relentless tyrant! cruel was thy sway,
> Hard to acknowledge, harder to obey,
> Had not sweet memory said, and promised true,
> That times so pleasant, ever shall be new,
> And penciled on the canvass of the mind
> In brightest colors all w'eve left behind."

My object is to speak of him as I knew him in 1834, after he had been twenty-six years a pastor. He was a robust, fleshy man, apparently, always in good spirits, with great social feelings, sprightliness of mind, frank and open in disposition, and ardent in his affections. At first sight, to a stranger, he appeared a little proud or aristocratic, all of which immediately disappeared upon entering into conversation with him. The first intimacy I had with him was soon after the " Village church" was organized. Supplying that half the time and his, the other half, I had opportunity to understand him thoroughly. He was kind and tender hearted. He loved his friends ardently. His home was ever open to them, and his companion was as kind hearted, friendly and frank as himself. It was a delightful family to visit. One never feared not meeting a kind reception at that beautiful palace-like house, upon one of the finest hills in the vicinity of Boston. So kind and loving was Dr. Codman, that if any one of his friends came near his residence and did not call on him, he felt really grieved. His regard was sincere, and so cordially expressed, that no man could doubt his sincerity.

In a memoir written of him by his class-mate and life-long friend, Rev. Joshua Bates, President of Middlebury college, we find the following item to the credit of Dr. Codman's friendship and kindness. Dr. Bates says in his Journal: —

"How great is the goodness of God in giving me such a friend as John Codman! He has presented me with an Interleaved Bible, Cruden's Concordance, and Brown's Dictionary of the Bible. He has requested me to consider his property as my own. " God, said he to me, has blessed me in giving me more money than I want to use; you have but two hundred dollars a year; you cannot live upon it; let my money be your own.' Never have I known a friendship so pure and fervent. May God reward him; and may our friendship, which is founded on the religion of Jesus, be lasting as eternity."

At the time he offered me Cruden, I hesitated in receiving it, saying that he conferred obligations which I could never repay. He wrote on a piece of paper as follows: — I am surprised to hear you speak of the reception of favors which cannot be repaid. If I have ever conferred a favor upon you, it has been amply and doubly repaid. I enjoy what is to me of infinitely more value than silver or gold, the pleasure of your society, and, I must hope of your friendship. Let me- I beseech you, return a little of the debt, by sharing together what a merciful God has been pleased to give me. 1t would be my highest happiness, if we were so intimately united as to supercede all those ideas of obligation: that we were one in heart, and life, and in all our interests."

This speaks the man exactly as he was for his social and friendly characteristics; and this continued with him to the end of his eventful life. It, indeed, grew sweeter and more abounding as age increased upon him.

My intimacy with him was, probably, as great as that of any of the young ministers of the vicinity. He was Moderator of the Council that installed me, and, also, of that which dissolved the pastoral relation. In the meantime, we often exchanged, and oftener still, did I preach for him in his own pulpit. Being in his near neighborhood. he was moderator of many ordaining and installing Councils of which I was scribe. As the Doctor was thoroughly "old school," he could not brook any thing in the examination of a candidate that looked even towards any new-fangled notions in theology, and oftener than once, when we were acting in the capacity just named, in a low voice, did he say to me, "I cannot vote to settle this man. He is not clear upon these points. Why did they call such a man?" But, when Dr. Storrs interceded, as he often did, by saying " he will come right. I know him, and his piety," Dr. Codman, would say, " well, since brother Storrs is so well satisfied, if you will put the motion in this form, " we are so far satisfied that we proceed to ordination, I will vote for it, though I cannot say, I am fully satisfied."

Dr. Codman was a truly pious and devoted man. He was a " good shepherd, and cared for the flock." He loved to preach. Situated as he was, with large worldly means, and in the immediate vicinity of Boston, and with an extensive acquaintance, on both sides of the water, he was subject to many ministerial calls. I remember being at his home one Saturday, when a brother minister, from a distance, called and offered to preach for him. The Doctor thanked him cordially, and then added, a little facetiously, " I want to preach myself, for I have a new sermon, and I don't have such an one very often? This, perhaps, was not strictly true, for, considering the many calls upon his time, he wrote more sermons than could have been well expected he would.

Dr. Codman had two horses, one of which he called ' Old School' and the other, ' New.' I asked him, Dr. which is the better horse? His reply was characteristic and conveyed much. He said, " the new school is the swiftest; but the old school is the safest."

Dr. Codman was remarkable in encouraging and speaking well of young ministers. The first time, Rev. William M. Rogers, ' one of his boys,' as he called him, preached in his Church, there had been a death of a young man whose father lived abroad. There was no Atlantic Telegraph then. Mr. Rogers, in his prayer, said, " thou hast stricken him and he knoweth it not," referring to the father. Dr. Codman said to me, after service, "how beautifully brother Rogers applied that text! Did you ever hear anything more so?"

While I was supplying the "Village Church," he had invited Rev. Mr. Blagden, then settled at Brighton, to preach one Sabbath evening. In giving the notice, he said to me, "Tell them, he is one of the most popular young men in the land."

REV. RICHARD SALTER STORRS, D. D.

Dr. Storrs first Sabbath's preaching in Braintree was brought about by the following incident,—late at night, after Mr. Samuel Nott, then with Mr. Storrs, at Andover, had engaged to preach in Braintree, while splitting wood, for exercise in the yard of the Seminary, he cut his hat so badly by an unlucky blow, Mr. Nott said to him, Storrs, now you *must* go to Braintree and preach. He did go, and after preaching two Sabbaths, the following took place, an account given us by Dr. Storrs himself.

1811. April 26. The Church met, and voted " to set apart the first Wednesday in June, for the ordination of Mr. Storrs." also " to send letters for assistance in the ordination" to certain pastors and Churches.

The "letters missive" were responded to by the following pastors and their churches viz., Rev. Mr. Niles, Abington ; Rev. Mr. Williams, Weymouth; Rev. Mr. Norton, N. Weymouth ; Rev. Mr. Strong, Randolph ; Rev, Mr. Codman, Dorchester ; Bev. Mr. Gile, Milton ; Rev. Mr. Storrs, Longmeadow ; Rev. Mr. Reynolds, Wilmington ; and Rev. Dr. Griffin, Boston.

Rev. Mr. Williams was chosen Moderator and Rev.

Mr. Norton, Scribe, with Rev. Mr. Codman, assistant Scribe.

After the usual devotional exercises, the proceedings of the church and parish in relation to the call were read, and a verbal declaration of acceptance was made by Mr. Storrs before the Council; who also presented a written confession of his faith, "The Council, having attended to these things, and having obtained satisfaction, that Dr. Storrs is a regular member of the Church of Christ, and that he has been licensed by the Presbytery of Long Island to preach the Gospel, voted to proceed to ordination."

The introductory prayer was offered by Rev. Mr. Strong; the sermon was delivered by Rev. R. S. Storrs, Sen; the consecrating prayer was offered by Rev. Mr. Niles; the charge to the pastor, by Rev. Mr. Williams; fellowship of the Churches, by Rev. Mr. Norton; concluding prayer by Rev. Mr Gile. The irrelevant service of "a charge," or "address to the people," in those days was an unknown work of supererogation.

Mr. Storrs was born in Longmeadow, Feb. 6, 1787; graduated at Williams College, 1807: first studied theology with Rev. Dr. Woolworth, of Bridgehampton, L. I.: was licensed by the Suffolk Presbytery: supplied the then collegiate pulpits of Smithtown and Islep six months: afterwards spent a year and an half in the Theological Seminary at Andover, leaving that institution in September, 1810.

July 3., 1861, Rev. Dr, Storr's Church celebrated the Fiftieth Anniversary of his settlement, and he preached from the following text:—

Having therefore obtained help of God, I continue unto this day, witnessing both to small and great, saying none other things, than those which Moses and the Prophets did say should come. Acts xxvi, 22.

It is well, if in the multitude of our thoughts on occasions like the present, God's comforts delight our souls. Sure I am, that unless the Lord had been our help, we had this day dwelt in silence. Scarcely more distant from mind fifty years ago, was the thought of reaching the period of an antediluvian life, than of seeing the day God has now opened upon us. Verily, he is our God, and we are the people of his pasture; strength and beauty are in his sanctuary; give unto him, O my soul, and all ye people, the glory due unto his name.

Fifty years ago this day, in this place, an honored father addressed his eldest son, in those words of Paul to Timothy, "Hold fast the form of sound words which thou hast heard of me." On the basis of this injunction he affirmed "the form of sound words" to embrace God's existence in three persons; his sovereignty over all creatures, and universal providence; the certainty of all events as fixed in the counsels of eternity; the entire moral depravity of man, the necessity of Almighty influence to create him anew unto righteousness; the immutability of the Law's obligations and sanctions, salvation only through the righteousness of Christ, and that by faith alone; the resurrection of the dead, the final judgment, and the awards of eternal life or death, according to the deeds done in the body. These, and other logically connected teachings of the Holy Spirit, were charged on your pastor by parental and apostolic authority, to be held fast in all circumstances of place and time.

The following were the heads of this memorable Sermon :—

1. No help can come from Him, but through combined prayer and prudence; both are commanded, and neither can be safely neglected.

2. Help obtained from God will allot to him a healthful locality.

3. God's "help" secures a competent supply of means for personal and family support.

4. Help obtained of God preserves from pastoral connection with a people given to change.

5. Help from God will surround the minister with able friends, whose sympathies shall never fail him.

6. Help from God will inspire warm love for his work, however difficult and self-denying.

True, Braintree is not the paradise that God prepared for the first human pair, nor the Elsyium of poetic fancy, nor even the loop-hole of retreat from each vile passion that degrades humanity, yet,

"With all thy faults, I love thee still!"

And when it is remembered that fifty years ago, and for many after years, no post-office blessed the town, nor public conveyance for letters, papers or persons, was to be had, even semi-weekly, except through villages two miles distant; that but for the occasional rumbling of a butcher's cart, or a tradesman's wagon, the fall of the hammer on the lap-stone, or the call of the plowman on his refractory team, our streets had well nigh rivalled the grave-yard in silence, it can scarcely surprise one, that our knowledge of the outer world was imperfect, nor that general intelligence and enterprise were held at a discount; and if powder, kettle drums, and conch-shells, proclaimed the celebration of a wedding; or if wine, and "spirits more dangerous than any from the vasty deep," were imbibed at funerals to quiet the nerves and move the lachrymals of attendants; or if rowdyism and fisticuffs triumphed over law and order, on town meeting, muster and election days, in illustration of Falstaff's valor, or Tom Morton's revelry, it was but the legitimate outflow of combined ignorance and Heaven daring recklessness. Those days are passed, and shame throws its thick mantle over them. Light has fallen from heaven, and darkness flies. The drunkard, the pugilist, and the veteran in sin, hide their diminished heads within the folds of night's dark drapery, conscious of their vileness in religion's eye, and their desert of universal scorn and indignation. Better days have come.

The following is the modest account which Dr. Storrs gives of himself:

As to personal items 'tis enough to say that, I was the eldest son of Rev. Richard S. Storrs, and Sarah (Williston) Storrs, born at Longmeadow, Mass., February 6th, 1787; graduated at Williams College, in September 1807, and at Andover in September, 1810; spent seven months in missionary labor in Georgia and South Carolina; was ordained pastor of first church

Braintree, July 3, 1811, and here continued till the present time by the help of God.

Beside the pastoral labors here performed, various services, at various times, have been rendered to the American Education Society, the Massachusetts Missionary Society, and the American Home Missionary Society, as their agent in collecting and distributing funds, for successive months and even years.

In one instance, Rev. Edwards A. Park was settled as a colleague pastor, and continued in that relation during two years, when failing health compelled his resignation of the office; and within a few months after, the health of the senior pastor gave way, and the ministrations of the sanctuary fell into the hands of Rev. Paul Jewett, and one or two others, for some two years more. During many subsequent years the pastor has been enabled to discharge many of the duties of his office, with a measure of comfort to himself, and acceptance to the church and people. But a year since he felt it his duty to decline all further responsibilities of the pastorate, and at present the supply of the pulpit is in the hands of the parish committee. As in former days, " God hath shined out of Zion," so in these later times, may his glory appear unto his people, and his salvation to their offspring!

We then, added the following, which we have no reason now to change. We knew Dr. Storrs many years, even from our youth up. Settled near him, we had an opportunity of becoming acquainted with his influence, the weight of his character, the power of his preaching, the estimation in which he was held by his ministerial brethren, and the kindliness and sympathy of his heart.

No man in the church had a wider influence than Dr. S. Were the feeble churches of Massachusetts (and there were many made feeble at that period), by being compelled " for conscience sake," to leave their places of worship, funds and church furniture, and go out and commence anew, under the rulings of the judges of those degenerate days), to be strengthened, and new plans planted, Dr. S. was the man to do the work. He knew every rope in the ship, from the great cable that held the sheet anchor, to the smallest strand of the light rigging, and he must leave his people and voyage the Commonwealth.

The *Boston Recorder,*—(almost, but not quite, the first religious newspaper in this, or in any land :) if it was in failing circumstances, he was the man to put his strong hand and giant mind under it, bear it up and send it abroad to labor for Christ and the church. Thus, neither once, nor twice, did he lift it out of the mire, and send it on its way rejoicing.

The weight of his character was felt in the building up of the Congregational Churches, from the sands of Cape Cod to the hills of Berkshire; nor was it limited by the boundaries of old Massachusetts, which the South say now rules the nation, but it extended through the Home Missionary Society, to planting the religion of the Pilgrims at the far West, and " to the uttermost ends of the earth."

As a preacher, he had no superior in these parts. Perhaps we cannot convey our ideas on this better than by telling the following:—A village had grown very rapidly through the *traffic in leather* (as most of the towns around Boston have) till its inhabitants felt as though they were of some importance in this little world. They were in want of a pastor, and report said, they visited Dr. Woods, of Andover, to secure one. The old Profsssor, in the very quiet way for which he was noted, inquired what kind of a man they wanted? The committee said, they had grown to be of some importance, their society was large, and they wanted a first-rate minister. One who stood six feet in his shoes, of good proportions and commanding appearance, and, finally, " one who could out-preach Dr. Storrs of Braintree."

The old Dr., with his usual shrewdness, said, we have the man who will answer all your descriptions, but the last one, but I can't say but in process of time he may do that.

Dr. Storrs influence upon his brethren and the estimation in which he was held by them was vast. We may illustrate this, also, by the following: It was our lot to be scribe of more than one ordaining council of which the eminent, urbane and dignified Dr. Codman was moderator. The Dr. could not well bear any stumbling in the examination of a candidate upon " Orignal Sin," or, the condition of infants, being born in sin ; and, oftener than once did he say, in a low voice, when some want of clearness was exhibited in a candidate upon this point, "I can't vote to settle this man."

Dr. Storrs would say, "I know the young man—he has been in my family; he is pious, and will come out right."

Dr. Codman would say, "I did think I could not vote for this man. But since Brother Storrs has said so much, and I have unbounded confidence in his opinion, I will vote for his ordination."

Nor was it with Doctor Codman alone that his opinion had influence. It reached all his ministerial brethren.

The kindness and sympathy of Dr. Storrs towards his younger brethren was unbounded. "We speak that which we know." Located but two miles from him, and young and wanting wisdom, and needing advice, we found one in him, who was ready and willing to give; not grudging, but as our great necessity required,

We have every reason to believe that we were not an exception to his sympathy among the younger ministers, and know that it extended to all. A genial smile and a kind recognition he manifested for all his younger brethren in the ministry.

He always had a word for every one, and often it was a pleasant retort of which we might give many instances.

Dr. Storrs has had three wives, and but one child, the Rev. R. S. Storrs, D. D., of Brooklyn, N. Y., and we have often thought in connexion with him, of the fabled reply of the lioness, when told that she bore but *one*—" but a lion."

We have just visited the Doctor and spent an hour with him. His mind is bright, his hearing good, but bodily strength impaired. He reminded us of the appropriate line—"Nature must fail, but grace must thrive." The same kind recognition and genial smile, and kindliness of heart, as in former years, are still manifested, and our visit was remarkably pleasant.

I now add, Dr. Storrs died at his residence in Braintree, Monday, August 11th, 1873, aged eighty-six years and six months. The sermon, preached by Rev. Edwards A. Park, gives a brief history of his lineage and labors, in a style which could have been given by no other man within our knowledge.

The writer of this sketch saw him near the close of his life and though feeble, he was the same gracious, meek and loving friend he had ever been for forty years.

It should be remarked of this eminent and excellent man, that he would never change from his first flock. He could have had any parish in any city, but he came to Braintree to stay, and was a Pastor there for sixty-three years. He acted from principle, and when his only son, was dismissed from his pastorate in Brookline, Mass. to go to Brooklyn, New York, Dr. Storrs, the father, voted against the dismission of the son.

Rev. Jonas Perkins.

Rev. Jonas Perkins was born in North Bridgewater (now Brockton) in 1790, and was the son of Josiah Perkins and Annie (Reynolds) Perkins. He was a descendant of Mark Perkins who came from Ipswich 1741. Jonas Perkins graduated at Brown University, 1813, and had the A. M. three years after. He studied Theology with Rev. Otis Thompson of Rehoboth. He was ordained Pastor of the Union Church of Weymouth and Braintree 1815, where he remained till his death, which took place in 1874. He gave us the following sketch himself.—

This church was organized August 14th, 1811. It consisted of members from the first and second churches of Weymouth, the first in Braintree, and the first in Quincy—twenty-eight members in all—eight males and twenty females. The first pastor was Rev. Daniel A. Clark, ordained January 1st, 1812, and at his own request dismissed October 20th 1813. The same year I received my diploma at Brown University, and immediately entered upon my theological course under Rev. Otis Thompson of Rehoboth, September 1814, in connection with the late Rev. Alvan Cobb of Taunton. I was licensed by the Mendon Association, Dr. Emmons presiding.

On the moral wrong of American slavery, I was from the beginning of my ministry decided. In my Fast-day sermons, years before the formation of the Anti-Slavery Society, in referring to national sins, I represented slavery as a national sin, of flagrant turpitude, exposing the nation to the judgment of Heaven.

During my ministry the number received into the church was three hundred and nineteen. The greater part were received at times when no special religious interest prevailed in the parish. The others were the fruits of revivals. In 1828, there was a general revival, and fifty-four persons were added to the church. In 1832 another general revival was enjoyed, resulting in the addition of forty-five to the church. Another revival in 1842 brought into the church thirty-seven individuals.

The number of infant baptisms which I administered was three hundred and forty-four.

The number of persons united in marriage by me during my pastorate, was eight hundred and eighty-six.

The number of funerals which I was called to attend was six hundred and seventy-eight.

In attending meetings on the Sabbath, and other meetings during the week, I have travelled the distance between my residence and the place of worship more than nineteen thousand times,—amounting to over six thousand miles.

Soon after my settlement, I joined the association. The name which it then had was the " Association of Boston and Vicinity." The place of meeting when I joined was South Reading. The body consisted of the Congregational Evangelical clergy from Braintree to that town inclusive, being about ten persons.

Some few years since, hearing a person exultingly

say that the ranks of the orthodox were diminishing, and that soon there would be none left, I called his attention to the fact, that, within the territorial limits of this association, the number of churches had increased more than four-fold within forty years, and asked him how long it would be, according to that ratio, before his prediction would be fulfilled. Since the Norfolk Association adoped its present name, which was several years after my settlement, eighteen new churches have been organized within its present limits, and there are four associations in Boston and vicinity where there was then only one. Fifty years ago it was the prevailing opinion, expressed in diverse forms, that New England was almost the exclusive soil congenial to the growth of this branch of the Christian Church. While the churches of New England were contributing liberally to evangelize the growing population at the West, their own eclesiastical polity, whose practical results were thus evinced, was deemed unsuitable to the churches gathered by their own missionary!

We met a man upon the road, who learning that they were going to the ordination, and not knowing that they were my parents expressed his kind sympathy for the young candidate, and said that "No minister could remain with the society at Weymouth Landing more than three years." (No one save Mr. Perkins would have been likely to.)

In reference to my settlement here, I have endeavored to seek direction from God and have received the advice of wise and good men; and when by ordination I had been consecrated to the work of the gospel ministry as pastor of this church, I resolved, relying on divine grace, to labor here as long as God should permit my pastoral relation to last.

In my review of past events I have been led thus briefly to allude to subjects of national and universal interest, because whoever has occupied a place, however humble, on the Christian watch-tower these fifty years, cannot but have felt that responsibilities resting upon him, not only in relation to his particular charge, but in relation to all for whom Christ died. J. PERKINS.

The above modest sketch, written by our good brother, speaks forth just the prudent, kind characteristics of the man. It embodies sound common sense, good knowledge of human nature, a quiet spirit, faithful preaching, and speaks as a minister of the meek and lowly Saviour should speak. We have known no better adviser; no one whose counsels could be more safely followed, or opinions adopted, than brother Perkins. He never sought "pre-eminence," but always stood in his lot, and no man could find aught against him, "except concerning the law of his God." Here he was firm. The great fundamental doctrines of the Bible were the sum and substance of his preaching. Still this was always done with "the wisdom of the serpent, and the harmlessness of the dove." No man could be more prudent.

His salary was always small, yet he brought up, in a highly respectable manner, a large family. It should be mentioned in this connection that Mrs. Perkins was ever a prudent wife, and like Solomon's Wise Woman, thus "built up her house." Indeed, we know not where to look for a pastor's wife who more fully answers the wise man's description of the "virtuous woman;" or Paul's directions for the wife of a bishop, or deacon, than Mrs. P. has ever been.

Had he had some other woman for his companion, with all his meditative quietness, in which he might well be compared with Isaac of old, he would hardly have remained Pastor of "the Union Church of Weymouth and Braintree," forty-five years, for human nature is very similar there to what it is in other places, as was evinced by the short stay which Rev. Mr. Dickerman, the immediate successor of Mr. P., made among them. Never was the truth of the declaration more verified than in Mr. P.'s case, "a soft answer turneth away wrath, while grievous words stir up anger."

We say these things not unadvisedly, for, having been located in the immediate vicinity of his church, we always found him a cordial friend, a faithful brother, and a safe counsellor. The people of his parish were from a heterogeneous population, among whom a minister of the gospel, especially, one of the good old Puritanic School, had to walk very straight; and, even then, no man could walk on a bee-line, or, keep on a straight one, without being sure to bi-sect the path of some one else, for where paths were so numerous, as they were in this parish for half a century past, their crossings and interlacings formed a pretty good net-work on the face of the moral soil. Indeed, the classes and sects were as numerous as those of "Athens," when Paul preached on " Mar's Hill," and was encountered by herds of Grecian Philosphers. Here, were Hopkinsians, Old Calvinists, Unitarians, Universalists, Baptists, Methodists, Sweedenborgians, Abolitionists and anti-Abolitionists, Federalists and Jacobins, Whigs and Democrats, Free Soilers, Liberty and Slavery parties, besides the little, local squabbles, more or less of which are always rife in a country village, and, especially, where the border-line of two towns runs through the same village. Then, Mr. P., was always a temperance man, and (strange to say) some of the people there were not always temperate.

Now, I think my readers will generally admit, that any man who could steer a barque, so public as that of a gospel minister, for nearly fifty years among so many breakers, and keep clear of them for that long period, must have been possessed of more than ordinary prudence; or, to change the figure, one who could walk among so many fires, for so many years, and not get singed, nor "have even the smell of fire pass over him," must be worthy of the name of "Prophet," with honor, in his own place.

It is true there were redeeming qualities, " cases" among the Weymouthites and Braintreites, in Mr. P.'s parish. There were, here and there, men of character and principle, of property and standing, among Mr P.'s parishioners.

Of these, Deacon Jonathan Newcomb was one. He

was prosperous in the granite or stone-cutting business, as it was called. He was a benevolent man and often gave considerable sums to foreign and domestic missions, to erect meeting-houses (there were no churches then,) in various places, and to help out, or add something to Mr. P.'s salary.

REV. DAVID SANFORD.

Was settled as Pastor of the Village Church, Dorchester, in 1830. He was the son of Mr. Philo Sanford, Pastor of the church in West Medway. He graduated at Brown University in 1825, and A. M., in regular course. He studied theology with Rev. Dr. Ide, and at Andover Seminary. He preached a short time in the city of Lowell, and in Somersworth, New Hampshire. May 22d, 1828, he was installed in New Market, N. H. He was dismissed June 1830, to take charge of the church in Dorchester, over which he was installed Pastor, July 14th, 1830. He was again dismissed, September 1838, to take the pastoral charge of a new church, in his native place, Medway Village. He was installed there, October 3d, 1838, and there he has remained " to this present," 1871.

Mr. Sanford's early education was a religious one by his pious parents; and when they were removed, his eldest sister took their place in giving him instruction from the Assembly's Catechism and the Bible.

We have been intimately acquainted with Mr. Sanford since 1823. In Brown University our acquaintance commenced, where he was one of the most active in the devotional and theological meetings and societies of the students. While pursuing his theological studies at Andover Seminary, he was among the most active in religious matters, both in, and out, of the Seminary often walking ten miles Saturday evening to be present at Sabbath School meetings and other religious services. In Lowell, where he often went, his meetings were greatly blessed, and after he was licensed to preach, the people there would have been pleased to have retained him permanently. At Great Falls, and New Market, N. H., his labors were greatly blessed. From New Market, he came to be Pastor of the Village Church, in Dorchester, where he remained several years, and was the honored instrument of building up that Church, and of accomplishing much good in the neighboring churches. By a singular providential coincidence, we were thrown into near proximity to him in College, at New Market, and again, at Dorchester, as we labored with him in the same town in New Hampshire, and near him in Quincy, while he was in Dorchester, so that " we speak that we do know."

His extreme activity of body, warmth of heart and fluency of speech enabled him to make more family and parish calls, and to more profit, in the same time than any other minister of our acquaintance. He always had a word " in season," for every one.

His kindness and sympathy for the afflicted were remarkable. "He became all things to all men," in the best sense of that passage of the great Apostle, strengthning the weak, reclaiming the erring, confirming the strong and making every body better with whom he came in contact.

His health was ever delicate, and often, he was apparently, near heaven, but he had one of those elastic constitutions which will arise, as it were, to a new life, aided always, and very much by an active, energetic and ever hoping mind. Considering his frail body, it is truly wonderful that he should have accomplished so much. The Lord has used him as an instrument of great good to the church, and, now, though feeble, he is still doing good, both by his tongue and by his pen. "He is a good man, and goes about doing good." May he yet continue many days on earth.

Rev. Dr. Gile.

We have not the date of his settlement in Milton. He was there many years; was an eloquent and popular man. He was among the last to come out from the Unitarians, and continued to exchange with them long after many of his brethren had refused to do so. He justified his course by saying, "he thought, he could do more good by preaching in their pulpits than they did harm by preaching in his." Why, "said he," I exchange with Rev. Mr. Whitney, of Quincy; and his people meet me at the door and say, Mr. Gile, why don't you come oftener? We are so glad to hear you, we wish you would come once a month."

He did not give up exchanging with them, till they held a Council in Milton, of which Rev. Peter Whitney was Moderator, which Council decided that "Rev. Dr.

Gile's usefulness was at an end." After this decision, Dr. Gile ceased exchanging pulpit-services with that denomination.

Dr. Gile was an exceedingly gifted man in prayer. He died in a good old age, venerated and greatly lamented.

Rev. John Phillips.

Mr. Phillips was settled over the first parish in Weymouth when I came to Quincy. He was a descendant from the old and honorable Governor Phillips family, and his father was the first Mayor of Boston. Mr. Phillips is a brother of Wendell Phillips. He graduated at Harvard, and studied theology at Andover. He was settled several years in Weymouth, was greatly beloved for his amiability of character and fidelity as a pastor. He left Weymouth, and was dismissed at his own request. He was afterwards settled over the Orthodox Congregational Church of Methuen, and remained there many years. His health became impaired and he resigned his pastorate and removed to Boston where he still resides, with a very pleasant family, amidst a large circle of friends. No one can know Mr. Phillips, but to admire and love him so amiable and christian is his demeanor.

Rev. Ebenezer Burgess, D. D.

Was settled in Dedham, at the time I came to Quincy He was born in Wareham, Mass., April 1st, 1790. He died in Dedham, Deccember 5th, 1874. He graduated at Brown University, 1809. He was for sometime, Tutor there, and afterwards Professor in Vermont University. In 1817, he was one of the original founders of the Colony of Liberia. He studied theology both at Andover and Princeton, and in his religious creed, he was a Princetonian. He was settled over the Orthodox Congregational Church in Dedham, 1821. He was the Author of the " Dedham Pulpit, ' and the " Burgess Genealogy," in 1865.

Dr. Burgess to strangers, had the appearance at first of being a proud man; but he was really, just the reverse. As one became acquainted with him, it was evident he was humble, kind and sympathizing. He was a good pastor, a wise and kind husband and father, and for many years was greatly beloved by his Church, by his ministerial brethren and in the community. Dr. Burgess was remarkable for the neatness and good order in which he always left the room in which he had slept. Every thing was in its place, and all neatly arranged. He was benevolent, but always accompanied his gift with the gentle remark, " Mrs. Burgess had a little money left and she thought she would make you a sharer in it." This seemed the more proper, as Mrs. Burgess inherited a much larger fortune than the Doctor.

Rev. Wm. M. Rogers.

Mr. Rogers was born in the Island of Alderney, near the coast of France. Left without parents he was sent to this country, and was brought up by his uncle, Capt. W. M. Rogers of Dorchester, where he became a member of Dr. Codman's Church. His name was Joseph Kettelle. He graduated at Harvard University, in 1829. He was ordained and installed over the Congregational Church in Townsend, Massachusetts, where he remained five years. In 1835, he removed to Boston, and took charge of the Franklin Street Church. This was a new church then just organized. and worshiped in the Odeon, the name of which had been changed from that of the old Federal Street Theatre, which stood at the corner of Franklin and Federal Streets. The church took its name from Franklin Street. It was removed to Winter Street in 1841. Mr. Rogers died August 11th, 1851, aged nearly 45 years, and was buried at Leominister. The new church was a pleasant and commodious edifice, occupying the site where Chandler and Co's store now stands. Mr. Rogers was very popular and every seat in the house was taken. He was an eloquent and fluent speaker, and rarely if ever wrote his sermons. He took a deep interest in the cause of seamen. No minister of Boston for the last fifty years stood higher than Mr. Rogers. He was in some respects a politician and a zealous Whig. He ruled his people and carried out his own plans in every particular. When two men had driven Rev. Hubbard Winslow from the pastorate of Bowdoin Street Church, where he had been prosperous for twelve years, one of them came to the Winter Street Church, A gentleman who had known how they had used Dr. Winslow, said to me, I am glad that man has joined Roger's Church, for, he is the right man to "put a hook in his nose and a bridle in his mouth and turn him into the way in which he ought to go." This proved to be a fact. He was as quiet under Mr. Rogers management " as a weaned child." Occasionally, some others came there who had been restless eleswhere. But. who became very docile here, and the reason was, Mr. Rogers had the entire confidence of his people. and his Church was full to overflowing—this last is, and has ever been, an indispensable qualification for a Boston minister. It matters not so much how, or what he preaches, if his house is full and it pays. The writer once took tea with Mr. Rogers, where he was to lecture before the Boston Lyceum. He drank several cups of strong green tea, and ate nothing. I gave him some hygenic advice upon this point, which, probably, was not followed. It was the way to be brilliant and to live a short life only; and he died of paralysis before he was forty-five. But, he rested from his labors with honor, and with the praise and admiration of thousands.

EDITORIAL RECOLLECTIONS OF BOSTON.

CHAPTER XII.

CONTENTS.—Visit to Boston in 1816—Jesse Smith's Stages—Stop in "Bromfield Lane"—Boston then, and now—Value of land then, and now—Central Court and Winter Street—Benjamin Russell—Rev. C. G. Finney—Rev. Mr. Dodd, the Mesmerizer—The Old Winter Street Church and Rev. Wm. M. Rogers—Millerism and the End of the World—Old Relics of Boston—The Common, and its Fences—The Ministers of Boston—The Public Schools.

In 1842, I removed to Boston. My first visit to the city was in 1816, the cold summer, when there was a frost in New England, every month in the year. Well do I remember that summer, for, I was a boy working upon a farm. The sun would rise in the morning, and not a cloud could be seen, and every one judged, we were to have a beautiful summer day. About nine A. M., a cloud would appear in the North-West, the wind would begin to blow from that quarter, the clouds grow blacker and thicker, and by the afternoon, the weather would become so chilly that an overcoat would be very comfortable. The season had been late and cold in the Spring, and early in September, a hard frost killed all the Indian Corn; but rye and potatoes were never better than they were that year, and upon these, the greater part of the people lived. Flour was twelve dollars a barrel, which had never been above five dollars before, except during the war with England from 1812 to 1815. Had we then been told that flour would be from twelve to fifteen dollars a barrel in 1874, with all the facilities we have now for raising wheat, we should not have credited the statement.

I came from Taunton, in one of Jesse Smith's stages, and "Nat Blake" was the driver. We came to Shepard's Tavern, in "Bromfield Lane," which might then be well called a "Lane," for it was not wide enough for two carriages to pass abreast.

Here I wish to recount the endurance of first impressions, for, to this day, "Bromfield Street" seems the most familiar of almost any one in the city. From that old "Tavern," I then a boy, reconoitered and made observations, being very careful to note each departure from it, that I might make a safe return through the crooked and short streets and lanes of this Capital of New England. The Boston of that day was a very different one from that of the present (1874). There were no North and South Market Streets then. In fact, there was not much of anything south of Bromfield Street. There was the "old Marlboro Hotel;" but it was a small, one story house, with a large garden around it. Farther south, was the "Lamb Tavern," on the site where the "Adams House" now stands.— Here the "country people used to leave their horses," while they went "down town shopping." The "Boylston Market" was then built, and this was considered the extreme "South End." There was an old building on the corner of Washington and Essex Streets, called then, as now, the "Liberty Tree" Corner.

From thence, to Roxbury line, there were very few houses and no stores. The "Neck," where Washington Street now is, was a long, narrow, winding strip of land over which the waters of the "South," and the "Back Bay," at high tides, mingled the one with the other; while on either side, at low water, nothing but muddy, grassy flats were visible. School, Milk, Water, Franklin, Summer, Pearl, and many others, where now the greater part of the business of the city is done,— were all occupied with dwelling houses. Indeed, most of these streets were thus occupied to a much later period.

"Fort Hill" was the "Court End" of the city. There lived, in splendid houses, the most wealthy and retired "merchant princes." Mr. Waterson, Edward and William Reynolds, Samuel K. Williams, and many others there had their palaces. Edward Reynolds, the father of Dr. Edward Reynolds, Sen., told me, "when I bought the land where this house stands (on Fort Hill) I could have bought the land where the State House now stands for one-quarter of what I paid for the land here; and now, the land at the State House is worth four times as much as it is here." This was a change of eight times in the value of the land on Fort Hill and Beacon Street, during the active life of one man, say, sixty years.

As great changes as this, in the value of land have taken place even since I removed to Boston, in 1842. Then, I was offered, and urged to take the land, at the the foot of the Common, where Dr. Keep's house now stands, at seventy-five cents a foot, and the land at the corner of Boylston and Tremont Streets, where the "Masonic Temple," now stands, at one dollar a foot, and I have no doubt but that I could have had it, at seventy-five cents a foot. Now, I suppose, it could not be bought for ten dollars a foot; so great has been the change in its value in little over thirty years; and I doubt not, as great changes will transpire in the next thirty years. A little more than thirty years ago, every body said, land would never command a higher price in Boston, than it did then; and most supposed, it would be cheaper in the future.

When I removed to Boston, I first rented a new house in "Central Court," where the store of Jordan, Marsh & Co., now stands, of Ebenezer T. Andrews, who then lived in Winter Street. At that time, Winter Street was chiefly filled with dwelling houses, and these were occupied by Doctors. I recollect, Mrs. Andrews said to me one day, "yesterday, our girl was taken suddenly ill, and I sent for all the Doctors in the street. It was about eleven o'clock, A. M., but not one of them was at home. But, in about an hour, twelve doctors gave us a call."

Mr. Andrews was a printer, by trade; one of the old settlers at that profession, and he told me, "once, we had the whole Bible in type, in our office, (stereotyping had not then been invented), a thing that could not be said of any office either in England or Europe. " Central Court", said Mr. Andrews, " was my garden, and when I bought it, it was considered, quite " up town." This platt of land alone, was enough to make him rich, as it did. I have been told that his son, who owns it, rents the premises occupied by Jordan, Marsh & Co., for forty thousand dollars a year.

At the time I moved into this " Court," Benjamin Russell, the famous editor of the "*Columbian Centinel*," occupied a house at the head of it, and I used to see him looking from the window towards Washington street, every morning, like a ' caged bird' apparently, anxious to get out. He was a very old man, and had fought many battles with Jeffersonisan Republicans and Democrats, who had dared to attack the old lion, Federalism, in his den. Mr. Russell was as staunch a defender of Federalism, as was old John Adams, the second President of the United States. Each of them thought, if Federalism died, the " Republic was done for." Political lying was never carried to greater perfection than it was in those early days of our history; not even all the lies told about old Andrew Jackson, (whose fame has been growing brighter from the day of his death to the present) equaled those in the day of this old Federalism and Republicanism.

The winter of 1842-3, was an eventful one. Our residence in Boston was a " new departure" from our former country life, and was very pleasantly spent.

Rev. Charles G. Finney preached at the old Marl

boro Chapel, (now the Lowell Institute.) I had known Mr. Finney from 1831, when I attended a "protracted meeting" with him at father Wilson's, in the Beneficent Church, in Providence. At that time, he was very strong and robust. Afterwards, he had a severe fit of sickness, and after it, he never regained his former physique and never weighed so much, by several pounds. Then, too, he was stern and denunciatory of all that he did not approve. Good Deacon Snow, of Providence, son of the former minister, offered a prayer, of the old fashion, and Finney said, "a few more such prayers would freeze hell over." Deacon Snow never got over this stern rebuke.

I never saw a greater effect produced upon a congregation than Mr Finney produced upon this congregation. He was refering to salvation by Christ; and, in the sweetest language, representing all the redeemed as singing praises to the Lamb, when he stretched himself up, looked over the audience, and exclaimed, in a voice of thunder, "Hark! what's that? It's all hell come up. We've served out our time in the State's Prison of the Universe. We demand admission into Heaven. No glory to the Saviour. Glory to hell-fire, which has purified us."

The whole audience were astounded and started from their seats in astonishment The Restorationist minister challenged him to a public discussion the next day, which he did not notice.

He had been in Boston, often during these ten or twelve years, and preached in Park Street, to the admiration of many; and, in his lectures in the winter of 1843, he was completely subdued. He had been repudiated by some of the Boston Congregational clergy, but not a word of reply was heard from him in all his sermons this winter. They were plain, simple, gospel sermons—thus, he evinced a true catholic and forgiving spirit.

This winter, also, witnessed no small amount of humbug. A certain Rev. Mr. Dodd, a Universalist preacher, hailing from Fall River, came to Boston to lecture on "Animal Magnetism." There were a number of ministers of this denomination, that winter, in the Legislature, and the notices through the papers, went out, as though he was invited by the Legislature to come here and lecture on this mighty subject. He held forth, also, in the Marlboro Chapel. His lectures were well attended, and he cleared five thousand dollars in two weeks. He then, had a call to Salem, and when he returned in two weeks, the spell was broken, and he could scarcely raise a "baker's dozen" of deluded hearers. So much for leaving Boston at "high tide." The poor man did nothing in Salem, and lost his hold on Boston. He was the veriest quack that ever filched money out of a Boston audience, which is the most prolific field for deceivers and adventures on our planet. There are turning points in this business, as well as in getting an honest living.

The first Sabbath after we removed to Boston, we started out in pursuit of a church; and, as I was more or less acquainted with all the Boston Congregational ministers, we made for the nearest port, which was Rev. Wm. M. Roger's Church, in Winter Street. Ascending the many steps, which we well remember, we met Mr. Cook, the very gentlemanly sexton. I asked him, if he could accommodate us with seats, in the utmost suavite in modo, that I could command? He said, "if you will wait till the congregation are seated, I will accommodate you, if I can; but every seat in the house is let." I said to my wife and her sister, who was with us, we will go to another port, and we started down the steps, intending to go to Park Street Church. As we were descending the steps, some one took hold of my shoulder and said, "are you going away?" I turned and saw it was Rev. Mr. Rogers, the Pastor. I said yes, there are no seats in your church. "Come to my pew," said he, " and sit there, till you can get seats." We did so, and it was several weeks before we could get a seat. The house continued full as long as Mr. Rogers was pastor,

It was one of the greatest mistakes ever made in removing this Church to the "Back Bay." It was done by one or two men, and there has been no lack of seats since. It has, also, been a mistake in huddling together all the churches upon this territory, not half of which can be said to have at present a decent congregation.

In our judgment, it was a great mistake in over filling up the "Back Bay." Had the people, who now live there, gone out and bought the whole territory upon the Roxbury and Brookline Highlands, and erected their palaces, there, they would have cost less, and been worth much more; and, whoever shall be here fifty years hence will find these large houses occupied for Mechanic's boarding houses and inhabited by the Irish, as was "Fort Hill," and the present dwellers upon the Back Bay and their descendants will be on the Hills just named. An old farmer once told us the following story.—'I had a flock of sheep, and they were frightened by a dog, when one of them ran and jumped into a well, and all the rest followed, till the well was full." This is the way the "Back Bay" has been filled. One rich man went there first, and all the rest followed.

In 1843, the winter after I removed to Boston, was the time of "Father Miller's" end of the world. We had one family in "Central Court" of this persuasion, called "Second Adventists." I never knew why they were entitled to this name, as all Christians are both First, and Second Adventists, for, they all believe Christ has already come once, and will come again, which will surely be His "Second Advent." One family kept boarders in this Court. Many people were around at that time, and the stage-loads that came pouring in to board with this family, kept the Court lively. They, the family, gave away all they had. The last thing the lady gave up was her watch. It had been given her by her mother on the day of her marriage, and she did not want to part with it. But she was told, "she could never go up, till she gave that, to the Lord." So, she gave it. Whole families were ruined by this excitement. A merchant, of my acquaintance died and left but a small property. His widow and an only daughter kept a few boarders, and managed to live comfortably, till this fever broke out among the inmates; the final result was, the daughter died of consumption, induced by excitement and anxiety, and the mother found refuge in a lunatic asylum.

One of their preachers got up a great Tabernacle on Howard Street, where the Athenæum now stands, which would hold several thousands! It was finished about a year before the end was to come, and he went to an Insurance Office to get it insured for *seven* years. Said the Insurance Agent, "Mr. H., you will not, of course, expect us to insure beyond the great conflagration!" "Well," he said, "he thought it would not cost much more, and he might as well get it insured for seven years."

A meeting was held in a Hall. just as you entered into Temple Place, from Washington Street. (Temple Place was not then made into a street). I attended a meeting one day, in this Hall. It was "confusion worse confounded." One man said, "the end of the world would certainly come in six weeks from that day." Another said, "it could not possibly be put off more than three weeks." A woman said, "I do not think it is wise to fix any particular day; for my part, it is my privilege to wait till my Lord comes." I thought this one woman had more sense than both the men. A large, colored woman said, "I have been into the country, and called on a priest, and he shut the door in my face. I then turned, and warned his people." A man then said, "the town where the sister had been was Dorchester, and the minister was the Rev. Dr. Codman, and proposed that they should pray for the Rev. Dr. Codman." Another man commenced praying in a very energetic manner, but in his great zeal entirely forgot to remember the Doctor. But the former one seemed determined that the Doctor should be prayed for, and remembered him most zealously, telling the Lord that all his money would never get him into heaven, as long as he refused to hear the good sister who had visited him.

There were two little boys there, one about seven, and the other five years old. The elder one had a snap-rattle, and when the shouting was at its height, he would shake the rattle. He thanked the Lord that "he had got his little brother onto the 'anxious seat,' and he should not leave it, till the end."

The floor was covered with men, women and children, some prostrate, some kneeling, some sitting and others standing. It was the most perfect "Babel," I ever saw. After the day for the predicted end had passed, I asked one woman, that had sat in her robes all night, expecting to go up, but who didn't, what she supposed it was, and she said, electricity.

Some made money out of this fanatical excitement. One old man built a Tabernacle on a back-lot out of Jackson Place. I tried to purchase it, and not come into possession till after the day appointed for the end; but the old Scotchman was to shrewd to sell cheap on these conditions.

Notwithstanding all this vast amount of wild fanaticism and delusion, there were some good, pious, devoted christians mixed up with these errors, and some educated and really christian ministers.

As late as 1812, there were several of the old relics of Boston to be seen that have since disappeared. The old house on Milk Street, in which Benjamin Franklin was born, was then standing. The "Old Hancock House," which Governor Hancock built in the woods then remained. An old lady, living in Chatham, on the Cape, told me the following:—"I was born on the spot where St. Paul's Church now stands, and from there to where Governor Hancock built his house, it was all woods, and everybody wondered why the Governor should build a house away off in the woods."

Boston Common was made such by an order passed as early as the 30th day of March, 1640. Let it be remembered, this was but ten years after the settlement of Boston. So, the Common is an old affair. Some of the early records of the town about this piece of land, are very curious, and curiosity has not yet ceased (1874), about it. In 1646, the following votes were passed, showing the State and use of the Common at that time.

"At a Generall townes meeting upon the Lawful warnings of all the freemen it is graunted yt all the inhabitants shall have equall Right of Comonage in the Towne. Thos who are admitted by the Towne men to be Inhabitants.

"It is ordered, yt all who shall after the dat hereof come to be an Inhabitant in ye Towne of Boston shall not have right of Comonage, onless he hier it of them yt are comoners.

"It is ordered, yt ther shall be on the Comon yee by Inhabitants of ye Towne but 70 Milch Kine.

"It is ordered, yt ther shall be no dry cattill, younge cattill or horse, shalbe free to goe on ye Comon this year but on horse for Elder Oliver.

"It is ordered, yt noe Inhabitant shall have power to all his righte of comonage, but only to let it out to hire from year to year.

"It is ordered, if any desire to keep sheep, hee may keepe four sheep in his liew of a cow."

Perhaps there is more force in the following *order passed the same day, than has been generally noticed in it. It is undoubtedly the origin of all the votes and orders as well as clauses of city charters, preserving the power of control of the Common with the legal voters:

"It is ordered, yt noe comon marish and Pastur Ground shall hereafter bye gifte or sayle, exchange, or otherwise, be counted onto ppriety without consent of ye major pt of ye inhabitants of ye towne."

If the order of the thirtieth of March, 1640, established the Common, there can be little doubt that the foregoing perpetuated its existence.

From time to time, a person was appointed to "keep the cowes which goe on the Common," for which he had "two shillings and sixpence the head for every cowe that goes there;" and a few years later a shepard was also appointed.

The following order, passed on the thirty-first of May, 1852, seems to indicate a great abuse of the Common, and perhaps also the streets of the town. Our ancient Selectmen were not very choice in the use of language, but the words of the record give a much better idea of old times than any substitute for them that can be made by the writer. The record is as follows:

"At a meeting of all the Select-men it is ordered, that noe person inhabiting within this town shall throw forth or lay any intralls of beast or fowles, or garbidg, noe carion, or dead Dogs or Catts, or any other dead beast or stinkeing thing, in any hie way, or dich, or Common, within this neck of land of Boston, but or inioynd to bury all such things that soe they may prevent all anoyance onto any.

Further it is ordered, that noe person shall throw forth dust, or dung, or shreds of cloth or lether, or any Tobacko stalks, or any such things into the streats."

These orders were evidently the commencement of internal health arrangements, and may have had a good effect for some time; but it is very apparent that they must have peen forgotten or overlooked, as it became necessary on the thirtieth of March, 1659, five years later, to make the following record in the town book:

"Whereas ye Comon is all times much anoyed by casting stones outt of ye bordering lotts and other things yt are offensive, Itt is therefore ordered, yt if any person shal hereafter any way anoy ye Comon by spreading stones or other trash upon itt, or lay any carrion upon itt, every person so offending, shall bee fined twenty shillings."

Thus, from this ancient record, it appears that the Common was to be ever sacred. It was neither to be monopolized by individuals, cut up into house-lots, or streets, nor encroached upon in any way.

But Young America makes no stop in this day to pay obeisance to any of her ancestors, or, to respect any of her antique relics, What are they to us? Suppose somebody did wish to preserve the "Old Hancock Mansion," the house in which "Ben Franklin" first breathed, the "Paddock Elms," the "Common" intact, and many other items, reminding us of "old Boston."— Who cares for that? All must give place to the "Almighty Dollar." The day will come when the destruction of these old landmarks will be deeply regretted. Such remembrances of by-gone days are valuable, as they teach the flight of time, the record of the past, the arts and things that were here before we were. But Vandalism pays no deference to age, no respect to antiquity, but looks solely to present profit and pleasure. America has quite enough of this reckless going ahead irrespective of whither they go, or where they go, or where they will land.

The "Old State House," at the head of State Street, was erected in 1712; Christ's Church, in Salem Street, was dedicated in 1723; the Corner Stone of the "Old South Church" was laid the 31st of March, 1729; King's Chapel was dedicated in 1773; the present State House was built in 1798.

The Ministers of Boston in 1842, were Rev. Dr. Blagden, at the Old South Church; Rev. Hubbard Winslow, D. D., was Pastor of the Bowdoin Street Church, to which Dr. Lyman Beecher preached. Mr. Winslow was a very successful pastor, until dissatisfaction arose among some few of his parishioners, which resulted in his dismission, the breaking up of his health, and the death of the church. Rev. Silas Aiken, D. D. was pastor of the Park Street Church, a very good man, and quite as good a preacher, when they drove him off, as he was when they settled him. Rev. William Jenks, D. D. was pastor of the Green Street Church, a very learned, worthy and excellent man, and the Author of the "Comprehensive Commentary." Rev. Dr. Towne was pastor of the Salem Church, and then, a very popular preacher. Rev. Joy H. Fairchild was pastor of the Phillips Church, South Boston, against whom afterwards there were many charges, but who was acquitted by the court. Rev. Wm.

M. Rogers was then pastor of the Central or Winter Street Church, and very popular, with a full house. Rev. Dr, Kirk, about that time, went off with the best half of the Park Street Church, and formed the Mount Vernon Church, of which he was the Pastor till his death, in 1874. These, I think, constituted the Orthodox Pastors of the city at that time.

Of the Unitarian clergy at that time, we had Rev. Dr. Lowell, of the West Church, Rev. Dr. Gannett, the popular successor of Rev. Ellery Channing, D. D. Rev. John Pierpont, D. D. at the Hollis Street, a Poet, a Lecturer, a keen, shrewd man, who fought the greatest moral battle ever fought in Boston with the Distillers and rum-sellers, of that day. He gained his case in the courts, and received $14,000, at one time, of his back salary.

I must relate here, the experience of Mr. Pierpont, which he gave me the last time I ever saw him. He was in the Treasury Department, in Washington, and the following is his account of his seeking an appointment. "I had known Mr. Chase, who was Secretary of the Treasury, at that time. I had known him long, as an Anti-Slavery man—had visited him in Ohio, and he had visited me, in Boston. I was an old man and out of employment, and after he was made Secretary, I wrote him that I would like a place, as a clerk in his Department of the Cabinet. I received no answer. I wrote again, but again, I received no answer. When General B. F. Butler got up his Regiment, I volunteered to go as Chaplain, and was appointed. When the regiment arrived in Washington, almost the first man I met, whom I knew, was Mr. Chase. He appeared very glad to see me, and said, Mr. Pierpont, "you are too old a man for this service. I can give you a better position. I said, Mr. Chase, I wrote you two letters, and you never noticed them. He held up his hands in astonishment, and said, I never saw, or heard of them." They went into the 'waste basket,' where most office-seekers letters go. Such was my experience in writing for an appointment."

Of the Baptist Denomination, Rev. Dr. Sharp, " of blessed memory," was at the Charles Street Church; Rev, Dr. Hague at the old Federal Street, then Chauncy Street; Rev. Dr. Neale was Pastor of the same church, where he is now. Rev. Dr. Colver was at the Tremont Temple.

About this time, Rev. Mr. Knapp came to Boston, and preached as an Evangelist. A part of the Baptist ministers looked upon him, in the same light that some of the Congregational clergy did upon Rev. C. G. Finney, when he came to Boston, i. e. with disfavor.

Mr. Knapp was uncouth in his manner, his language was not of the purest English, some of his expressions sounded rather harsh upon polite, Boston ears; and Rev. Drs. Sharp and Hague; and, perhaps, some others, reproved him at one of their Monday morning meetings. When Dr. Hague had finished his remarks, of this character, it was Mr. Knapp's turn to speak; when, instead of a reply to the criticisms just made, he said, in that grave, solemn tone for which he was so famous, " Let us pray for our dandy brother."

He used to say. "I am the blacksmith to give the hard blows, and brother Kirk is the silversmith to put on the polish." Mr. Knapp's preaching did much to increase the Baptist denomination, and they built two new churches while he was here, or, soon after.

The Boston Public Schools at that time were as good as they have been at any subsequent period. The teachers were well qualified and did their work thoroughly. The greatest fault that could be found with them was, the brain-pressure. Several things combined to enhance this evil. In the first place, there was a rivalship among the teachers from the highest to the lowest. Each felt that his, or her, pupils must compare favorably with the other pupils, who were to be advanced to a higher position, and hence, they drove them forward without stint, and irrespective of health. They must do so much, and if sick, that did not excuse them. They must study the harder when they were well. Rivalship among the teachers crushed the life out of many of the pupils.

Another thing that aided in carrying on this work of destruction was, the stimulus of *getting a medal.* This was an unmitigated evil. It ruined the health of many, destroyed the happiness of more, and set the pupils at variance with each other, and the parents at odds with both teachers and the school committee. It was often difficult for the committee to decide between pupils, as to which really ought to have a medal; and let them be distributed as they might, some, even a majority, were always displeased. While on the committee, we made a Report, in print, in favor of discontinuing the giving out of the city medals; but, it was like beating the air, and some considered us half insane. To say a word against that time honored custom indicated a "softening of the brain," if, indeed, such an one ever had a brain. We had the satisfaction, however, of knowing that the same board, composed largely of the same men, twelve years afterwards, voted almost unanimously to dispense with giving out these medals. It was a joyful day for the children, the parents and the committee, when they adopted this course.

Another evil attending the administration of the Public Schools then, (and it still prevails), was the election of unsuitable men to the School Board. The question was not asked, is he fit for the place? Does he know anything about Schools? Has he had any experience in them? Did he ever teach? Will he attend to the duties devolving upon a member of the School Committee? But, the question was, is he of *our* party? If so, this was enough. Under this rule, men have been elected to superintend these Schools, who knew nothing, and cared nothing about them, and who had not interest enough in them to even attend the meetings of the Board. Often, several meetings would be appointed, and no quorum would be present, and, consequently, no business could be done. Long since, we said, and are still of that opinion, that it would promote the welfare of the schools, if the School Committee should be appointed by the Supreme Court, or, by the Governor and Council, of the Commonwealth. It would lift the cause of education in Boston, out of the slums of politics, and tend to keep brawling politicians out of the Board.

Boston has always boasted too loudly of her public schools. They do not fit our youth for business, as they ought. They neglect what would be useful, and teach much that is valueless.

No man knows the age of the "Old Elm," on the Common. It was, undoubtedly, a product of the ancient fourts, and is known to have been an old landmark as early as 1722, ninety-two years after the first settlement of Boston.

The first fence on the Common enclosed a part of it only, and consisted of a row of posts with a rail on the top of them. This fence was built in 1734. But, as this left many openings for carts to pass through and over the Common, by which the herbage was destroyed, another was built after the first one was destroyed to warm the British while they were encamped in Boston. The wooden fence, which was standing around the common, in my first visit to Boston, fifty years ago, enclosed three sides of the common only. This second fence was built in 1784. This second fence remained till the great gale of September 23d, 1815. That part of it which was then destroyed, was rebuilt in the next month, October. The last of the wooden fences was to enclose the Mall from the cow pasture, and was built within the other. This was removed while Harririson Gray Otis was Mayor, for the reason that it was unnecessary, as the cows were no longer to feed upon the Common.

Next, and last, came the iron fence, which was built in 1836, which was 5,932 feet long, and cost $92,159,-85. Now, 1874, the Goths and Vandals have removed a part of this fence, indeed, all of it from Park to Boylston Street, for no other conceivable purpose, but to encroach upon this ancient domain; and, it looks probable, that the next generation will scarcely ever know that there ever was a "Boston Common," so mightily grow the avarice and worship of the "Almighty Dollar." This fast age has no reverance for antiquity. It would dig up the old stones, which Joshua placed in Jordan, where the Priests feet stood, when the Israelites passed over against Jericho, if it could sell them to underpin stores.

Rev. Charles Cleveland.

He is named in these sketches both because he was a Minister of Boston, and, because he exemplified the true principles upon which men ought to live, if they would obey the laws of nature, which are the laws of God.

I have often visited "Father Cleveland," in his own home. I knew his habits and manners, and often conversed with him of them, and he requested me to take his place after him, if I survived him, which I have done, in some measure, in carrying aid to the poor from such men as Amos A. Lawrence, Albert Feasing and other benevolent persons who have furnished me the means.

He was born in Norwich, Conn., June 21, 1772. He was placed in the family of his uncle, William Cleveland, of Salem, Mass., in March, 1784; sailed on a voyage to the Cape of Good Hope in November 26, 1785; was Clerk and Deputy Collector at the Custom House in Salem, from September, 1789, to 1802. While occupying this position he saw the handwriting of Washington every week. From 1802 to 1809, was clerk in the store of Stephen and Henry Higginson, in Boston. From 1809 to 1816, was stock and exchange broker in Boston. While in this business, he prepared and published a set of exchange tables, giving, in United States money, the exchange from one penny to £5,000; and from par down to 25 per cent. discount, and up to 10 per cent. advance, varying one-fourth per cent. on each sum. These valuable tables are still in use, both in this country and in England; and a copy of them is carefully preserved in the British Museum.

From 1846, for nine years, he was engaged in mercantile pursuits under the firm of Cleveland & Dane, on Market Street, now Cornhill. It was about this time Mr. Cleveland became deeply interested in the city poor, and set about devising plans for the formation of a society for their amelioration. For thirteen years, he was Chaplain of the House of Correction, South Boston.

For nearly half a century, he has been known as "Father Cleveland, Missionary to the Poor." He was married at the age of twenty-six, living forty-three years with his first wife; re-married, living twenty-seven years with his second wife, who died November 21, 1869, in the seventy-fifth year of her age. He was the father of but three children—sons—and but one of them is now living.

His ancestors were not long-lived, his mother living but to the age of thirty-five, and his father to seventy-one. He attributes his longevity to his mode of living and, although it has been a life of constant, uninterrupted activity, it has been one replete with joy and happiness, as his bright, cheerful, radiant face and sparkling countenance of to-day will testify. His diet has been simple, nourishing food, plainly prepared. His supper is invariably light, consisting of a few crackers, which he prefers to any thing else, and are always kept on hand for him at this meal. Eats very sparingly of best beef or mutton-steaks, making breakfast his principal meal. Every morning in the summer season, rising at 5 o'clock, he can be found with toilet perfectly arranged, down stairs in his cosy, little room or office, at the desk writing or reading, or both. After breakfast he spends the entire forenoon, or till nearly 2 o'clock—the hour at which he dines—in visiting the abodes of wretchedness, degradation, and misery, in the by-ways and lanes of the city, relieving the wants of the occupants, feeding the hungry, clothing the naked, and ministering spiritual comfort and cheer as well as temporal salvation. I can not tell you how surprised I was when I was ushered into his presence. Instead of finding the decrepit old man my mind had pictured out, I saw the cheerful, agile, supple semicentarian. I had been somewhat prepared for this change, inasmuch as I was obliged to call the third time in order to find him in; but my imaginary photograph had not been worked up in glowing colors enough I was sstonished to find none of the tremor and nervousness usually attendant upon old age. He writes a beautiful, legible hand. In early manhood, he told me, he used tobacco—chewed, and then smoked for many years, until he became convinced that the noxious weed was feeding upon and sapping, not only his vitality, but his enjoyment, happiness, and equanimity of mind. He abandoned it at once, and forever. Ere long, his nervous system was restored, and his sweetly refreshing sleep and happy frame of mind returned.

Said he, "Suppose I had continued the use of tobacco, and taken a little stimulant of some kind occasionly, do you think I would have lived to be the hale old man that I am?" His health is very good and has been all his life, with the single exception of a severe attack of pneumonia twenty-five years since. He knows nothing of biliousness, nor has he ever experienced anything like dyspepsia, with its innumerable train of attendant ailments and evils. He regards gluttony, or intemperance in eating or drinking, as the prime cause of disease, and thinks there are few who do not eat to satiety. One of the things upon which he lays much stress, is, attending to the demands of nature instanter, particularly, that of evacuation. Said he, "My friend, it is the fashion of the world to go out night after night, (especially during the long winter evenings), in quest of pleasure, to the theatre, the ball-room, or some other place of excitement, where the best hours of the night are spent in a sleepless and highly-wrought condition."

He remarked that, he could see no valid reason why any one should be worthless, useless, or inactive in old age that his mind is very nearly as vigorous and active as ever, and can now readily memorize whole chapters of the Bible, and paragraphs, or, entire poems from Milton, Young, or the modern poets. He recited for me a choice selection from Young, his favorite poet, and added that, when he retired at night, these memorized thoughts or verses were his anodyne. He would repeat a chapter or two from the Bible, until, lost in the gentle, soothing arms of Morpheus, he was released; and awoke ever in time to greet the early morning hours. These persons, said he, go out to seek pleasure or happiness, but, virtually, they never find it, and always return home empty; whereas, if they would but spend their evenings properly at home, instead of keeping these "late hours," that which they are constantly seeking and never finding, except in the transitory joy of an hour, would come to them in an abiding form. Wisely and justly does he condemn these so-called evening entertainments. With a conscience void of offence toward God and man, sleep to him is sweet, refreshing, and invigorating.

Sabbath, May 27, he preached to the inmates of the institutions on the Island—an audience of one thousand or more persons. For the 25th inst., the Sabbath next following his ninetieth birthday anniversary, he has already made two appointments. In the forenoon he preaches at the Seaman's Bethel, and in the evening at the Old Ladie's Home, in Charlestown, at one or both of which places, I expect to hear him. He remarked that no idle or indolent man ever was or ever can be happy. His eyes are good—clear and sparkling yet—although he has used glasses more or less for nearly half a century. He lost his natural teeth some fifteen or twenty years since. These were preserved by the free and simple use of pure water. I think he and his walk and work of nearly one hundred years in virtue's paths has proved a *perennial feast.* Now he is *all alone,* biding his Father's time for the pale boatman to come, to guide him safely over the shadowy stream to that land unseen by mortal eye, where darkness or shadow never comes. He died fourteen days short of his one-hundredth birth day, in hope of a glorious resurrection.

His whole life has been one of *ceaseless* activity, is about five feet six or seven inches in height, and weighs perhaps 140 or 150 pounds.

CHAPTER XIII.

CONTENTS.—Matters Relating to the Health of Boston —The Professors of Harvard and Jefferson Medical Colleges and the Doctors of Boston—Dr. J. C. Warren—Visit from the Legislature—Dr. John Ware— Dr. George Hayward—Dr. Walter Channing—The Medical and Clerical Professions combined—Practice in Boston—Fifty years ago—Then and Now.

Dr. John C. Warren, Professor of Anatomy and Surgery, in Harvard Medical College, filled this chair or forty years, as his father had done before him. He was an eminent surgeon, and though a slow lecturer, was always sure. One winter, while I attended medical lectures, we had considerable rowdyism about the old Mason Street College. There was singing, shouting, and some swearing—medical students are generally not renowned for decency and good behavior ;— I judge so, from the fact that this was the case not only in Harvard, but also in the Jefferson Medical College, in Philadelphia, where I also attended lectures. The students would leave Dr. Webster's lecture on chemistry, in which they never took much interest, and go up to the door of Dr. Warren's room, and stand and kick against it half an hour before the time of lecture. One day Dr. Warren gave us a very pleasant lecture on good manners after the following tenor : " There has been considerable disturbance about this building, in the way of singing, shouting, and such like. I am fond of singing, and if any of you wish to sing, I will stop in my lecture; and afterwards proceed with it. Then, as to kicking my door, it is no use to do that. It will not open until twelve o'clock; that is, making allowance for different time pieces; for, though the "Old South" clock and the "Park Street" clock are both orthodox clocks; yet they don't run exactly alike."

The next day, as Dr. W. was lecturing on the eye, and while holding the artificial eye in his hand, a large wad of paper was thrown from an upper seat of the amphitheatre, and passed directly between the Doctor's eyes and the artificial one in his hand. The Doctor laid down the eye; turned pale; attempted to speak; and choked up; but finally said, "I don't know who threw that, and I don't want to know, but if I ever do know, I will treat him like a rascal;" Then, as though this expression from one of his age and dignified calling did not come with a good grace, and seemingly upon second thought, he added, "but if he will confess it, and ask forgiveness, I will forgive him." A brother of ex-Governor Clifford, a member of the class, knowing who threw the paper, arose and said, "It is well known who threw it, and he had better confess it and ask Dr. Warren's forgiveness" A young man, apparently not more than eighteen or twenty arose and said, "I threw it,—Sir." "Well, why did you do it?" said Dr. Warren. "I don't know, Sir," said the young man; "others had thrown things, and I did it thoughtlessly." "Well."

said the Dr. with a good deal of emphasis, " I forgive you." He then said, " After the pleasant lecture which I gave you yesterday, and which I did not at my own option, but at the request of my colleagues, I being the oldest Professor, it was a gross insult." As the students revered Dr. Warren more than any other one of the Professors, this broke up the rowdyism for that winter, and they behaved decently.

Up to that time, it had been very difficult to obtain subjects for dissection; and sometimes the resurrection-boys had been caught in stealing bodies from the graveyard. One day, Dr. Warren said, " Young gentlemen, I am to have some invited guests at my next lecture, and I want you to leave three or four of these lower seats vacant."

The next day, some thirty members of the legislature, with old Dr. Buck at their head, (he then being a member of that body) entered and occupied these vacant seats. Dr. Warren's object in inviting them, was to obtain a law by which subjects for dissection could be better secured. Whether by design or not, I am unable to say; the Dr. was lecturing upon an old subject, which had begun to smell, and which, consequently, is not very agreable, except to those who love ammonia. Soon, some of the invited guests began to hold their handkerchiefs to their noses; and ere long, one of them arose and left; another and another followed suit, until none of them remained, save Dr. Buck; and, as the last of his colleagues disappeared through the door, Dr. Buck looked at Dr. Warren and smiled. Suffice it to say, the Dr. obtained the law he desired, and which is still in force. By it, the bodies of paupers, who die at the Institutions of the city and have no friends to claim them, are delivered to the faculty for the use of the college.

During two or three of the last years of Dr. Warren's life, he invited the Doctors of Boston to his house for an evening's entertainment. On these occasions, he took us from the cellar to the attic. In the former, we saw the bird-tracks on the stones taken from the bottom of the Connecticut River, or somewhere else; where, when made, it was a soft material, and afterwards became hardened into stone. As we ascended from room to room, they were filled with various specimens, such as Doctors love to collect. Indeed, we here saw, not what Dr. John C. Warren had himself collected; but, also, many things which his father had gathered during the forty years that he filled the same Professorship. When we had inspected everything, and came to the collation, which consisted of oysters and other good things, which Doctors love, the old Dr. would say, " There are a great many things in this house;" which was, indeed, very true.

Dr. Warren had a fine set of gold plate. But this was not produced, when he used to invite the Students, once each winter, while he lectured; nor, on the occasions above named, near the close of his life, when he invited Doctors. I was, however, once invited there, when an English lord visited this country; and, at that time, the table was spread with gold Plate.

Dr. J. C. Warren descended from an aristocratic family. He valued himself highly upon his successful operations, and very justly, for, he was a skillful surgeon. On one occasion, he was taking up the Subclavian artery—a very nice operation to be sure. But, he mistook the artery twice, and took the vein of the same name. Each time, he was informed of his mistake by an assistant. It was a mistake readily made even by a good operator. The next day, the Doctor occupied the whole hour of his lecture in apologizing for his mistake. This showed how much he felt it.

Dr. W. was in many respects a very remarkable man. He did much for the cause of temperance, and was for many years, the honored President of the Massachusetts Temperance Society.

He was, also, a pious man, and in the two volumes of his Biography, recently presented to me by his Grandson, Dr. J. Collins Warren, a son of Dr. J. Mason Warren, who occupies the old homestead, I find several prayers written by him, in admirable style and an excellent spirit.

Dr. John Ware, our Professor of Theory and Practice, was meek; apparently, humble; a gentlemen of sterling common sense, an acute observer, rarely mistaken in his opinion, and one of the most reliable physicians that Boston has ever had since it has been known to the writer. Whenever I wanted counsel in any medical case, Dr. John Ware was my first choice. Next to him, came Dr. Marshall S. Perry; who, though not a Professor, was a perfect gentleman, of sterling integrity.

above all trickery, and one who never stole patients, In this last respect, he was *toto celo*, above some physicians with whom I have come in contact within my thirty years practice in Boston.

Of Professor Webster, when suspicion first rested on him as the murderer of Dr. Parkman, I said, I did not believe it, for, he was to indolent too murder any man.

Dr. George Hayward was another of our Professors. He was a good lecturer, a very passable operator ; and evinced his self-complacency by the manner he struck the heels of his boots into the pavement as he walked. He belonged to the old Hayward family, and had a good share of the stamina of that substantial race. Dr. H. was a man of considerable reading, had travelled abroad, and felt that he was not a whit " behind the chiefest," be they whom they might.

Professor Walter Channing was another of our teachers. He amused us with many funny stories, and sometimes said more than he meant. This was the case at one of the meetings held to stir up the citizens to bring the Cochituate water into the city. Several meetings were held in " old Faneuil Hall" to get the steam up ; and, at one of them, Dr. Channing made an address, in which he undertook to prove that the water would cost the owners of real estate nothing, as the tenants would have to pay for it. By way of illustration, he said, I own a house in Tremont Street, (that being where he lived, and one which he owned as was well known.) I own another in Beacon street, and so on. The next morning, the papers came out with these statements, with comments. "We did not know Dr. Channing was so rich." So, the Dr. hastened from office to office to have these statements rectified, as they contained more than he meant to say, " Why, I don't own but one house in the world," said he. Well, but you said you did, replied the men of the quills. "Oh! but I was speaking hypothetically," said the Doctor.

Dr. Channing was an amiable gentleman, and he is still living at a very advanced age.

Professor Jacob Bigelow was considered perhaps, the most scholarly man of all our Professors in Harvard Medical College at that time. He still lives at nearly ninety years of age. He is too well known as a writer and a learned man to need commendation from us.

In the Jefferson Medical College of Philadelphia, Prof. Muter was an excellent lecturer, and greatly loved and admired by the students.

Prof. Dungleson was correct, a little heavy, but on the whole, a good instructor.

Prof. Mitchell was calm, clear, and a fine lecturer. At the old Pennsylvania Medical University, where I also attended one course, we had Professors Wood, the Author of the U. S. Dispensatory, a wonderful man; Jackson, Rogers and other eminent men.

A word must, also, be said of Prof. H. H. Childs, of the Berkshire Medical Institute. He was a man of great activity and indomitable perseverance, a true friend and a most excellent man.

Under such men, and at four Medical Colleges, I attended lectures; so that if I was not posted in medicine, it was my own fault, and must be ascribed to my own obtuseness of faculty, for, I certainly sat at the feet of a sufficient number of " Gamaliels."

Having been previously engaged in another profession, I had an opportunity to compare the two, which many never have. There is some difference in the general temperament and manner of speaking in these two professions—the clergy are more excitable, loud and boisterous in the their manner, and deliver their messages more in the form of a harangue and, hence, work more upon the passions. The Medical Professors are calm, moderate, and philosophical in their addresses, plainly stating what they have to say, and letting it pass for what it is worth : while many clergymen seem determined to beat, by main strength, their sermons into the heads of their hearers, forgetting that " bodily exercise profiteth little,"

Both professions are about equally dogmatic and tenacious in their opinions—both denounce almost all who differ from them in sentiment and opinion, and both wax warmer and more zealous in proportion to their ability to sit as judges upon the merits of others. On the whole, from a survey of these two learned and liberal Professions, for forty years, attending upon their instruction, and mingling with them in all their clerical Associations, Presbyteries, Assemblies, and Medical Societies from " Suffolk District" to the " American Medical Association," though in both there have been some hot headed, and aspiring, yet, the clergy have rather taken the palm from the " Medicine men.'

In a word, there has been no small smattering of human nature, of its foibles and follies in both,—surely, sufficient to lead one to say—

"I've seen an end of all perfection here below."

As I lived in Boston, I began to practice in Boston. It is no easy matter for a young physician, unless he have a father, or uncle, or some influential man to introduce him, to get a practice in a city like Boston. A multitude of physicians commence practice in the city and soon leave—are starved out. There are physicians who will aid a young man, though he be not a relative; but their number is, comparitively, small. Such, however, were Prof. John Ware, Marshall S. Perry and Winslow Lewis. All of these aided me.

I never made any pretentions to surgical skill, my taste being altogether for Medical practice. But some times, a surgical case would o come in, that it could not well be avoided. Early in my practice, an old lady, more than four score, fell down stairs and broke one of her legs. I was called, and set it as well as I knew how. But, that night I felt very much as Dr. Channing used to tell each class, the story of his first patient. She was a lady, and he gave her an emetic, (it was more customary to give emetics then—fifty or sixty years ago—than now, 1875) and, said he, " I could not sleep any that night for fear I had given enough to kill her," so I could not sleep, lest I might not have set the broken leg well. The next morning, therefore, I met Dr. Winslow Lewis, one of our best Surgeons, a most polite man, and told him my trouble. "Oh!" said he, "I will go and see it." What was my gratification when, after examining it, he said, "You have set this leg as well as I could have done it." In six weeks, the old lady was able to walk, which was a very short time for a fracture to unite in so old a person.

I shall never forget the following case which occurred in the early days of my practice. A young man, recently married, boarding in a large house, where, also, lived many others, was taken sick with typhoid fever. He was a very sick man, and no Doctor even, could tell whether he would live or die. I attended him, and everything went well for some fifteen days, save only that he was very sick; and, of course, grew no better. One day, when I made my regular visit, I found his yonug wife in tears; and on examining the patient, and finding him no worse, I inquired the cause of her grief. She said, the boarders in the house are urging us to have another Doctor, but, both myself and my husband are satisfied with you. Whom do they want, said I? Dr. Perry, said she. Well, said I, send for Dr. Perry, either with, or without me. She said, We would prefer to have you present. Dr. P. was sent for; came and examined the case—I told him all that I had done. He told them, I was doing just as he should do—that the man was very sick, and it could not be known whether he would recover or not.

Then, all went well so far as I was aware for another week, when, I learned that the same meddlesome boarders had sent for Dr. P., to attend the patient, which he declined to do, telling them that I was doing all, he thought, that could be done in the case.

Dr. P., was again sent for to see the patient with me, which he did. The young man, after thirty-five days of fever, recovered.

When I contrast this treatment of Dr. P., with that of some other physicians, I can but thank him, though, from the depths of my soul, I despise them.

Let me tell you of one of this latter class I was attending an old lady in my neighborhood, when I found him there. He was a distant relative of the family, and the daughters of the lady had called him merely on that account. He came, while I was there; and to the disgust of them and myself, too, he immediately proceeded to treat the case. He treated me as though I had been an outlaw, and had no business there. He died in an Hospital for the Insane—and if boorishness and want of decency are concomitants of insanity, he was always insane.

I have met with some such boors in my later practice but it has not disturbed me as it did then. There are certain Doctors (fal.ely so called) who keep their barkers out, and who, when they find a person sick, especially, with some lingering disease, are ever on the alert to inquire, Who is your Doctor? Why don't you have Dr.— ? He will cure you in less than no time—every body has him, &c. All this kind of management is too mean and detestible in "a learned and liberal profession."

I made *chronic* Diseases—those of the lungs, skin

and nervous system a prominent study. I was led to this rather by the fact that I belonged to a consumptive family; and, also, from another fact, to wit, that I had been compelled to abandon a profession that required public speaking, by a chronic enlargement of the vocal chordes, which prevented me from using my voice. At one time, I had, as patients, twenty clergymen with bad throats. Diseases of the Throat, Lungs, Skin and Nervous System occupied considerable of my attention.

Still, general practice took enough of my time to give one a taste of its pleasures. Three times, in one of the coldest nights of our rough climate, has the door bell aroused me, just as renewed sleep was creeping over me. On no occasion, by day or night, did I refuse to go at call. In some respects, there was not much merit in this, for, necessity was laid upon me to go, or starve; and, in a vast number of cases, going did nothing towards preventing starvation.

Any physician who goes to all the calls made for him, performs more gratuitous labor than can be found among any other class of men. There is a satisfaction in doing this—in relieving pain, in succoring the needy, and in doing good.

A physician in a great city occupies a peculiar position. He is the confidential friend of all his patients. He is entrusted with their secrets. If he were to divulge them, it would produce trouble and consternation in Society. He is made the depository of them, that he may have the better understanding of their diseases, and be the better able to treat them. The clergyman approaches the physician, but does not reach the extent and importance, as to secrets, which the physician does. The lawyer may be entrusted with the secrets of his client, and is not compelled to divulge them even in a court of justice. Nor, should the physician be. Upon this princple, some of the most eminent physicians have refused to divulge them, even in court. Dr. Abernethy said, " I will rot in jail before I will do it." The celebrated Borehaave took a similar position. Some courts have decided that physicians must tell all that is communicated to them, while fulfilling their duty as the medical adviser. But, this requirement is a bad one ; and should never be insisted on, as, if for no other reason, it may criminate others who are not concerned in the case.

Besides, were the physician to be loquacious—were he to be open mouthed, he would soon destroy himself. He would blast all his attempts to get practice. A Doctor, who cannot hold his tongue, ought to have it cut out, or abandon his profession. I have known a young physician ruined in his practice, by his own loquacity.

No man goes through so many, and so great changes in so short a time as does the physician. Now, he is in the palace of the rich, and the abode of the honorable, rejoicing with those who rejoice that "a man child is born into the world." Anon, he is called to a den of infamy, where life is ebbing away by the vice of the poor sufferer ; and into all the intermediate circles between these extremes. He needs to be a man of unshrinking principle, indomitable perseverance, vigorous health, courageous, fearless, gentle, and possessed of a dumb tongue. All this, and more will be acknowledged by any one who shall accompany him on his visits for a single day or night in a great city. After all, the Doctor of to-day, cannot do like the Doctor of fifty years ago, as will be seen in the sequel. Old Dr. John C. Warren said to us, among some of his closing remarks, which were always good and of vast moment,—" never attend a patient that will not mind you. I was called last night to see a Beacon Street lady and prescribed for her. I saw her this morning and she said, Dr. I didn't take that medicine you prescribed last night. " Well, why didn't you take it ?" I didn't know as it would do me any good. "I took my hat and walked out. That is the way to do." It might have have done for Professor John C. Warren, but it would not do so well for a young Doctor in 1875.

EIFTY YEARS AGO, THEN AND NOW.

Then men lived temperately eating pea-porridge, and lived long, too, and were healthy. Now, they live fast, eat everything, and die young, or live on as miserable invalids. Then they drank water, cider, small beer and old Jamacia-rum, and rarely died drunkards. Now they drink tea, coffee, ale, and liquors poisoned with drugs, and die at an early age of paralysis. Then we had boys and girls, and children were taught to obey and reverence their parents, and to " honor the old man," Now, there are no boys, and girls, but young men and young ladies, and parents obey their children, and old men and women are soon made to know, that they have no more business on earth, than a mole above ground. Then, children learned more useful knowledge by six months schooling in a year, and that only till they were a dozen or fourteen, than they do now from four to twenty years. Then, what they studied was useful, spelling, reading, writing, arithmetic, their mother-tongue. Now, it is a smattering of everything, and not much of anything,—a little Latin, a little French, less German,

"To gain other tongues,
And lose their own."

Then, farming was honorable, and a trade necessary and durable. Now, cultivating the ground is despised, and what we learned from Noah Webster's spelling book, to wit,—" all mankind live on the fruits of the ground; the first and most necessary employment, therefore, is to till the earth,"—is practically false ; and to be a popin-jay in a store, jump a yard-stick, be a man-milliner, and make egg-shell bonnets, seems to be the glory of our young men, and to wear them and other gew-gaws, the sole wish, rather than occupation, of the young women, and old ones, too.

Then, ministers were reverenced, and supposed to know everything, and no one doubted the truth of what they said ; and when they settled in a parish, they came to stay.

Then ministers honored each other, and always made the oldest, moderator, and gave him the head of the table. Now, the merest stripling, if chance has placed him in the biggest parish ; or brass has brazed his face, or self-conceit elevated his soul ; or, spiritual pride filled his heart, is the presiding deity, and holds the highest rank. May be this is one reason, why ministers have lost the influence they once had, for, no profession can be respected by others, that does not respect itself.

Now, because they are like Sampson, shorn of his locks, weak, and more despised than any other class; "speckled birds, at which all the birds of the forest (and all the birds of the city) do peck,"—they are rolled from place to place as if on wheels, and stay nowhere, the place where the Methodist minister's daughter said, she was born.—So many of them are out of parishes that, four or five are sometimes found hired, in one Insurance office, and, if a parish becomes vacant, the deacon or elder, (who holds a standing office), in a single month, has fifty applications for the empty pulpit. —Brother Sargent, good, obliging man, on Saturday, has twenty ministers, and but five pulpits. Yet thousands of ministers are wanted, really and truly, if the whole heathen world is to be converted; but, not such, as must have the sunniest place in Zion.

Then, Lawyers were somebody. They were not all mischief-makers—they had ability. Old Jeremiah Mason, when he wished to put Gabriel on the stand, and make him swear, knew he could do E. K. Avery no good, unless he would swear, and so he spoiled the heavenly vision—and Daniel Webster, (though when a boy, he only helped his brother " Zeke " do nothing), could get a murderer even, clear, though he confessed his guilt; and Rufus Choate with whom lingered even to our day, a spark out of "Hervey's meditations among the Tombs," of the old fire, could prove that Tirrell was a somnambulist, even. Now, lawyers are; well, I mus'nt say what they are, only I heard some men talking the other night about a lease, drawn by one in their interest, who made fools of them all; and, the Weymouthians might have been right, when they objected to Parson Smith's daughters marrying John Adams, " because he belonged to a useless profession."

Then, Doctors, too, were of some consequence. Every old woman would trumpet " what the doctor said," from one end of the parish to the other, quick as no time; then, too, no one could be a doctor, who didn't know something; or, if he were, he had to go farther, and could get no pay for what his tom-foolery· Now, who cares for what the doctor says? And, who *is* a doctor? Jonney, who drove my hack yesterday, is as much a doctor to-day; has as big a shingle, and more patients, than his master, who was fool enough to study all his life to make *him* a doctor—and the worst, I was going to say—no, and the best of it all, is, these jump-up-behinders get the largest fee, and laugh at the old fools who have spent the best of their lives to make themselves doctors. The women, too, but here my heart fails me, for, some of them are among the best of the whole pack; so, " let them slide."

Then, too, doctors, educated doctors, did not quarrel as now—were not divided into different sects, as now— " old school," (for, *we* have never admitted the nickname of *allopathic* which a certain class have endeavored to fasten upon us) Homœopathists, Eclectic. Thompsonian, Hydropathic, and a dozen other names. Then, a doctor *was* a doctor, neither more nor less. Now, this very day, February 21, 1875, a board of commissioners are in session, to expel one class from the Massachusetts Medical Society. Then, to be sure, there was, now and then, a quack, which has been the case from the days of Paracelsus Theophrastus Bombastus, the father of the whole tribe; but, then, if he found some fool to employ him, he had to whistle for his pay.

Then, we had " the one horse shay," which " Oliver Wendell" has attempted to describe and the old "stage-coach," which Lucius Manlius Sargent has immortalized in one of his " Temperance Tales." Now, we have fast horses, with all kinds of vehicles, from the phæton to the no-top buggy, with Jehu-like drivers, racing every Sabbath along Columbus Avenue, in spite of the Angell and his agents of the " Society for preventing Cruelty to Animals."

Then, we had no steam-boats to blow up, or burn down on the Sound—no rail-roads to send fast trains to smash up slow ones; no telegraphs to tell in London what was done in Boston half an hour before—as now. All these things have come up since our boyhood. Who will say, "the world don't move?" or, if he says so, who will believe him?

Then, the extravagance that now prevails in living— in houses, dress, equipage and everything else—was unknown. The writer is yet among the sixties, and still, he has lived long enough to see a complete change in ministerial influence, doctrine and practice, so far as permanency is concerned—also, a thorough change in Medical practice; from bleeding and calomelizing, to little medicine, and among many, to none at all. If these changes go on for the next half century as they have for the last, who can tell what will then be? Probably, men and women will fly like pigeons; breakfast in Boston, dine in London; sup in the palace of the Russian Bear; sleep in China, and dine at home he next day.

That there have been no improvements during this time is not denied. The world has made progress! Many of the old and crude notions and practices have changed for the better. One man can superintend the machinery of as much work as ten, perchance, twenty could have done. But, after all, as the lecture of Wendell Phillips—that old lecture on the " Lost Arts,'! which is over new, intimates, what has been lost, quite balances what has been gained.

We may think, as Job did of his friends, " doubtless we are the men, and wisdom will die with us." But, it will not. We shall do as our predecessors have—die and be forgotten, and the world will still go on—the sun will rise and set—the seasons go their rounds, " seed-time and harvest, cold and heat, day and night, summer and winter will not cease"—men and women will marry and be given in marriage, children come and go, and all the change will be, *we* shall not be here.

The writer has had an opportunity of seeing more than some others, in the fact, that he has seen the inside workings of two of the learned professions, and, been regularly inducted into both of them ; and, if teaching is a profession, into three of them. In all of these, he has found human imperfection.

> "Ambition, powerful source of good, or ill
> Has entered into them all."

But, it may be more prudent not to disclose the inside workings, and movements—the "wheels within wheels;" the strivings for power, honor, influence and place, than to lift the veil ; and so, let the curtain remain.

RECOLLECTIONS OF PHILADELPHIA.

CHAPTER XIV.

CONTENTS.—First Visit to the Quaker City—Camden and Amboy Rail Road—Contrast in the Streets of Boston and Philadelphia—Second Visit to that City—Our Boarding House—Medical College—Clinton Street Church—Lecturing in Private Schools—Visiting Public Places—The Place of Penn's Treaty with the Indians—His Second Purchase—Independence Hall—Fairmount-Water-Works—Fightings in—'52 and 3, in Philadelphia—Medical Colleges of that City.

My first visit to Philadelphia was made in 1843. I went there with a young gentleman, a teacher of one of the public schools of Boston. Our business was to reconnoitre in reference to opening a Female Seminary in that city. Previous to leaving Boston, I informed Benjamin Perkins, then of the firm of Perkins and Marvin, whom I knew to have a brother that was a bookseller in that city. Mr. Perkins said "you will have to pass over the Camden and Amboy Rail Road, and they will charge you double fare and treat you like a highway robber." Horace Greely used to call New Jersey, the state of Camden and Amboy, on account of the vast influence that corporation had over the state.

At that time, it was said, they were under obligation to the state to run one passenger train a day for three dollars, each; but they were careful to send off this train before the Eastern boats arrived in New York, so that all who came from the East had to go in the second train for which the fare was four dollars, each. Really, every person who lived out of the State of New Jersey was compelled to pay one dollar more for his passage from New York to Philadelphia, than those who lived in that State. Even down to a recent period, any person passing between these cities, who understood how this road was managed, could save a dollar by purchasing a ticket to some place in the State, and there securing another ticket to carry him through it. The sum and substance of it was, that, every person who passed through the State of New Jersey should be taxed one dollar extra; or, pay that sum more than a resident of the State.

The cars were of a peculiar construction, with the door at the side instead of the end. They were marked A. B. C. &c., and were proportionately dilapidated as we descended down the Alphabet. A gentleman who had a lady could enter the car A. but, as we had no lady we were waited upon into car D. The Conductor would come along every few moments and with a loud voice exclaim, "Show your tickets." Having done this several times, one of us had the impertinence to ask how often he wished to see them; for which we escaped only, as by the skin of our teeth from being put off the car. Thus Mr. Perkin's prediction came well-nigh being verified. Fortunately, under its new managers, the accommodations of this road have been greatly improved.

Upon arriving in Philadelphia, we were much interested in the laying out of that city. Having been long accustomed to the short, crooked streets and lanes of Boston, we were surprised at the long, straight streets of Philadelphia, crossing each other at right angles and thus making the whole city an immense checker-board On this visit for the first time, we saw Rev. Albert Barnes. We found him at his country house in West Philadelphia setting out strawberry vines in his garden. He did not encourage us much as to our contemplated school. He said Prof. Charles D. Cleveland had just opened a lady's school in that city which was very popular. I shall have more to say of Mr. Barnes hereafter.

My second visit to Philadelphia, was in Sept. 1852. I went there as Prof. of Physiology, Hygiene and Medical Jurisprudence in the Woman's Medical College, of Pennsylvania.

Philadelphia is the hottest place in the summer in North America, not excepting Charleston and New Orleans. Usually, September is as hot there as any of the summer months. My wife was with me. We took lodgings in a large boarding house in Third Street. The room was a large one, directly over the kitchen, under us were the puppies, which yelped all night, in the bed were the fleas and bed-bugs, and the room was filled with those enormous mosquetoes many of which would weigh a pound. Under all these annoyances, we could not sleep. The skin of my wife, being thinner than mine, and more delicate, it looked in the morning as though she were breaking out with the small-pox. The second night she wore her gloves and covered her face. This of course plagued the mosquitoes, but was no barrier to the fleas and bed-bugs. The next day, we removed to Fifth Street and took up our abode with a widow woman, who was a Quaker. There we had no annoyance from the pests which had afflicted us at the other place. When we told the good woman we were going to remove, she said, she was afraid we did not like our accommodations.

At our new boarding house, we made some pleasant acquaintances, among whom were Dr. Hayes, the Arctic explorer, then an under graduate, and a Mr. Asbury a great grandson of Bishop Asbury, and several other students. Our good Quakeress-provider was economical, as all good house-keepers should be; and, as Rebecca preferred Jacob to Esau, so she had her favorites, among the boarders, of whom Asbury was chief. She always sweetened the tea and coffee herself, and when any one wanted more sugar, she had one universal salvo.—"It is not stirred up." One day, Asbury called for more sugar. The good lady replied, "Asbury, It is not stirred up." Asbury retorted with a good share of the energy of the old Bishop from whom he descended—"Yes it is stirred up, I guess I know when it is stirred up." At this remark from her favorite, Hayes was so pleased that he wore an unusually pleasant countenance for a week.

I gave the introductory lecture at the College, which was printed. During this Winter, I became acquainted with many of the Philadelphians I preached several Sabbaths at the Clinton Street, Presbyterian Church, which was then without a Pastor. This house was originally built for a Congregational Church; and the Rev. John Todd was its Pastor. Under his ministry, Congregationalism failed in that city; and no effort was made to resusitate if for thirty years. The Presbyterians bought the house and turned it into a Presbyterian Church. As I became acquainted with the committee, appointed to select a candidate, they invited me to attend one of their meetings. They said, they wanted an Eastern man; and inquired who were some of the most popular ministers we had in Boston and Massachusetts. I named several, and among others, the Rev. Dr. Stone, then recently settled at Park Street. The Chairman of the Committee said, do you consider Dr. Stone a popular preacher? I replied, certainly, he became pastor of Park Street Church when the house was nearly empty; and has filled it to overflowing. "That is very singular," said he. "Mr. Stone was Agent of the Sunday School Union in this city; and when we wanted a supply and could get no one else, I engaged him, but I never did it but the people found fault with me for getting him." I asked a prominent clergyman how he accounted for this? He replied, "naturally enough. If the angel Gabriel were to come to Philadelphia, as a Sunday School Agent, Clinton Street Church would think him a very poor preacher."

This Winter, I lectured on Physiology and Hygiene

to a number of schools in Philadelphia; and among others, to that of Professor, Charles D. Cleveland. He had the most prosperous school in that city. It was limited to sixty pupils. Persons often waited two or three years for a vacancy. Mr. Cleaveland was strongly opposed to slavery, though a number of the young ladies of the school were from the South. I remember, a southern gentleman called upon him to secure a place for his daughter in the school: Mr. Cleveland said, "If your daughter comes to me, I shall teach her all the abominations of slavery." He replied, " I do not care what you teach her about slavery, provided you instruct her well in other things." I was lecturing one day on the constituent properties of the blood; when the Professor interrupted me by saying, "Is there any essential difference in the blood of a negro; and that of a white man?" I replied, there is no material difference. Then, addressing the school, he said, "You see young ladies, the Professor of Physiology says, "there is no difference between the blood of a negro and that of a white man. This harmonizes with the declaration of the Bible that, God has made of one blood all nations of men that dwell on the whole earth." This was the most perfectly organized school I ever visited.

This Winter, I visited the public buildings and prominent places of this old " Quaker City;" among which should be first named that in Kensington, called by the Indians, Shackamacon, near the famous old Elm under which William Penn made the following address

to the Red men. " We meet on the broad pathway of faith and good will. No advantage shall be taken on either side, but all shall be openness and love. I will not call you children, for parents sometimes chide their children too severely; nor brothers only, for brothers differ;—the friendship between thee and me I will not compare to a chain, for that, the rains may rust, or the falling tree may break; we are the same, as if one man's body were to be divided into two parts; we are all one flesh and blood." This speech of Penn's and conduct corresponding thereto were the reasons why perfect peace prevailed between the Indians and Penn's Colony, while every ten miles of New England soil was the scene of an Indian Massacre.

On one occasion only, did the Indians ever manifest any displeasure at the conduct of William Penn, or, any of his associates. This was, when Penn made his second purchase of land from the Indians. The contract was that, for a certain number of knives, beads, handkerchiefs, &c., he was to have as much land as a white man could walk around in a day. By the advice of Penn's associates, they engaged an Englishman, accustomed to travelling, who walked nearly as fast as a horse could trot. When Penn came to settle with them, the Indians were cross and sullen. Penn inquired the reason: and asked them if it was not their own bargain, and why they were displeased? They said, "yes, it was their own bargain, but the white brother took too big a walk. They never knew a man make such a walk before." Some of Penn's associates said, the Indians should be made to stand by their bargain, but Penn said, that would involve the spirit of war. He then asked them how many more beads and blankets he should give them, to make them satisfied. They stated the number, and he immediately complied with their request. When the Indians received them, they departed perfectly satisfied. Penn then said to his associates " how easy a thing it is to have peace."

No place in Philadelphia has more attractions for a stranger and lover of our history, than Indepencence Hall. This is a relic of the "Revolution." It was built in 1729-34. Visiting this relic of " ye olden time," and carefully examining it, we had peculiar sensations. In the Hall where the " Declaration of Independence" was signed, those old patriots, of " stubborn stuff," seemed to stand before us. We hear the silence, see the wavering, then, the resolution, and, at last, the final determination, " swim or sink, live or die," by which they arrive at the point of signing the immortal document. The first one to speak, is Rev. and venerable Patriot, *John Witherspoon*, of New Jersey. Like his old brother, John Knox before Mary, " the bloody," he does not quail. Bent with the weight of years, he rises and addresses his comrades, as he casts upon them a look of inexpressible interest and unconquerable determination, he speaks. "There is a tide in the affairs of men : a nick of time . we perceive it now before us. That noble instrument upon your table, which insures immortality to its author, should be subscribed this very morning, by every member in this room. He who will not respond to its call is unworthy the name of a freeman! Although these hairs must descend into the tomb, I would rather, infinitely rather! they should wither by the hand of the public executioner, than desert, at this crisis, the sacred cause of my country." He ceased. But, the fire of patriotism begun to burn brighter in every bosom, till JOHN HANCOCK, the President, noble representative of our " old Bay State," takes up the pen and signs his name in a large, bold hand; and, as he rises says, " There! John Bull can read my name without spectacles, and may now double his reward for my head. That is my defiance!"

Here, we saw the " Old Bell," which was cracked in ringing out the glad tidings of liberty to all the land. This Bell bears the following inscription, composed by Isaac Norris, a prominent member of the Colonial Assembly.

"The motto of our Father band,
Circled the world in its embrace;
'Twas Liberty throughout the land,
And good to all their brother race:
Long here—within the pilgrim's bell,
Had lingered—though it often peeled—
Those treasured tones that eke should tell
When Freedom's proudest scroll was sealed!"

The sturdy infant, born in " Independence's Hall,', July 4th, 1776, was rocked in the "old Cradle of Liberty in Faneuil Hall," and became too powerful and combative for all the troops of George the Third. Every

American, who visits Philadelphia and Boston, should carefully inspect these ever to be remembered edifices.

I visited FAIRMONNT WATER WORKS. These immense works supplied the City of Philadelphia with water, from the river Schuylkill. The water power was obtained by the erection of a dam across the river. The most wonderful thing about these works is, that the water is compelled to pump itself up into a vast reservoir 92 feet in a perpendicular height. I always considered this the greatest exploit, the Philadelphians ever accomplished; and I have wondered a thousand times how they had skill to do it; when they never knew how to teach the surplus water in the city to flow under the ground; but allowed it to run from their dwellings over the sidewalks, to produce ice in Winter, and bedraggle ladies' dresses in Summer. This dirty water, often remaining in puddles, and exhaling a noisome vapor, filled with pestilential effluvia, I believe, is looked upon by all strangers who visit that city as not only uncleanly; but also a great destroyer of health.

The ladies of Philadelphia, however, acquire a peculiar facility by habit of taking their dresses over these almost innumerable cess-pools; for, as they approach them by applying one hand to the dress, and a peculiar wriggle of the body, they pass over them with their dresses dry and clean; while a Yankee-girl, unaccustomed to them, would find her dress all bedraggled with mud and water. "The water-works at Fairmount were started July 1st, 1822, and from the commencement to December 31, 1850, including the

FAIRMOUNT PARK FROM PENNSYLVANIA BRIDGE.

cost of erection, and with the yearly additions to the works themselves, together with the extensions of the iron pipes in the city each year, they have cost $1,615,-169,82. The whole of the works (with the exception of the dam across the river). including the plan of distribution of the water in the city, were designed and executed by the late Frederick Graff, Esq.; and for efficiency and simplicity are not exceeded by any similar works now in operation. The city of Philadelphia was the first in the United States that possessed water-works, it being supplied by steam power previous to the erection of the present works at Fairmount; it has, therefore, served as a model for almost all public improvements of this kind erected in the country."

No one should visit Philadelphia, and leave it without spending some hours at these famous Water Works. I consider them the great wonder of the City. This water is much softer than the Cochituate, of Boston, or, the Croton, of New York. The great difference is perceived by simply washing one's hands in the water used in the " Quaker City."

What used to be called Philadelphia, and what was known to people abroad, as that city, was composed of three or four distinct municipalities. These all and each had its own city government, and in consequence of this, there were constant broils among the firemen and others. I witnessed several of these fights. I then considered Philadelphia very far behind Boston in this matter of squabbles, for, in the latter named city, I remembered but a single mob, to wit, that upon William Lloyd Garrison; while, in this single winter; I saw many of these mobocratic gatherings. The arch Street Presbyterian Church was near my boarding house, and the Rev. Dr. Wadsworth, a very popular preacher, had then just commenced preaching there. About as often as every other Sabbath, the firemen from the various cities would assemble near the Church, and with yellings and shoutings, keep up this disturbance almost the whole time of the service. I remember, I did not at that time, think Philadelphia a very orderly city; and, I said, such disturbances would not be allowed in Boston.

Happily, since the consolidation of all the separate municipalities into one, these disgraceful scenes have never transpired, and Philadelphia is now as well ordered, as any city in the Union. At that time, it was the cleanest and neatest city, I had ever seen. I fear, it has not always maintained this high reputation for cleanliness in all the years since 1852-3.

Philadelphia then had four regular, old School Medical Colleges, the old Medical University, the oldest; and, by many considered, the best Medical School in America, the Jefferson, founded by Dr. George McClellan, a New-England-man, to establish which, he had a long and bitter contest with the friends of the old University; the Philadelphia College, then managed by Prof. James McClintock, and the Pennsylvania Medical College. Of these four Colleges, the University and Jefferson, were the largest. I frequently attended the Lectures at each of these Colleges. I was very much interested in the lectures of Professor Jackson, on Physiology, and, also, those of Professor Wood, at the University. All the Professors, at this School, were men of great eminence and large attainments in the Medical Profession.

In the Jefferson, I was much interested in the lectures of Professor Muter. He was, I think, all things considered, the best, most thorough and pleasing lecturer, I ever listened to. Professors, Dungleson and Mitchell were, also, excellent lecturers; and, while I was myself lecturing in the Woman's College, as regular and as old School a College as any of them, I confess, I derived much information from the lectures of these other Colleges.

CHAPTER XV.

CONTENTS.—Girard College—Removal to Philadelphia—The private Schools of that City—The Public Schools and the School-Boards— Comparison between them and the Schools in Boston—Mischief of choosing Directors there, by Politicians: the same as in Boston—Ladies at the Head of the Grammar Schools—Voting Places in Philadelphia—Liquor Selling and Tobacco—Sabbath Schools, and Two Sessions in Phidadelphia—The Squirrels, the Worms and the Birds of Philadelphia.

Girard College·—This magnificent building is situated on the Ridge Road, about a mile out of the limits of the old incorporated city, of Philadelphia; and, since the consolidation, it is included in the city. It was founded by Stephen Girard, for the education and support of destitute orphans. Girard was born in France, and came to this country, at the age of ten years, in the capacity of a cabin-boy. By industry and economy, he accumulated a large fortune, the larger part of which, he bequeathed to the city of Philadelphia for the support of this Institntion. This College is one of the most beautiful edifices of modern times, a wonderful work of art, and the most wonderful monument of private munificence, to the cause of education, in the world. The corner-stone was laid the 4th of July, 1833, the buildings were completed in 1847; and the Institution went into operation in 1848. It is under the control of the city government. Girard was a peculiar and eccentric man. Many anecdotes are related of him. A full statue of him meets your eye, as you enter Girard College. This lasting monument to his memory will remain to the end of time. The Philadelphians, also, have taken much pains to perpetuate his name; thus, they have hitched to it Girard Bank, Girard Insurance Company, Girard Street, Girard Avenue, and more other Girard's than we have space to enumerate. The following clause in his will has tarnished his name among ministers and other Christians,—" I enjoin and require that, no ecclesiastic, missionary, or minister, of any sect, whatever, shall ever hold, or, exercise any station or duty, whatever in said College; nor, shall any such person be

GIRARD COLLEGE.

admitted, for any purpose, or, as a visitor within the premises appropriated to the purposes of said College.!' This article is immediately followed by this explanation,—" In making this restriction, I do not mean to cast any reflection upon any sect, or, persons whatever; but, as there is such a multitude of sects, and such a diversity of opinion amongst them, I desire to keep the tender minds of the orphans, who are to derive advantage from this bequest, free from the excitements, which clashing doctrines and sectarian controversy are so apt to produce." We think, ministers and christians ought to bewail their own selfishness and folly, in having divided themselves into so many sects, rather than find fault with Girard for these restrictions. It should teach them an important lesson; to wit, not to divide " the one body of Christ" into separate bands, by " one, saying, I am of Paul, another, I of Cephas, and I of Apollos;" or, for taking any other name than that of Christians.

The Girard Bank.—This is on Third, opposite Dock Street. It is a stately edifice, built originally for the " United States Bank," technically called, " Nick Biddle's Bank," or, " Old Nicks." After Gen. Jackson strangled this Bank, by refusing to renew its charter, Girard purchased the building, and called it after his own name. Here, from early morning until three o'clock, P. M., he transacted, in person, his extensive concerns, as a banker, and instructed. and received reports, from his numerous agents and captains of his vessels. After banking hours, he retired to his farm, where he enjoyed the pleasure of rural employments until the evening, when he again returned to his bank, where the midnight hour found him examining and scrutinizing the accounts of his clerks, with a keenness of inspection peculiar to himself. In the study of Girard's history, we cease to wonder at his magical success. His secret lay in the patient application of a sagacious mind to the single object of accumulation. It is in vain to say, that with some, all things seem to prosper, while beneath the touch of others everything withers and dies. The secret of success, so well understood by this remarkable man, is not so very difficult to solve after all; it lies in a word, and that is, Perseverance.

At this visit to Philadelphia in 1852, I first became acquainted with Matthew Newkirk, an eminent merchant of that city, of whom I shall have more to say hereafter.

In 1859, I removed with my family to Philadelphia. I had been so much pleased with that City, and my health so much improved by its genial air, that I resolved to take up my abode there. I resided there seven years, i. e. during the war and a year and a half after its close. My health was good during that whole time, and my old difficulty of the throat, which many years previous compelled me to leave off speaking in public, wholly left me. Very different, however, was the case of my wife. She lost her health, and on that account, we moved back to Boston in 1866.

The Private Schools of Philadelphia were numerous

and some of them very good. As before stated, in my visit to that city in 1852, I had lectured in Professor Clevlands. I opened a school for young ladies, and it prospered. I had pupils, both from the north and from the south. One young lady, from Louisiana, was with us during the whole war. Indeed, she had to remain, for, the simple reason that, she could not go home. She was the only one in the school who advocated the cause of the South.

There was one peculiarity about the teachers in these private schools. It seemed to pervade every school and sieze upon every assistant teacher. It was this,—as soon as he or she had entered a school to endeavor to gain the hearts of the pupils, as Absalom did the hearts of his father's subjects, and attach them to themselves; and then, open a school of their own. So general was this practise that, I do not know of an exception to it in a single school. Such a mean act would be frowned down in Boston; but, it was the order of the day in Philadelphia. Long custom had rendered it popular. I, among others, had a case of this kind. I took in, as a teacher, a woman who had been engaged in another school in Pennsylvsnia, at a distance from Philadelphia. This woman had some relatives in my school. At the end of one year, she opened a school of her own; and, I found, from the day she entered my school, through her relatives, she had been operating upon the pupils to steal them away, when she should commence a school for herself. She succeeded in getting a few of them. But, her course was short, for, the Lord removed her by death before she had operated for herself a single year.

The Public Schools of Philadelphia were better, in many respects, than I expected to find them. Their School-Board, unlike ours in Boston, was composed of two branches, or, a Senate and House of Representatives, the former and higher one, called "the Board of School Controllers," and the latter the "School Directors." The higher Board had control of the High Schools, and selected the school-books for the city. The latter supervised the Schools in each Ward, consisted of twelve members from the Ward, and were chosen by the Ward. The "Board of Control" consisted of one member from each Ward, chosen by the twelve Directors of the Ward.

There, as in Boston, the Directors were chosen from the slimy and dirty waters of the political arena; and, hence, many of them were but poorly qualified to perform the duties devolving upon them. Having a near neighbor, who was a politician, I found myself elected a member of the Board of Directors of Ward nine. I entered on the duties and found many things very different to what they had been in Boston, where I had served several years on the School Committee.

I soon learned, if I wished to introduce any change, or, new measure, I must conceal the fact that, it was a "Boston Notion," for, if this were once imagined, it would surely be defeated. There were some points in which I thought improvements could be made. The schools were not districted, and the result was, where a school was reported to have a good teacher, it would be filled to overflowing, while, in another, which was said to have a poor teacher, there would hardly be a "baker's dozen."

At one of our meetings, I ventured to suggest the propriety of districting the city, and of allowing none to send to a certain school, except those who lived within the District. But, I was immediately confronted by the following question, by a brother Director, "If you paid taxes in the City, and had children to go to school, would you not wish to send them to the best school?"

I replied, certainly, I should. But, it was evident all the children in the great city of Philadelphia could not go to one school; that we then had some schools altogether too large, while others were very small; that, in my judgment, it would be well to district the city, and endeavor to make each school the best. But, my suggestion went for naught, after telling them, the city of Boston was divided into Districts.

Philadelphia was ahead of Boston in one item connected with the Grammar Schools for Girls, to wit, they were all and each of them under the general superintendence of a lady-teacher; and, they were quite as well conducted, as the boys schools, were under a gentleman. I visited one of these schools where, a lady from New Hampshire, had been at the head of it for fifteen years, and the school was in excellent order.

Nothing touched the pride of the School-Board, or, of the teachers of Philadelphia, so keenly, as to intimate that, their schools were, in any respect, inferior to the Boston Schools. One teacher, esteemed the best lady-teacher in that city, said, " I have visited all the leading schools in Boston, and I never saw one there, so good as mine." This, it will be readily seen, was an unanswerable argument, especially, as she was a lady.

I have said, some of the school-directors were not qualified for their duties. It was the province of the member, who visited a school weekly, to sign the transfers, when a pupil went to another school. On one of these visits, a lady-teacher said to me, " here are some Transfers for you to sign." When I had done it, with a merry twinkle of the eye, she said, " I asked Mr —— to sign some last week, and he said, 'I don't write; you may put my name to them, if you wish.' "

Our Boston School Committee has been ignorant enough, but I have never known one of them, who could not write his name.

Much has been said in Boston, about there being no corporal punishment in Philadelphia. The fact was, this matter was regulated by the School-Directors of each Ward, and hence, in some Wards, it was practised, and in others, it was prohibited. In Ward nine, where I was a Director, it was not allowed, and the consequence was as follows.—a pupil, who offended, was suspended from the school till the Directors came, which was every Thursday. Usually, three of the Directors attended these weekly meetings; but, it so happened, that the first week after my duties commenced, I was the only one present, and the case of a boy, some ten years old, was to be adjudicated. The teacher said, this boy has been suspended, and you must decide if he is to be received back, or not. It was a rule that the parents, or, guardians of the children, on such occasions, should come with their children, and the mother of this boy was present. I pulled the little fellow towards me, and found he was stiff as a pole. I asked him how many times he had been suspended? With perfect indifference, he said, "he guessed a dozen times." I said, and, you have been reinstated every time, have you? "Yes;" and you promised to behave better each time, did you not? "Sposed he did:" and you didn't, did you? "Didn't know." Well, said I, my decision is, to reinstate him this time, and if he is suspended again, he must leave the school. You agree to that, do you? "Sposed he did." Turning to the mother, I said, and you agree to it, do you? She said, she suposed so, if the Directors said so. The next week, my coleagues were there, and the wayward boy was again brought before us, suspended. I told them my decision the previous week. They said, we could not afford to lose any more from the school, for, it was so small now that we draw very little money. I replied, the reason, it is so small is, it is not worth any thing. Nobody wishes to send to it. The pupils do as they please, offend every week and you reinstate them. Make an example of them. Either let them be punished, as they deserve in school, or, turn them out. Then, the school will be worth something. After considerable discussion, they agreed to my descision, and we cast out the refractory urchin, and from that time, the school began to improve, and, finally, became one of the best and largest of its class in the city.

In my visit to Philadelphia in 1852, the voting was done at a single place in each Ward. But there were so much quarrelling and fighting that, before my removal there, in 1859, they had divided the Wards, each into two or more Precincts, for voting purposes. But, so far as I was aware, the voting place in each Precinct, was in a tavern where liquor was sold. Certainly, in this respect, Philadelphia was behind Boston, for in Boston, we generally have a decent place for voting.

Before removing to Philadelphia, I used to think Boston was not behind any other city in the use of liquor and tobacco. But I found I was mistaken in this opinion, for, the " Quaker City" far outdid Boston in these matters.

In some streets, nearly every other house was either a grog-shop, or a tobacco-store. I was surprised to find what a large number of Irishmen and Irishwomen were allowed to maintain these nuisances. It had been said, when the yellow fever raged in Philadelphia, every body smoked, as a preventive of the contagion. Making this, a criterion, one would suppose this fever prevailed all the seven years I lived there, for everybody smoked. For rum and tobacco, Philadelphia takes the palm off Boston. But this was when Boston had a Prohibitory

Law, and Philadelphia lived under a License Law.

They had one excellent Association in Philadelphia, which has never existed in Boston, to wit, that of Sabbath School Teachers. It included all the teachers, of all the Evangelical Denominations, and numbered some two thousand. One winter, we had a course of Lectures, numbering seven or eight, by the prominent clergymen of the city. I should like to see a similar Association in Boston.

It was customary, in many of the churches, to hold two sessions a day of the schools; one at nine, A. M. and another at two, P. M. Some one proposed the following question for discussion before this association, "Is one or two sessions the most profitable for the schools?" A large committee, consisting of nine, one from each denomination, and the President and Secretary, constituted this committee. They were to write to the Superintendents and teachers of schools in all the principal cities of the Union, and ascertain, which, in their opinion was the most profitable, one or two sessions on the Sabbath? When the committee was appointed, I think, every one of them was in favor of two sessions. When they came to make their report, eight of the nine had been converted, and were in favor of one session·

Now came the "tug of war," in the discussion of this Report. Old men were there, who had attended two sessions a day of these schools for forty years, and their pleas and arguments were forty years strong. One prominent clergyman said, " If I must give up one service on the Sabbath, I would much rather relinquish one of the sermons, than one session of the school. Old men, lawyers, doctors, merchants said, "we have held these schools for forty years, twice on the "Lord's Day," and it would be sacrilege and going back to the "Dark Ages," to give up one session. The age of this custom seemed to be the chief argument in its favor.

On the opposite side, some of us contended that it was too much for both teachers and pupils—that they had no time for home-duties,—that children, who attended school all the week ought not to be confined so long on the Sabbath—that, if they had two sessions of the school, they would, and did, stay away from the afternoon sermon; and, while their parents were at church, they would be at play on the squares: and, lastly, that from all the schools from which the committee had heard, the general, and almost, universal opinion was, that one session was preferable to two. This last statement, was answered very summarily, by saying, of each of these other cities, *that* is not Philadelphia: and this was pronounced with an emphasis, which seemed to say, Philadelphia is the standard, and all other cities ought to conform.

After discussing the question three evenings till eleven o'clock, a vote was taken, and a small majority were in favor of two sessions. But, nevertheless, that discussion broke the back-bone of the two session—plan, and one after another of the churches gave it up, till in two years from that time, scarcely a school could be found where they had more than one session.

Shortly after this discuscion, I heard one of the pastors, who had been a strong advocate for two sessions, rebuking his people because they allowed their children to go home after the second session, and did not make them stay to the second service. But, really, it was this pastor's fault, or rather, the fault of the system he advocated, for, the children required this relaxation, and to make them attend church and hear two sermons, and stay at two sessions of the school was being "overmuch righteous," and causing the children "to die before their time."

In all my experience, I never saw people hold on to an old custom, with more tenacity, as it appeared to me, simply because it was old.

Philadelphia had long been famous for the squirrels in the squares. They were beautiful and tame, and would come up and eat sweet meats from your hand. I admired these little, docile animals. They were of a variety of colors, and their number seemed infinite.

At length, the span-worms appeared. They were as numerous as the flies of Egypt, and about as annoying, especially, to the ladies. Scarcely a lady dared to go through a square in the month of June.

If she ventured to do it, she was pretty sure to have her dress well covered with the worms. They became an unbearable nuisance. I think I was the first person, who suggested, through some of the papers, if they wished to be freed from the worms, they must destroy the squirrels. Then, the birds would return and devour the worms. It was a fact that not a bird was to be seen, or, heard in all the City. They had found that the squirrels destroyed their eggs and their young, and had entirely relinquished the city to the squirrels. At length, our suggestion was acted upon by the city fathers and a decree went forth that all the squirrels must be destroyed. This was executed, and the birds returned, and the worm-nuisance was abated, and now, in all those beautiful squares and in the tops of all those old trees, may be heard the singing of the birds when the Spring returns.

RECOLLECTIONS OF PHILADELPHIA.

CHAPTER XVI.

CONTENTS. Things and Prominent Men of Philadelphia—The Methodists and Education—The City Pro-Slavery—Southern Newspapers—The Union League—The Ladies' Work for the Soldiers—Rev. Albert Barnes—Rev. Drs. John McDowell—Henry A. Boardman—Henry Steele Clarke—George W. Musgrave—William Blackwood—Elias R. Beadle—Alfred Nevin—Jonathan Edwards—Charles Wadsworth—Edwin N. Nevin—John Chambers—James M. Crowell—Richard Newton—William P. Breed—Laymen—Matthew Newkirk—Alexander Whilldin—Matthias W. Baldwin—Stephen Colwell—George H. Stuart—George W. Childs—William H. Allen.

One of the first things that attracted my attention, after removing to Philadelphia, was to find all the men of eminence, Judges, Lawyers, Doctors, Merchants, &c., evangelical. In Boston, for a generation, it had been the reverse. In this city and State most of the men, famous for learning, had really been, or. had been classed, among Unitarians. Of these might be named, John Quincy Adams, (though this has been disputed) Edward Everett, Professor Sparks, Chief Justice Shaw, nearly all the Professors of Harvard College, in the Law, and Medical Schools, &c. So, also, the most prominent Congregational churches were all of this School of Theology.

In Philadelphia, there was but one little Society of this faith, and that was composed chiefly of those who had emigrated from New England. Dr. Furniss, their minister, was a perfect gentleman and a fine scholar.

It was very surprising to see all the officers and prominent stations filled by evangelical men.

Of the various Religious Denominations, I do not wish to make comparisons ; suffice it to say, the Baptists, Presbyterians, Episcopal and Methodists were all strongly represented.

It surprised me to find the Methodists taking the lead in education, because I remembered, when their first College, at Middletown, Connecticut, was started, there was great opposition to it among the good Methodist brethren. They protested that now, *we*, like other denominations, are to have *man-made* ministers, and our piety, which has hitherto shone brightly, will die. It is possible there was some ground for this apprehension, for, an excellent clergyman said to me lately, "I do not believe one young man in ten leaves the Theological Seminary with as much piety as he had when he entered it."

If this is so, it indicates that the good, pious, but unlearned Methodists of that day, were not very wide of the truth. But, the voices of a few prevailed over the many, and the Methodist College, above named, was chartered, and my old College friend, Wilbur Fiske, was appointed its first President. The change upon the subject of Education in this denomination has been astonishing.

Strange to say, and still stranger to be true, at the time of my removal thither, Philadelphia was thoroughly *pro-slavery*. It was just after the great revival, of 1858, was waning, after four thousand persons had attended at a time, a prayer-meeting, in Jane's Hall. The number was still great; but so intense was the feeling in favor of slavery that it was not allowed to be spoken of, or prayed against, in that meeting. "Father Cleveland," the almost centenarian of Boston (he lacked but fourteen days of a century when he died) visited his son, Professor Cleveland, of whom we have already spoken; and, in the "noon-day prayer meeting," prayed against slavery, and for its abolishment. He was taken to do, for this violation of the rules, and was told, "this is an interdicted subject, and must not be named in this meeting." The good old man replied, "why, I have prayed that slavery might cease for sixty years, and I can't stop now."

The writer had never been an ultra Abolitionist, and had been soundly basted by Garrison and his followers, as one of the signers of the famous "Clerical Appeal." But, he could not brook the pro-slavery proclivities of the Philadelphians. They were too gross.

It was a curious phenomenon, that, in 1859, just before the war, you could scarcely find a northern paper in all that city, except the Boston *Post* and *Courier*, while every southern town, that had a paper, was represented in every Hotel and Boarding-House of that city. Millions of property, in that city, were then owned by slave-holders, and multitudes of ex-slave holders resided there. The pulpits, save one or two, were all dumb on the subject of slavery. As no other city in the Union contained so many ex-slave holders, and so many run-away slaves, so, no other was so difficult a spot to speak out on this subject. It was not till sometime after the war commenced, and the people began to see their sons and their husbands brought home corpses, that they opened their eyes to the enormities of slavery.

Philadelphia, during the war, did more, I believe, for the soldiers than any other city. No sooner had it commenced, than I called together ten men, all originally from New England, and we organized the "New England Soldier's Aid Society." It was formed for the purpose of aiding the Soldiers from the New England States. It provided for their comfort, when they passed through the city, or, came to the Hospitals. Though this Society was first organized by men from New England, yet many others came to its aid, and contributed liberally to its funds. During the latter part of the war, and for some time after its close, (for it was needed till the Hospitals were closed) I was its President. I visited Massachusetts and collected funds for its use. It sent home to the New England States more than one hundred dead bodies to the comfort of their friends, besides many disabled soldiers. It, also, afforded aid to many who were not from New England.

The Union League, of Philadelphia, was one of the grandest Institutions ever devised. It numbered twenty five hundred of the most wealthy, influential and intelligent inhabitants of that city. It raised, equipped and sent to the war eight regiments at its own expense. It published pamphlets and articles of interest and sent them broadcast over the land.

It had Lectures at its Head Quarters weekly and kept alive the fire of patriotism. It poured out money like water. It was too expensive for most clergymen to be members, but through its generosity, the greater part of the ministers were made members gratutiously; and, of this number the writer was one. I gave them a lecture upon John Quincy Adams, who drove the opening wedge into slavery, by strenuously advocating the "Right of Petition," in Congress. The Union League Building, on Broad Street, below Chestnut, erected during the war, was one of the finest edifices, on that most splendid street, in the United States.

The Hospitals of Philadelphia, for Soldiers, were on a grand scale. There were more than twenty, in and around, the city. One of them, located at Chestnut Hill, it was said, would accommodate four thousand patients. One at West Philadelphia, had provision for three thousand, and there were smaller ones all over the city. The good Ladies of Philadelphia, took a deep interest in these Hospitals. They visited them daily, and I could name many who laid down their lives, that is, who died prematurely through their exhausting labors in visiting and aiding the thousands of sick and wounded soldiers. The excellent wife of Rev. T. W. I. Wylie, D.D. was one of them; the wife of my next door neighbor, William Struthers was another, and I could name many more; but how many will never be known till the judgment day.

It was a sight that angels must have watched, as we did, with delight, to see these delicate ladies, and little girls with baskets filled with sweet-meats and flowers, visiting these poor sick and wounded soldiers day by day. The soldiers, too, appreciated these favors. One summer, I came to Boston, and visited a little Hospital, at Readville. There I saw some who had been in a Philadelphia Hospital, and I told others, I was from Philadelphia. "Well," said one of them, Philadelphia is the best place on earth. I wish we were there now, instead of being in this "mud-hole." It had just rained and the place was wet.

Among the eminent ministers of Philadelphia, I name first, Rev. *Albert Barnes,* the distinguished commentator. He was one of the calmest, meekest, least self-conceited, and humblest men, in my judgment, that I ever saw. He used to tell a story of his early preaching, calculated to encourage young ministers, and to dampen the high aspirations of small parishes. " When I began to preach," said he, " I was in a small, country parish, where they expected to pay a salary of four or five hundred dollars" (four or five hundred dollars then, when we had money, was something). " I preached four Sabbaths. They held a parish meeting, and I did not get a call. They thought, I was hardly up to their parish."

Let no young minister, then, feel discouraged, if he fail to get a call in some little parish, in the country, where they think five hundred dollars a year is more than he is worth. Let them remember that this was thought of Albert Barnes, by such a parish, who was for forty years Pastor of the First Presbyterian Church of Philadelphia, and the foremost Commentator of America: and let such parishes learn the truth, and force of this declaration of Robert Hall,—" the disposition to set in judgment by parishioners upon ministers, is, generally, in inverse proportion to their ability."

One other amusing anecdote may here be told of Mr. Barnes. It was his custom to rise at four o'clock A. M , in the winter, and repair to his study in the church, and there write till breakfast at eight o'clock.

One very cold, stormy night, while he was trying to open the iron gate leading into the yard of the house, a police-officer laid his hand on him to arrest him as a burglar. Mr. Barnes, not being accustomed to such arrests, remonstrated—said, he was the Pastor of that Church, and was endeavoring to get into his study, &c. But the officer was inflexible and said, " you needn't think to stuff me with such corn as that. The ministers of Philadelphia are not fools enough to be fumbling about their church such a night as this, at four o'clock. You must go with me." Before the officer would release him, the good man was compelled to awaken an Alderman, who lived near by, to testify that he was not a burglar.

Mr. Barnes' power in the pulpit was great. His good sense, good will, and undaunted courage qualified him for a good preacher. He was not a genius ; would not be called brilliant. He was not eccentric, not ranting, never gave flings at creeds, and was never foggy. His manner was calm. A stranger, unacquainted with his preaching, would have been very likely to say, when he began, " there is not much in him," so quiet and unassuming was his manner. His matter was as quiet as his manner. As he stood like a statue, scarcely making any movement, so, his words were simple and his thoughts, or, the expressions of them, calm as a summer evening. As he proceeded, his voice grew a little louder, and his matter deeper, till you found he had fixed your attention almost beyond your control ;

and, as he progresed, every thought added to the preceding one, and every word enchained its predecessor, till you felt as though an inspired apostle was addressing you, the thoughts and words coming from his, and reaching your, heart. With the greatest modesty, meekness and simplicity, it might be said of him, as of John Knox, " he never feared the face of man."

He would pack more of God's thoughts into a single sermon than some ministers would in twenty. The keenest rebukes, the sharpest cuts, would come from his lips, that I ever heard, and yet, nothing like splenetic censure, or personal hatred was ever manifested in the slightest degree.

Of his being raised above " the fear of man," the noblest specimen appeared in his anti-slavery sermons. In these, (afterwards published in a book) he hurled the shafts of the Almighty, like thunder-bolts, against a system, which he characterized as " accursed, and one on which Heaven could never smile," while millions of dollars already won by slave-labor, and still being won by it, were owned by those seated along the aisles of his church.

I could write a whole book on this " Prophet of the Lord," but my present limits will admit no more.

REV. JOHN MCDOWELL, D. D.

At the time of my removal to Philadelphia, Dr. McDowell was Pastor of the " Spring Garden Presbyterian Church." I had preached for him in 1852; and, at the close of the sermon, he said to me, " this is good, old School, Presbyterian doctrine." This was said, because he had an impression that the New England Congregationalists, to which class, I then belonged, were not very " sound in the faith."

The Doctor's first Pastorate was over the Presbyterian Church of Elizabeth, N. J. While there, he wrote and published the first, and best " Question Book," on the Bible, of modern times. I felt almost acquainted with him, because we had used this book in our public School, and in the Sabbath School, of my native town, several years before.

Dr. McDowell was next settled over the " Central Church," of Philadelphia. Here he remained many years, but a division taking place in the parish, he was dismissed, and, with a portion of that Society and others, formed the "Spring Garden Church." He was Pastor of this church when I first knew him. He was a man of strong mind, sound in the faith, and of indomitable perseverance. A very interesting Memoir of him has been published, written by William B. Sprague, D. D. of Albany.

REV. HENRY A. BOARDMAN, D. D.

Dr. Boardman, Pastor of the " Tenth Presbyterian Church," was settled many years ago, and still remains as Senior Pastor. He is an excellent preacher, a gentleman of refinement, has had several calls, and appointment as a Professor, but has refused all of them; and, like a wise and good man,—as he is — has staid with his people, greatly admired and loved by them.

Probably, his congregation numbers more Lawyers, Judges, Doctors, Clergymen and other learned men than any other one in Philadelphia.

REV. HENRY STEELE CLARKE, D. D.

Dr. Clark was Pastor of the " Central Presbyterian Church." He was a good and faithful Pastor, exceedingly nice in his appearance, and in writing and delivering his sermons. A more amiable and kind-hearted man is not to be found. His labors were arduous, and he fell a victim to writing sermons, in the midst of his days. I admonished him, as a physician, as I had good Wm. M. Rogers, of Boston ; but, to no avail, in either case, for the zeal of the " Lord's House had eaten them up." There is something wrong in good ministers sacrificing their lives in this way. A memorial sermon, of Dr. Clarke, was preached by Rev. Charles W. Shields, D. D. then Pastor of the Second Presbyterian Church, now Professor at Princeton.

REV. GEORGE W. MUSGRAVE, D. D. LL. D.

My first acquaintance with Dr. Musgrave, was in the old Philadelphia Presbytery, the mother of all the Presbyteries in the United States. Dr. Musgrave was then one of the Secretaries of the Board of Home Missions. He was advanced in life, had been a Pastor in Baltimore many years, a man of strong mind, and one who would be prominent wherever found. As his eyes were bad, he generally spoke extemporaneously. He excelled as a debator, in which, he had few equals. Though he was in the combat, when the Presbyterian

Church was divided, in 1837, and, though he long wore the scars of that battle, yet, he was one of the most foremost in the re-union of these two branches of that church. "His voice was for peace," and the part he acted in uniting these churches was a very prominent one. He was chairman of the chief Union Committee, and the Moderator of the first General Assembly, that met after the two branches became one. His last pastorate was over the Penn Church, Tenth Street, above Poplar. He is a man of great parts, and a Bachelor, reputed to be very wealthy. His conversational, as well as his debating power, is equal to that of any man in the Church.

REV. WILLIAM BLACKWOOD, D. D. LL. D.

Dr. Blackwood was, and still is, Pastor of the ninth Presbyterian Church. It had the largest membership of any Presbyterian Church in the city. Dr. B., is a Scotchman, though my impression is, that he came from the north of Ireland, whence so many good Presbyterians have come. The Doctor is a remarkable man. He has large conversational powers, is a fine writer and a fluent speaker. Though sometimes in impaired health, he has held on, and labored efficiently in his pastoral work, and, in addition, has found time to write an elaborate commentary. Few pastors have done as well, and fewer, as much, as Dr. Blackwood.

REV. ALFRED NEVIN, D. D. LL. D.

When I first became acquainted with Dr. Nevin, he was pastor of the Alexander Presbyterian Church, 19th and Green Streets. It was then a new enterprise, and required great effort to sustain it. After leaving this pastoral care, Dr. N., published a new, religious newspaper, called the "Presbyterian Standard." Since then, he has been engaged in writing a Commentary upon various parts of the Bible, and has produced a very useful work for instruction to the church, and creditable to himself, as a theologian. The Dr. is of an active turn, and can never be idle. He was a chaplin of one of the United States Hospitals, in Philadelphia, during the War. He is a kind and obliging man.

JONATHAN EDWARDS, D. D.

Dr. Edwards was pastor of the West Arch Street Presbyterian Church. He is a man of excellent abilities; very "sound in the faith," has more than ordinary tact in transacting business, is a good christian brother, and now a successful pastor in Peoria, Illinois.

REV. CHARLES WADSWORTH, D. D.

Dr. Wadsworth was pastor of the Arch Street Presbyterian Church. He was a very popular preacher, and kept that large house well filled for twelve years. I think he would get more good material into a sermon than almost any other man of my acquaintance. He was peculiar. When he lived on Arch Street, he would walk down to his church on a little back street, and always seemed desirous of avoiding the company he might meet on a thronged thoroughfare. He rarely appeared at a meeting of his ministerial brethren, and performed but little pastoral duty. It was in the pulpit that he did his work, and there, he was a perfect success. His sentences were replete with beauty, all his words told; his imagination was exceedingly fertile, and one would seem to see the living spirits flitting about, of which he preached. For a long time after he came to Philadelphia, the house was thronged, and the aisles filled with seats, and even the vestibule. But, when the preaching was over, his work seemed to be done. To succeed in a city, a minister must be a very good preacher, or, an excellent pastor, or, fair, in both. Dr. Wadsworth possessed the first of these qualifications in an eminent degree.

ELIAS R. BEADLE, D. D. LL. D.

Dr. Beadle came to Philadelphia before I left. He was settled over the Second Presbyterian Church. He is a fine scholar, a splendid writer, a perfect christian gentleman, and an eloquent preacher. He was called to the Third Presbyterian Church, of Boston, but declined to leave his fine parish in Philadelphia. In every respect, our acquaintance with Dr. Beadle, found him a most lovely and amiable gentleman.

REV. EDWIN N. NEVIN, D. D.

Dr. Nevin is an eloquent man, a fluent speaker, a good debator, and always ready to advocate a good cause. He spent several years in New England, where we first made his acquaintance. He has now been for several years, the successful pastor of the German Reformed Church, Race Street, below Fourth, and successor of Rev. J. H. A. Bomberger.

REV. JOHN CHAMBERS, D. D.

Dr. Chambers is now the oldest pastor among all the Evangelical Churches of Philadelphia. His church is at the corner of Broad and George Streets. He has, I think, the largest congregation of any Protestant church in the city. He is an eloquent, zealous and stirring man, and makes his people work. He was not a zealous advocate for the union during the war. He has labored much in the good cause of temperance. When his people were taking a contribution, and the cents began to rattle in the boxes, we once heard him say, "I wish strangers to undertand that we don't take up coppers here. My own people know it already."

REV. JAMES M. CROWELL, D. D.

Dr. Crowell was pastor of the Seventh Presbyterian Church. He was a good pastor, and a faithful preacher. There was no more amiable and lovely man of our acquaintance in the city. He left and took charge of a church in Buffalo, New York, but has since returned and become pastor of a church in West Philadelphia.

REV. RICHARD NEWTON, D. D.

Dr. Newton needs no commendation. "His praise is in all the churches," not of his own denomination only, but, also, of all others. He is a most efficient "workman that needeth not to be ashamed." In the Sunday School, in temperance, in the prayer-meeting, in the pulpit, everywhere, he is ever ready to any good work. He came to the "Church of the Epiphany," when it was in a low state. The Sunday School was run down, and in a single year, everything wore a new aspect. The school was soon the largest in the city. Such a man can never be held in the leading strings of any one denomination. His soul is to large, it will overleap all sectarian bounds and go out for the elevation and conversion of the world. He is the " right man, in the right place to edit the publications of the Sunday School Union."

REV. WILLIAM P. BREED, D. D.

Dr. Breed is pastor of the " West Spruce Street Church." This was formed chiefly by a colony from Rev. Dr. Boardman's Church. Dr. Breed is a laborious and excellent pastor. He never lags, but is always up to the work, whatever work he may have to do. He is very courteous and kind, and ever knows the state of his flock. We found him always the same, " ready to every good work."

MATTHEW NEWKIRK.

I became acquainted with Mr. Newkirk in 1852, on this wise, I was introduced to him by Rev. H. S. Clark, his Pastor, in his Sabbath School, and at Mr. Newkirk's request, addressed the School. By invitation, I went home with him and dined.

When I removed to Philadelphia, seven years later, I hired a house of him, and attended the "Central Church," of which Mr. Newkirk was an Elder.

The family, from which Mr. Newkirk sprung, was of the Huguenots of Holland, and the North of France. He was born May 31st 1794, in Pittsgrove, Salem

County, N. J. From early boyhood, he improved his time in industry and in acquiring information. In 1810, he came to Philadelphia and entered the dry goods store of Joseph and Collins Cooper. There, he remained five years, till he was twenty-one. He became a volunteer soldier in the war of 1812. In 1816, he commenced business for himself, in company with a sister. May 1st, 1817, he married Miss Jane Reese Stroud, and in twenty-one months, followed her to the grave. July 2d, 1821, he married Margaret Heberton.

Mr. Newkirk, in 1821, formed a partnership with his brother-in-law, W. Y. Heberton, and went into trade at 95 Market Street. During his whole Mercantile life, he took a special interest in young men. In this respect, his influence was great in aiding them in forming habits of industry, economy, morality and religion. His second wife died in 1841, and two years previous to her death, he retired from active business to give his attention to her health. In July, 1846, he married Miss Hetty M. Smith, who still survives him. She is a devoted christian, one of "the salt of the earth."

Mr. N. was one of the most efficient Directors in the U. S. Bank; built the Philadelphia, Wilmington and Baltimore-Rail-Road, furnishing a large share of the capital, and, as he once said to me, " walked his floor often till midnight to think where he could get $20,000, the next day to carry on the work." The plan of checking luggage originated with him. He did as much, if not more, than any other man, to open up to commerce the vast coal-beds and iron-mines of Pennsylvania. He, probably, owned more real estate, and more dwelling houses than any other man in the city of Philadelphia, At one time, he owned land in eleven different states.

He ever took a deep interest in Education, was one of the City Council to erect Girard College, and the planner of those fine, architectural Buildings. The Polytechnic College owed its existence to him. He was for several years President of the Female Medical College; and, at his own expense, educated a lady who practiced medicine successfully, till her death. He was the oldest Trustee of Princeton College, and presided at the meeting, when Rev. Dr. James McCosh was elected President. For forty years, he gave his earnest and cordial support to the cause of temperance, and was President of the " Pennsylvania State Temperance Society."

But it was the *religious* life of Mr. Newkirk in which he most excelled. He was long an Elder and the Treasurer of the General Assembly, had the best Sunday School in the city, and was ever "ready to every good work." If our limits allowed, we could say much more of this eminently good man.

ALEXANDER WHILLDIN.

Mr. Whilldin is another of Philadelphia's noblemen. He is a whole-souled man, a prominent merchant, the President of several Institutions, an Elder of the

North Broad Street Presbyterian Church, and a good citizen in every sense of the word. He took his Pastor, Rev. E. E. Adams, to Palestine and paid all his expenses. I was with him in the Sabbath School, commenced in the Wagner Institute, which formed the Nucleus of the Presbyterian Church, of which Rev. Mr. Robbins is now Pastor.

MATTHIAS W. BALDWIN.

No man in Philadelphia gave more occupation to her citizens, built more churches, or, did more good than Mr. Baldwin, so far as one could judge. His business was profitable and the money he made was readily and willingly given to erect houses of worship, aid good objects, and succor the poor. It was a pleasure to ask him for money, for, he never " gave grudging, but of a ready mind." I had occasion to go to him several times for aid for the poor, the soldiers, and benevolent societies. He always met me with a smile, and asked, " what do you need now ?" I think seven Presbyterian Churches owed their existence to this good man.

STEPHEN COLWELL.

Mr. Colwell was one of the great men of this city. He was an iron-merchant, liberally educated, a student, and wrote a book entitled "New Themes for Christian Ministers," which made much stir in the comunity. He was an eminent financier, and in those days of the war that " tried men's souls," as well as their bodies, when Judge Chase was Secretary of the Treasury, he often came to Philadelphia and spent a night with Mr.

Colwell, to confer and get his advice on what to do about our country. He was the principal Editor of all the Publications of the "Union League," which did such good service for the country duriug the war, and which erected that splendid edifice on Broad street, called after the name of the League. In all difficult questions, no better adviser could be found in the "Quaker City," nor, indeed, in the whole country, than Stephen Colwell. No man took a deeper interest in the welfare of the prisoner, or, of the poor than he.

GEORGE H. STUART.

Mr. Stuart is an eminent merchant, a devoted and large hearted christian, whose zeal and love for "the Master," outstrip, and go beyond all sectarian or denominational bounds. He was the Chairman of the "Christian Commission," which did very much good to the bodies and souls of the soldiers. No man living is better calculated to get up a great meeting for any benevolent object, or, to give to it a better, more earnest and effective address, when gathered, than George H. Stuart. No meeting was ever known to fail of which he was the projector. Meetings got up by others, no matter how good, might be their object, often failed. But, I never knew one to fail in which George H. Stuart was the manager.

GEORGE W. CHILDS.

Mr. Childs held the same place among Publishers that Mr. Stuart did in gathering a vast audience.

When Mr. Childs took hold of an enterprise, everybody felt that it would be a success, and it was. Witness the vast circulation of the *Public Ledger*, and go through the immense edifice where it is published.

WILLIAM H. ALLEN, M. D. LL. D.

Dr. Allen was a New England man, a graduate of Bowdoin College, and seems to have been raised up by Providence to fill the place of President of Girard College. A very good man was appointed, as the first President of this College ; but he soon resigned, feeling that he was not the man to manage this class of boys. Dr. Allen was then appointed, and everything went on like clock-work for thirteen years. Then, some city political matters came up, and Dr. Allen resigned. Another gentlemen was appointed to the Presidency, but in two years, he resigned, and Dr. Allen was re-appointed. He knows how to conduct just such an Institution. Moreover, in him, the devil seems to have been defeated in his attempt to keep the religious instruction of the pupils out of this College, for, Dr. Allen is a religious man, and though not a clergyman, preaches better sermons and expounds the Bible better than half the clergy in the land.

CHAPTER XVII.

THE CENTENNIAL EXHIBITION.

CONTENTS — Opening Day — Concourse of People — Philadelphia the Right Place — Bishop Simpson's Prayer — Whittier's Centennial Hymn — John Welch's Address — Cantata by Sydney Lanier — Address by Gen. Hawley — President Grant speaks — Concluding Ceremonies — — Starting the Great Engine — Sabbath Law of Pennsylvania — Some of the Centennial Buildings.

The 19th of April, 1876, was fixed as the day for opening the great Exhibition. But it was soon discovered that this was too early a day; and as the time drew near, and every thing was in confusion, another day, the 10th of May, was agreed upon. The trumpet of this mighty affair had been sounded the world over, and all nations had been summoned, as once at the dedication of the golden image in the plain of Dura. When the expected day came, all the arrangements having been completed in an admirable manner, a vast throng of people assembled to participate in the festivities, and give *éclat* to the opening ceremonies. The arrangements had been so wisely made, that all moved like clockwork from the first assembling of the grand procession in the morning to the final dispersion late in the afternoon. The day itself was a perfect one, of just the right temperature, neither too hot nor too cold. The refreshing showers of the preceding day had laid the dust; and the freshness of early spring shone forth from the beautiful lawns, trees, and shrubbery of Fairmount Park.

The site for an American Exhibition that is connected with our Centennial celebration had been well selected. Of all our great cities, Philadelphia had the first part in the work of the Revolution, and, consequently, the associations are with her to a greater extent than they are with any other place of the kind. Boston led in the time before the war began; but, after the English left her territory, early in 1776, her Revolutionary position diminished, at once, as it were, and it never was regained. New York early fell into the hands of the enemy, the victim of overwhelming force by sea and land. Charleston was too far to the south to take that lead to which she had good title because of her importance and the spirit of her people. Philadelphia became the first place in the Colonies in a political sense, as she was in most other respects. She was the largest of our municipalities, having, it is believed, almost as large a population as would have sufficed to equal the united populations of Charleston, New York, and Boston. She was the social capital of the Colonies, and had much wealth and a various society; and, in the books and letters of those years, she often is spoken of, and alluded to, in ways that show how high she stood both at home and abroad, as well in England as in America. The first meeting of the Continental Congress took place there, and most of that body's sessions were there held. There it was that the Declaration of Independence was written, discussed, and adopted, and put forth to the world, more than a year after Washington had there been appointed to the command of the country's armies, and placed on the road to achieve the purest immortality ever won by mortal man. Then Philadelphia had her part in the military history of the contest, being threatened by the English in 1776; and it was through her streets that Washington led his army to the field of Brandywine, when Howe had taken his command to Pennsylvania, at the close of the summer of 1777. The city was taken by the invaders in the last days of September, and they held it for almost three-fourths of a year; and, during their occupation of it, it was the scene of the greatest gayety, so that it has been considered as Howe's Capua. There was much hard fighting in the vicinity of Philadelphia, for weeks after the place had fallen. For years after they left it, it was the seat of the American government; and for the last decade of the century, it was the seat of that government under the present Constitution; and it should have continued to be the national capital until now. All things considered, no place can be named that has better "claims" to the honor that has been awarded it than Philadelphia.

THE OPENING OF THE GRAND EXHIBITION.

PRAYER BY BISHOP SIMPSON.

ALMIGHTY and everlasting God, our heavenly Father, heaven is thy throne, and the earth is thy footstool. Before thy majesty and holiness, the angels veil their faces, and the spirits of the just made perfect bow in humble adoration. Thou art the Creator of all things, the Preserver of all that exist, whether they be thrones or dominions, or principalities or powers. The minute and the vast atoms and worlds alike attest the ubiquity of thy presence and the omnipotence of thy sway. Thou alone art the sovereign ruler of nations. Thou raisest up one, and castest down another; and thou givest the kingdoms of the world to whomsoever thou wilt. The past, with all its records, is the unfolding of thy counsels and the realization of thy grand designs. We hail thee as our rightful Ruler, the King eternal, immortal, and invisible; the only true God, blessed for evermore. We come on this glad day, O thou God of our fathers, into these courts with thanksgiving, and into these gates with praise. We bless thee for thy wonderful goodness in the past; for the land which thou gavest to our fathers, — a land veiled from the ages, from the ancient world, but revealed in the fulness of time to thy chosen people, whom thou didst lead by thine own right hand through the billows of the deep; a land of vast extent, of towering mountains and broad plains, of unnumbered products and of untold treasure. We thank thee for the fathers of our country, men of mind and of might, who endured privation and sacrifices, who braved multiplied dangers, rather than defile their consciences, or be untrue to their God; men who laid on the broad foundations of truth and justice the grand structure of civil freedom. We praise thee for the closing century, for the founders of the Republic, for the immortal Washington and his grand associates, for the wisdom with which they planned, and the firmness and heroism which, under thy blessing, led them to triumphant success. Thou wast their shield in hours of danger, their pillar of cloud by day, and their pillar of fire by night. May we, their sons, walk in their footsteps, and imitate their virtues. We thank thee for social and national prosperity and progress; for valuable discoveries and multiplied inventions, for labor-saving machinery, relieving the toiling masses; for schools, free as the morning light, for the millions of the rising generation; for the books and periodicals, scattered like leaves of autumn over the land; for art and science; for freedom to worship God according to the dictates of conscience; for a Church unfettered by the trammels of State. Bless, we pray, the President of the United States and his constitutional advisers, the judges of the supreme court, the senators and representatives in Congress, the governors of our several Commonwealths, the officers of the army and navy, and all who are in official position throughout the land; guide them, we pray thee, with thy wisest counsels, and may they ever rule in righteousness. We ask thy blessing to rest upon the president and members of the Centennial Commission, and upon those associated with them in the various departments, who have labored long and earnestly amidst anxieties and difficulties for the enterprise. May thy special blessing, O thou God of all the nations of the earth, rest upon our national guests and our visitors from distant lands. We welcome them to our shores, and we rejoice in their presence among us, whether they represent thrones or culture, or research, or whether they come to exhibit the triumphs of genius and art in the development of industry and in the progress of civilization. Preserve thou them, we beseech thee, in health and safety; and in due time may they be welcomed by loved ones again to their own native lands. Let thy blessing rest richly on the Centennial Exhibition; may the lives and health of all interested be preserved in thy sight. Preside in its assemblage. Grant that the association in effort may bind more closely every part of our great Republic, so that our union may be perpetual and indissoluble. Let its influence draw the nations of the earth into a happy unity. Hereafter, we pray thee, may all disputed questions be settled by arbitration, and not by the sword; and may wars forever cease among the nations of the earth. May the new century be better than the past; more radiant with the light of true philosophy, warmer with emanations of a world under sympathy with thee. May capital, gains, and labor be freed from all antagonisms, by establishment and application of such principles of justice and equity as shall reconcile diversified interests, and bind in imperishable bonds all parts of society. We pray thy benediction especially on the women of America, who, for the first time in the history of our race, take so conspicuous a place in a national celebration. May the light of their intelligence, purity, and enterprise shed its beams afar, until in distant lands their sisters may realize the beauty and glory of Christian freedom and elevation. We beseech thee, Almighty Father, that our beloved Republic may be strengthened in every element of true greatness, until her mission is accomplished by presenting to the world an illustration of the happiness of a free people, with a free Church, in a free State, under laws of their own enactment, and under rulers of their own selection, acknowledging supreme allegiance only to the King of kings and Lord of lords. And as thou didst give to one of its illustrious sons first to draw the electric spark from heaven, which has since girded the globe in its celestial whispers of "Glory to God in the highest, peace on earth, good-will toward men," so to the latest time may the mission of America, under divine inspiration, be one of affection, brotherhood, and love for all our race; and may the coming centuries be filled with the glory of our Christian civilization. And unto thee, our Father, through Him whose life is the light of men, will we ascribe glory and praise, now and forever. Amen.

Then came the singing of Whittier's Centennial Hymn, set to the music of J. K. Payne of Massachusetts. The words could hardly be caught, of course, by the vast throng; but the music could be heard as distinctly as though it were being performed in a hall. It was noble choral melody, admirably performed, and at once caught the ear of the audience, who set up a tremendous cheering when it was concluded.

CENTENNIAL HYMN.

BY JOHN GREENLEAF WHITTIER.

Our fathers' God, from out whose hand
The centuries fall like grains of sand,
We meet to-day, united, free,
And loyal to our land and thee,
To thank thee for the era done,
And trust thee for the opening one.

Here, where of old, by thy design,
The fathers spake that word of thine
Whose echo is the glad refrain
Of rended bolt and falling chain,
To grace our festal time, from all
The zones of earth our guests we call.

Be with us while the New World greets
The Old World, thronging all its streets,
Unveiling all the triumphs won
By art or toil beneath the sun;
And unto common good ordain
This rivalship of hand and brain.

Thou who hast here in concord furled
The war-flags of a gathered world,

Beneath our Western skies fulfil
The Orient's mission of good-will;
And, freighted with Love's golden fleece,
Send back the Argonauts of peace.

For art and labor met in truce,
For beauty made the bride of use,
We thank thee; while withal we crave
The austere virtues strong to save,
The honor proof to place or gold;
The manhood never bought or sold.

Oh! make thou us, through centuries long,
In peace secure, in justice strong;
Around our gift of freedom draw
The safeguards of Thy righteous law;
And, cast in some diviner mould,
Let the new cycle shame the old.

Hon. John Welch, President of the Centennial Board of Finance, was then introduced, and spoke inaudibly as follows: —

ADDRESS OF JOHN WELCH, ESQ.

Mr. President, and Gentlemen of the United States Centennial Commission, — In the presence of the Government of the United States and of the several distinguished bodies by which we are surrounded, and in behalf of the Centennial Board of Finance, I greet you. In readiness at the appointed time, I have the honor to announce to you that under your supervision, and in accordance with the plans fixed and established by you, we have erected the buildings belonging to us, and have made all the arrangements devolving on us necessary for the opening day of the International Exhibition. We hereby now formally appropriate them for their intended occupation; and we hold ourselves ready to make all further arrangements that may be needed for carrying into full and complete effect all of the requirements of the acts of Congress relating to the Exhibition. For a like purpose we also appropriate the buildings belonging to the State of Pennsylvania and the city of Philadelphia, erected by us at their bidding: to wit, Memorial Hall, Machinery Hall, and Horticultural Hall. These and other substantial offerings stand as the evidence of their patriotic co-operation. To the United States of America, through Congress, we are indebted for aid which crowned our success. In addition to those to which I have just referred, there are other beautiful and convenient edifices which have been erected by the representatives of foreign nations, by State authorities, and by individuals, which are also devoted to the purposes of the Exhibition.

Ladies and gentlemen, if in the past we have met with difficulties, disappointments, and trials, they have been overcome by a consciousness that no sacrifice can be too great to occasion us to ever forget the memories of those who brought our nation into being, or the events of 1776. It excites our present gratitude. The assemblage here to-day of so many foreign representatives uniting in this universal tribute is our reward. We congratulate you on the occurrences of the day. Many of the nations have assembled here to-day in peaceful competition; and may each profit by the association! The Exhibition is but a school. The more thoroughly its lessons are learned, the greater will be the gain; and when it shall have closed, if by that study the nations engaged in it shall have learned respect for each other, then it may be hoped that veneration for Him who rules on high will become universal, and the angels' song once more be heard, " Glory to God in the highest, and on earth peace, good-will toward men."

The cantata by Sydney Lanier of Georgia, music by Dudley Buck, was finely rendered by the grand chorus; and it too proved entirely worthy of the occasion. The solemn opening chorus at once captivated the listeners. The bass solo, admirably given by Mr. Myron W. Whitney of Boston, was enthusiastically received, and Mr. Whitney was obliged to respond to an encore. Following are the words of the cantata: —

CANTATA.

BY SYDNEY LANIER.

The Centennial Meditation of Columbia.

I.

From this hundred-terraced height,
Sight, more large with nobler light,
Ranges down yon towering years;
Humbler smiles and lordlier tears

Shine and fall, shine and fall,
While old voices rise and call,
Yonder where the to and fro
Weltering of my Long Ago
Moves about the moveless base
Far below my resting-place.

II.

Mayflower, Mayflower, slowly hither flying,
  Trembling westward o'er yon balking sea,
Hearts within, "Farewell, dear England!" sighing,
Winds without, but dear, in vain replying,
Gray-lipped waves about thee shouted, crying,
    "No! it shall not be!"

III.

Jamestown, out of thee, —
Plymouth, thee, — thee, Albany, —
Winter cries, "Ye burn: away!"
Fever cries, "Ye freeze: away!"
Hunger cries, "Ye starve: away!"
Vengeance cries, "Your graves shall stay!"

IV.

Then old shapes and masks of things,
Framed like faiths, or clothed like kings,
Ghosts of goods once fleshed and fair,
Grown foul bads in alien air,
War, and his most noisy lords,
Tongued with the light and poisoned swords,
  Error, Terror, Rage, and Crime, —
  All in windy night of time

Cried to me from land to sea, —
"No! thou shalt not be."

V.

Hark!
Huguenots whispering "*Yea*," in the dark;
Puritans answering "*Yea*," in the dark.
"*Yea*," like an arrow shot true to its mark,
Darts through the tyrannous heart of Denial.
Patience, and Labor, and solemn-souled Trial,
    Foiled, still beginning,
    Soiled, but not sinning,
Toil through the sterterous death of the night, —
Toil, when wild brother-wars new dark the light;
Toil, and forgive, and kiss o'er, and replight.

VI.

Now praise to God's oft-granted grace!
Now praise to man's undaunted face!
Despite the land, despite the sea,
I was; I am; and I shall be —
How long, good angel? oh, how long?
Sing me from heaven a man's own song!

VII.

"Long as thine art shall love true love,
    Long as thy science truth shall know,
Long as thine eagle harms no dove,
    Long as thy law by law shall grow,
Long as thy God is God above,
    Thy brother every man below, —
So long, dear land of all my love,
    Thy name shall shine, thy fame shall glow."

VIII.

O Music, from this height of time my word unfold;
In thy large signals all men's hearts man's heart behold;
Mid-heaven unroll thy chords as friendly flags unfurled,
And wave the world's best lover's welcome to the world.

Then came President Hawley's address of presentation, which he read from manuscript held in his hand. He spoke as follows: —

ADDRESS OF HON. JOSEPH R. HAWLEY.

Mr. President, — Five years ago the President of the United States declared it fitting that "the completion of the first century of our national existence should be commemorated by an exhibition of the national resources of the country and their development, and of its progress in those arts which benefit mankind;" and ordered that an exhibition of American and foreign arts, products, and manufactures, should be held under the auspices of the Government of the United States, in the city of Philadelphia, in the year 1876. To put into effect the general laws relating to the Exhibition, the United States Centennial Commission was constituted, composed of two commissioners from each State and Territory, nominated by their respective Governors, and appointed by the President. Congress also created an auxiliary associate corporation, the Centennial Board of Finance, whose unexpectedly heavy burdens have been nobly borne. A remarkable and prolonged disturbance of the finances and industries of the country has greatly magnified the task, but we hope for a favorable judgment of the degree of success attained.

July 4, 1873, this ground was dedicated to its present uses. Twenty-one months ago this Memorial Hall was begun; all the others, one hundred and eighty buildings, within the enclosure, have been erected within twelve months. All the buildings embraced in the plans of the Commission itself are finished. The demands of applicants exceeded the space, and strenuous and continuous efforts have been made to get every exhibit ready in time. By general consent the Exhibition is appropriately held in the City of Brotherly Love. Yonder, almost within your view, stands the venerated edifice wherein occurred the event this work is designed to commemorate, and the hall in which the first Continental Congress assembled. Within the present limits of this great park were the homes of eminent patriots of that era, where Washington and his associates received generous hospitality and able counsel. You have observed the surpassing beauty of the situation placed at our disposal.

In harmony with all this fitness is the liberal support given the enterprise by the State, the city, and the people individually. In the name of the United States you extended a respectful and cordial invitation to the Governments of the other nations, to be represented and to participate in this Exhibition. You know the very acceptable terms in which they responded from even the most distant regions. Their commissioners are here, and you will soon see with what energy and brilliancy they have entered upon this friendly competition in the arts of peace. It has been the fervent hope of the Commission, that during this festival year the people from all States and sections, of all creeds and churches, all parties and classes, burying all resentments, would come up together to this birthplace of our liberties, to study the evidence of our resources, to measure the progress of a hundred years, and to examine to our profit the wonderful products of other lands, but especially to join hands in perfect fraternity, promise the God of our fathers that the new century shall surpass the old in the true glories of civilization; and furthermore, that, from the association here of welcome visitors from all nations, there may result, not alone great benefits to invention, manufactures, agriculture, trade, and commerce, but also stronger international friendships, and more lasting peace. Thus reporting to you, Mr. President, under the laws of the Government, and the usages of similar occasions, in the name of the Centennial Commission I present to your view the International Exhibition of 1876.

At the conclusion of Gen. Hawley's remarks the President arose, and a subdued cheer went up as he began to read his address. The President put on his eye-glasses, drew his manuscript from an inside pocket, and read it in schoolboy fashion, almost without taking his eyes from its pages in so doing. He wore buff kid gloves, and his voice to the few who could hear was husky.

ADDRESS OF PRESIDENT GRANT.

My Countrymen, — It has been thought appropriate upon this Centennial occasion, to bring together in Philadelphia, for the popular inspection, specimens of our attainments in the industrial and fine arts, and in literature, science, and philanthropy, as well as in the great business of agriculture and of commerce. That we may the more thoroughly appreciate the excellences and deficiencies of our achievements, and also give emphatic expression to our earnest desire to cultivate the friendship of our fellow-members of the great family of nations, the enlightened agricultural, commercial, and manufacturing people of the world have been invited to send hither corresponding specimens of their skill to exhibit on equal terms in friendly competition with our own. To this invitation they have generously responded. For so doing we render them our hearty thanks. The beauty and utility of the contributions will this day be submitted to your inspection by the managers of this Exhibition. We are glad to know that a view of specimens of the skill of all nations will afford to you unalloyed pleasure, as well as yield to you a valuable practical knowledge of so many of the remarkable results of the wonderful skill existing in enlightened communities.

One hundred years ago our country was new and but partially settled. Our necessities have compelled us to chiefly expend our means and time in felling forests, subduing prairies, building dwellings, factories, ships, docks, warehouses, roads, canals, machinery, &c. Most of our schools, churches, and asylums have been established within a hundred years. Burdened by these great primal works of necessity which could not be delayed, we yet have done what this Exhibition will show in the direction of rivalling older and more advanced nations in law, medicine, and theology, in science, literature, philosophy, and the fine arts. Whilst proud of what we have done, we regret that we have not done more. Our achievements have been great enough, however, to make it easy for our people to acknowledge superior merits wherever found. And now, fellow-citizens, I hope a careful examination of what is about to be exhibited to you will not only inspire you with a profound respect for the skill and taste of our friends from other nations, but also satisfy you with the attainments made by our people during the past hundred years. I invoke your generous co-operation with the worthy commissioners to secure a brilliant success to this International Exhibition, and to make the stay of our foreign visitors, to whom we extend a hearty welcome, both profitable and pleasant to them. I declare the International Exhibition now open.

The entire proceedings occupied somewhat more than two hours, and were attentively listened to.

CONCLUDING CEREMONIES.

At precisely twelve o'clock the signal was given, and another national flag was run up on the Main Building, amid the wildest enthusiasm and the cheers of the multitude. The orchestra rendered the Hallelujah Chorus, and it seemed to inspire every one with wild enthusiasm. The booming of cannon was now heard, and the ceremonies were drawing to a close. During the chorus the great body of invited guests arose, and began to move into the Main Building; and the passage through the throng from Memorial Hall to the Main Building was opened and kept clear by files of military and the police. The procession of officials was preceded by military escort, and headed by President Grant, who conducted the Brazilian Empress on his right arm, and was accompanied by Director-General Goshorn on the left. Following came the Emperor Dom Pedro, escorting Mrs. Grant; then the President's Cabinet, several members of which the people soon recognized and cheered; next the Judges of the Supreme Court, Congressmen, the States Governors, and army and navy officials. In leaving the stand erected for them, it was necessary for the distinguished party to descend a short flight of steps; and when Secretary Bristow, Gen. Sheridan, ex-Speaker Blaine, Gen. Hancock, and others were spied here by the crowd, they were cheered as they passed down and into the aisle. The passage could be kept open only by the herculean efforts of the police officers. The jam at the doors of the Main Building was tremendous.

THE PARTY IN THE MAIN BUILDING.

The narrow entry was completely packed by the surging mass of men, women. and children, which followed close upon the heels of the departing guests. The Presidential party entered the northern transept, and turned down the eastern nave, following which they had the immense display made by the United States on their right, and the rich and elegant contribution of France on their left. The exhibits of these countries were hurriedly glanced over by the party; and the President was received by the individual owners and exhibitors with enthusiasm, and was introduced by the director, Gen. Goshorn, to many of them. A rapid view was next taken of the exhibits in the western nave; and the party passed up to the centre of the building, viewing the rich German collection, and shaking hands with its managers. The Empress and Mrs. Grant showed great interest in the rich display of china, bronze, rare laces, and dry goods, and expressed their enthusiastic admiration of the beauty of the exhibits. The other large displays were taken in, and a brief stop was made at the Spanish contribution. The party proceded alone then to the main entrance, and passed out.

STARTING THE GREAT ENGINE.

The procession to Machinery Hall was through an imposing military array, drawn up on either side. Upon entering this building the party passed up the central aisle to the giant Corliss engine. Here the military reserved a broad space from invasion by the crowd, and the President and his party walked on to the platform. Here he spent some time informally examining, with Dom Pedro, the great mechanical monster; and both these gentlemen were introduced to Mr. George H. Corliss, who chatted pleasantly with them about his engine. The ladies of the party, too, seemed to share the general admiration for the engine, and walked around it with as much interest as any of the gentlemen. At a quarter past one o'clock the Exhibition was formally opened, when President Grant and the Emperor Dom Pedro grasped the levers, and opened the throttles of the mighty machine, and set the massive and complicated mechanism of the building in motion. A buzz of admiration arose from the vast multitude as the great wheel turned round with increasing speed, and the responsive echoes came back ringing and ticking, whizzing and buzzing, announcing the activity which the giant had diffused through the machinery for almost every manufacturing purpose, from many countries, and connected by two miles of shafting, thus making a remarkable and memorable array. The formal ceremonies were now over, and the Centennial Exhibition successfully inaugurated. After leaving Machinery Hall, the President and his party drove directly to the residence of Mr. George W. Childs.

THE MASSACHUSETTS BUILDING.

Immediately after the opening ceremonies, Gov. Rice, accompanied by his staff and the Executive Council, proceeded to the Massachusetts Building. The party were welcomed by Dr. Loring, who in a few words presented the building to the Commonwealth. Gov. Rice responded with a few remarks highly complimentary to the Massachusetts Commission, consisting of Col. Saltonstall, Hon. Hamilton A. Hill, and Hon. Joe V. Meigs, on the advanced state of Massachusetts exhibits.

A GLORIOUS SUCCESS.

This evening the points of interest centre in the hotels, the corridors of which are thronged with people busily engaged in discussing the events of the day, and the attractive features of the Exhibition so far as they could be inspected in a single day. The crowd of visitors has not diminished in the least; and it is altogether probable that the throng will increase, now that the attractive features of the Exhibition have been published to the world. Those already here cannot possibly gain an adequate conception of the vast display of exhibits in less time than a week, so that a still greater rush may be confidently looked for in the immediate future. The opinion is everywhere expressed, that nothing approaching the extent and magnificence of the display within the Exhibition grounds has ever been witnessed in this country; and it may well be doubted whether any of the world's fairs held in the past in the great cities of Europe has equalled ours in extent, or surpassed it in variety or general interest. Several departments are yet to be finished, and it will doubtless require several days to arrange the exhibits of each nation so that it will appear at its best; but there is already enough and more than enough to absorb the attention of the most fastidious visitor, and to enable him to realize the beauty, grandeur, and significance of the great undertaking that has brought together here the greatest achievements of the world's genius, skill, and industry.

THE EXHIBITION GROUNDS

will not be open for visitors at night at any time during the season. To-night the larger halls are all lighted and guarded by the Centennial Corps. The arrangements for closing, as per official order, are as follows: "A signal is given at six, P.M., when all visitors must retire from the buildings; and exhibitors are required to clean their spaces each evening. The second signal is given at half-past six, when the admission gates to the buildings are closed. The exits are closed at eight o'clock."

In addition to what has been said of Philadelphia, it was appropriate that this Exhibition should be held in Pennsylvania, because of her good laws for keeping the sabbath, and thus securing it from being opened on the "Lord's Day."

William Penn landed upon the shores of the Delaware in the year 1662, and afterwards moved from there to New Castle, and from there to Chester, where he held the first great Assembly, and gave to this Commonwealth its first great law. It is a singular and providential circumstance, that not only in that great law, but in its first and leading section, he laid the foundation of this vast Commonwealth upon the religion of Almighty God, and that the first and greatest stone upon which he depended in that foundation was the sabbath which we revere.

It is as follows: —

"*Be it therefore enacted*, That these following chapters and paragraphs shall be the law of Pennsylvania and the territories thereof, Almighty God being only Lord of Conscience, Father of Lights and Spirits, and Author as well of all Divine knowledge, faith, and worship, who only can enlighten the mind and convince the understandings of the people in due reverence to his sovereignty over the souls of mankind, it is enacted by the authority aforesaid, that no person now or at any time hereafter living in this Province, who shall confess and acknowledge one Almighty God to be the Creator and Ruler of the world, and who professes himself to be subjected to and to live peaceably and justly under the said government, shall in no ways be molested, but shall be permitted to have his or her conscientious persuasion or practice; nor shall he or she at any time be compelled to frequent any place of religious worship contrary to his or her mind, &c.; and, if any person shall interfere with his or her persuasion of practice in matters of religion, such shall be looked upon as a disturber of the peace, and be punished accordingly."

There is the broad platform upon which every true religion in the world may rest, and those who do not, in our opinion, hold the truth in its entirety, may dwell for ever. You may remark that it invites the people of God to come here, and promises them that protection which they could not enjoy in any land in Europe. Now, mark what follows; for this is the stone to which I allude, and which the builders of our own day would have us reject. While giving the widest liberty it goes on to say, —

"*Be it further enacted by the authority aforesaid*, That according to the good example of the primitive Christians, and for the ease of creation, every first day of the week, called the Lord's day, people shall abstain from their common toil and labor, that, whether masters, parents, children, or servants, they may the better dispose themselves to read the Scriptures of Truth at home, and to frequent such meetings of religious worship abroad as may best suit their respective persuasions."

That has been the law of Pennsylvania from that moment until this, without a moment's intermission; the very first law that was ever passed, and I trust it will be the last one ever to be abrogated. When the control of this Province to a certain extent passed into the hands of the Legislature, when they met in 1700 and 1705, what did they do? Why, they passed a law confirming what Penn had enacted, and applying penalties for its infringment.

In 1705 they passed a law entitled, "An act to restrain people from labor on the first day of the week;" and they affixed severe penalties to the breaking of that law.

Thus, in accordance with this law, the Exhibition was closed to visitors on the sabbath.

SOME OF THE BUILDINGS.

THE MAIN BUILDING is 1,880 feet long, 460 feet wide, 70 feet high, and has a central tower 120 feet high. This building with its towers and projections covers an area of twenty-one acres and a half.

THE HORTICULTURAL HALL is a permanent edifice. It is a fine, beautiful building. The conservatory with which the angles are adorned, with eight fountains, is 230 by 80 feet, and 55 feet high, with a lantern 170 feet long, 20 feet wide, and 14 feet high.

THE ART GALLERY, or Memorial Building, is designed to be a permanent hall, and is built of iron, granite, and glass. It is 365 feet long, 210 feet wide, and 59 feet high. It has a central dome 150 feet high, on which stands a figure of Columbia.

THE AGRICULTURAL BUILDING is made of wood and glass. The nave is 820 feet long by 120 in width, and the height 75 feet from the floor to the point of the arch.

MAIN EXHIBITION BUILDING.

ART GALLERY.

CHAPTER XVIII.

BROWN UNIVERSITY FIFTY YEARS AGO. — RECOLLECTIONS OF COLLEGE-LIFE.

CONTENTS. — President Messer — Professors at that Time — Dr. Messer's coming to the Point — Dr. Wayland's Advent — Inspection of him — The New Order of Things — One Mistake — Tristam Burgess and Professor DeWolf — Dr. Wayland's Success — The Manner of his Teaching, and his Interest in the Pupils — His Compliments to our Class — Our Regard for him.

Here let it be stated, at the outset, that some men of talent and eminence graduated immediately preceding President Wayland's presidency, though those were revolutionary days with the college.

President *Messer* was a man of ability, though in some respects peculiar. He might have been considered uncouth in some of his manners and expressions; but his questions and remarks were generally to the point, and he always made himself understood by the pupil and the class. Let it be remembered that our class was under his administration nearly four years, and during these years there was an entire change of officers, from the president down to sweeper Williams, whom many of the students of that day well remember.

Dr. Messer, either for or without cause, was suspected of holding religious opinions not in harmony with those of the Baptist denomination, and consequently had become unpopular with a number of the trustees. This led some prominent students of the class of 1825, who were Baptists, to take exception to the president; among whom were Stone, Newton, and Sears, the last-named since president. Two of these were expelled, Stone and Newton. Sears remained and graduated. Dr. Messer knew he was unpopular, and in conversation with the writer, about the time he resigned, said the Baptists were determined to make the institution strictly a Baptist concern, and therefore he would have nothing to do with it.

It was a fact, that, up to that time, a majority of the faculty had been of other denominations. Professor Adams was an Episcopalian; Rev. Calvin Park, D.D., a Congregationalist, and a man of ability; Professor DeWolf, if of any, of the Episcopal; Tristam Burgess, a Baptist; one of the tutors a Congregationalist, the other a Baptist.

In the class of 1826 graduated Edwards A. Park, now Professor Park of Andover; also George Burgess, the late Episcopal Bishop of Maine; and John Kingsbury, afterwards an eminent teacher, and one of the curators of the college. These and others of that class have become eminent. The class of 1825 graduated forty-eight. No other class reached so large a number up to 1852, on the catalogue now lying before me; and I am unable to say whether any one since has gone beyond it in numbers. I said President Messer usually came to the point, and made himself understood. The following item may serve for many of its kind. Our class were reciting from that uncouth book, "Stewart's Intellectual Philosophy." One of us, perhaps not of the quickest apprehension, was asked, "How do we gain a knowledge of external objects?" Apparently not comprehending the question, and standing by a post in the old chapel, Dr. Messer said, "How do you know there is a *post* before you?"

"Because I see it," was the reply.

"Very well," said the president: "suppose you ran your head against it, would you know it then?"

"Yes."

"Why?" said the president.

"Because I should feel it."

"That's right," said Dr. Messer.

I used to admire Dr. Messer, and many interesting items of him do I well remember. Among other things, he was the best detector of counterfeit money in the land. I once had a five-dollar bill which several of the bankers in Providence said was counterfeit. I took it to Dr. Messer to pay a tuition-bill. He pulled down his glasses, and looked at it; then took it to the window, and, after carefully inspecting it, put it in his pocket. I never heard from it.

These remarks are not made to disparage what President Wayland did, as will fully appear in the sequel.

Dr. Wayland came to Brown in the winter of 1827, at the age of thirty-one. He commenced hearing recitations with our class in the month of February of that year. He had removed to Providence during the then long winter vacation, which was six weeks. My chum, who was familiarly called "Old Zach," and myself, had returned the day before the term commenced. We, of course, were anxious to see the new president; and in the evening we made an errand to go to his house. Our real object was to scan him, and make up our minds what kind of a man he was, and whether he was the right man for the place. We introduced ourselves as members of the senior class; were politely received, and entertained for half an hour. The president said he should expect much from our class, for we would be his *pioneers;* a name which he often gave us afterwards, and which I find he used in his autobiography. We left him, satisfied that he would do.

Dr. Wayland says, "The first business which I undertook was to frame a new set of laws for the college." One of these laws was, that the officers should occupy rooms in the college. Dr. Wayland says, "None of them, I believe, had previously occupied a room in college." If by the *officers*, the doctor meant professors only, this was the fact; but, if he meant to include the two *tutors* among the officers, he was mistaken in his belief. The tutors had always, up to this time, occupied rooms in the college. I am perfectly satisfied of this. One of them, at the time Dr. Wayland came, was tutor Crane, a townsman of mine, whose room I often visited. They also boarded in "The Commons," as it was called, for the purpose of keeping order at the table. One little incident fixed this point in my mind. Mr. Cady, the steward, had been there many years, and become probably a little negligent. I boarded out of the college. There was considerable fault found with the steward's providing; and one of the tutors said to me, " I wonder the students bear it. I can't live so."

I said, " They are probably afraid of the faculty."

He replied, " I don't believe the faculty would injure them for it."

I suggested this idea to my chum, who boarded in " Commons." This was sufficient. The next day, but three out of the whole number went in to dinner, and the same number to supper. The next day Mr. Cady resigned. But he had some feeling about it; and, when he passed any of those students who left him, he did not see them, while he would cross the street to speak with one who boarded out at the time. This feeling lasted a long time; for, when the new South College was to be erected, the trustees, to straighten the line which is still crooked, wanted to purchase a part of Mr. Cady's garden, he said, " Brown University is not able to buy a foot of my garden."

One other incident I well remember, which shows that the tutors resided in the college. One night the college-bell commenced ringing, as it was wont to do in Dr. Messer's reign (for many strange things then happened; so many, indeed, that Dr. Wayland might well feel that discipline had to be commenced anew). As one of our class has well said, "Theatre-going was prohibited, and a late supper was no longer considered a valid excuse for an imperfect preparation for a recitation." The old farmer up north of the college no longer lost his fine flock of turkeys, which he raised for the college boys several years in succession. Strange as it may seem now, it happened in those days, that the doorstep of President Messer's house often sustained a large crop of chicken and turkey-bones. When the bell thus set itself to ringing, Dr. Messer would often get over to the college before the tutors were out of bed, and sometimes the students heard him reprove them for their sluggishness.

There were two or three points in Dr. Wayland's management which did not commend themselves to the students. One of them was the removal of "several gentlemen who had performed some service at the same time that they lived at home, and were engaged in other avocations." One of these was the Hon. Tristam Burgess, then a member of Congress. Though he had been with us but half the year, yet his services were invaluable. He was our "professor of rhetoric, or belles-lettres and elocution;" and no man could have performed the duties of such a position better, or to the more general satisfaction of the students. We learned more from him in these branches in half, than we could have learned from any other man in a whole year. He would go out upon the stage, and speak, as no other man could, the piece, —

" At the close of the day, when the hamlet is still," —

to the delight and admiration of the class. I have now all my college-compositions, with his criticisms upon the back of them; and I often review them with delight, both to see my own simplicity and his acuteness. He was the man that skinned John Randolph, the great Virginia wit. Randolph had compared the girls who worked in our New England cotton-factories, to their Southern slaves, and represented them as unchaste. Burgess took up the gauntlet, and said, "They are pure as the water that flows from their snow-capped mountains. It is a mercy that monsters cannot propagate their kind. One monster is enough for one Congress, — quite too much for one Republic." Randolph never entered Congress again. Another was Professor DeWolf. He was our lecturer on Chemistry, and one of the best I have ever known in that science. He was in independent circumstances, a genial and kind-hearted man, resided at Bristol, and, though he received a small salary, yet he expended the whole of it, and more, upon apparatus for his lectures, and the means of rendering them more useful. These two were among the best instructors we had, and their removal from the college was justly lamented. No doubt, that had a tendency to lessen the classes to which reference has already been had.

One other circumstance, that tended to the same result

was, the college was considered to have been put more exclusively under Baptist influence. This the Baptists had a perfect right to do, and I do not name it as any fault on their part. Williams and Amherst were understood to be controlled by the Trinitarian Congregationalists; Harvard, by the Unitarians; and it was perfectly right that Brown should be a Baptist college. When our class was there, a majority of the pupils were from Congregational churches. I saw no proselyting spirit there, and President Wayland was truly Catholic. Still this impression, together with the increasing influence of Williams and Amherst, aided in diminishing the number of students; so that it was not wholly the new laws, that rendered the classes succeeding ours smaller than they had previously been. The only thing about Dr. Wayland to which we then objected was, he was a *free-trade* man. But all learned men are now for free trade. The only difference was, Wayland was half a century in advance of them. The two things that gave Dr. Wayland his popularity were *his mode of teaching*, and *his personal influence with the students for their good*.

His mode of teaching was entirely different from that to which we had been accustomed. Up to that time, we had taken our books with us into the recitation-room, and some — not the most studious class — had often continued to get a squint at them even when reciting. When a pupil could repeat verbatim from the books, it was considered a good recitation; and in rhetoric and Stewart's Philosophy, one of our class usually committed the whole lesson to memory. He, when called upon to recite, would rattle off two or three pages of that peculiar uncouth style of Stewart, without stopping to breathe, or without a question; and he was considered a good recitation-scholar. But, if a question happened to be asked that involved the *principle* of the lesson, he floundered like a fish on dry land.

When we studied Euclid, we drew the diagrams on paper, in a book for that purpose; and some read the demonstration from the same book, which they had written out. This order of things was reversed by Dr. Wayland. Our class was under him but one term; for in those days we had six weeks vacation, immediately preceding commencement, which took place the first Wednesday in September. We were surprised, when we commenced the study of " Kames's Elements of Criticism," that we were directed to leave all our books in our rooms. But we did it. The first recitation-hour was chiefly occupied by the president in telling us *how* he wished us to study. We were advised to write out an analysis of each lesson, study it, and come to the recitation without either the writing or the book. The novelty of the thing gave impetus to our study. We very soon began to like it. To all who were *thinkers*, it afforded great pleasure. I have that written *analysis* now, and several times have I read it over; and, especially when teaching young ladies, I have since taken it as a guide for my questions. But this manner of reciting did not suit three or four of the class, who, parrot-like, had previously rattled off a page or two with great fluency. It very soon threw them into the shade.

In the same way we recited *political economy*. The great mass of our class was delighted with the change, for we soon saw that this was the way to make us *thinkers;* and we did what we could to sustain the new system. President Wayland gives us the following commendation in his autobiography, which in a good degree we deserved: "The example of the senior class, which came more immediately under my instruction, was worthy of all praise. They comprehended their position, and knew that on the exemplification of the new system by them depended greatly the future success of the college. Their conduct, both as students and as young gentlemen, was high-minded and exemplary. At the close of the term, they greatly distinguished themselves." In another place he says, "The senior class, especially, acted a most honorable part, and were the pioneers of the new movement. Among them were several men of fine talents and highly estimable character."

Since that time I have prepared several pupils for Harvard and other colleges, two for West Point, taught a young ladies' school both in Boston and Philadelphia, had several medical students, and in all these cases have carried out in teaching what was then called *the new system;* and they have liked it much better than they did the old plan. This was one instance in which President Wayland was *the* great man of his age, — *the manner of his teaching.*

The other item in which he excelled was his personal influence with, and his individual power over, young men. He was naturally rather austere; not always the most urbane in the recitation-room. But all this disappeared when he sat down alone to counsel and advise a young man. Of this I had personal experience. My health was bad; I was dyspeptic, and my eyes were weak; I was also *poor*.

Just previous to the close of the term, Dr. Wayland called me to his room, inquired about my health, spoke of his having studied medicine, and gave me the following advice: "My father is a Baptist minister at Saratoga. I advise you to go there, and spend the six weeks of vacation. I will give you a letter to him, and he will find you a place where you can board cheap. Drink the water, and take care of your health, and you will come back better."

As I was about to leave the room, knowing my pecuniary circumstances, he said, "Don't wear your best clothes when you are travelling. You can save a good deal by being careful. *I* always wear my old clothes on a journey, and carry my good ones in my trunk, and put them on when I get to my journey's end."

This was very simple but very useful advice. I took the letter to his father, and found him a true Englishman, a man of integrity, careful, sound, active, and truly pious. He had a fine garden in which he worked every morning, and I worked with him. I wore green glasses. One morning the old gentleman said, "It seems to me all our young men are becoming blind."

"Why?" said I.

"Because," said he, "I see you wear glasses."

I replied, I had been advised to wear them because my eyes were weak.

"For that very reason," said he, "I advise you to leave them off."

I took the advice, and put them in my drawer, where they remained quietly for twice the length of time that old Troy was besieged. When age began to creep over my eyesight, I exchanged them in part for gold-bowed spectacles, which I valued very highly both because the glasses were good, and the bows the best-wrought and the handsomest I had ever seen. One day I was called but a few steps from my residence to see an old colored woman, had my glasses, and wrote a prescription. When I had returned home the glasses were missing, and I never saw them since. I always supposed I laid them down, and she kept them. But I learned a lesson; to wit, never to get another pair of gold-bowed spectacles.

I said Mr. Wayland was cautious. He had ceased to be the pastor of the church in Saratoga, though he usually preached on the sabbath somewhere. We heard a young man preach a lecture, one evening, to his old flock; and the next morning I asked him what he thought of him. With great gravity he replied, "I never make up my mind from hearing a man once." I thought this a wise remark.

He found a boarding-house for me with a widow by the name of Lee, where I was very comfortable during my stay of six weeks in that village. It was a pious family; and one of her daughters, then deceased, had been the wife of the missionary Graves.

I shall be pardoned for relating one or two anecdotes from which I learned something, and which are now well remembered, though more than fifty years have since rolled away.

There was then boarding there an old gentleman who had been a sergeant in the army under Washington. He was tall, and straight as an arrow; seemed to feel his importance very much; and said but little unless when some men of consequence called on him. His room was adjoining mine; and one morning the youngest daughter of Mrs. Lee had entered it, and was putting the room in order. The table was covered with papers; and, as she was dusting, the old sergeant entered, and with a very stern and loud voice said, "I'd thank you, marm, not to *derange* my papers." She was young and timid, and flew out of the room like a shot; and I never saw her in it again.

I used to work with Mr. Wayland in his garden, and found it a healthy exercise. He was a first-rate gardener; and I have since recommended this exercise to many others.

I must say one word about Mrs. Wayland, sen. She was then over sixty, but as active as ever; and dressed elegantly, not to say *gayly*. She was remarkable for decision.

I took tea there; and we had no plates, knives or

forks, or cloth, upon the table. This was something new to me; but I have since learned that it is very common in England. The toast was spread, and we laid it on the hard and highly-polished table.

Such was the result of Wayland's fatherly care, that I returned in better health than I had enjoyed for some time.

Another instance of his personal conversation was with my classmate Frederick Parker. Parker, being the son of John Avery Parker, one of the rich whalemen of New Bedford, had plenty of money. He had an amiable disposition, but was not a student. He was what some would call *wild*. He was rusticated three times, six months each; once to Mr. Holman's in Douglas, which place was far away from anybody, the church standing in the woods, and the parsonage the only house near it. This was a sore affliction to Parker, because he could find no company. A second time he was sent out to Rev. Mr. Cobb of West Taunton. Parker was so pleased with the change, that, when Dr. Messer pronounced the sentence, he said, "*Thank* you, *Dr. Messer; anywhere but Douglas.*" A third time Parker was sent out to Rev. Mr. Perkins of Braintree.

I have named these several rustications to prepare the way to say that Dr. Wayland, I think, would have done differently with Parker.

In our senior year he was very much as he had been. He had too much money. He would go to his father; and when *he* told him, "Frederick, you have had all the spending-money I shall give you this term," he would go to his oldest sister, Mrs. Timothy Coffin, and she would supply him.

I distinctly remember those items, because, being one of the poor boys, I always kept a little money by me; fearing, if I got out, I might never get any more. Parker, rooming near me, often said, " Cornell, lend me ten dollars." He was sure to pay, and I always did it. On one occasion he had been home. When he returned, I said, *Fred*, did you get any money?"

"No," said he: "my old man was cross, and won't give me a cent." (But putting his hand upon his pocket) he added, " Mother gave me a hundred dollars."

Now, Dr. Wayland managed differently. I remember, Parker had done something amiss. Wayland called him into his room. Some of us watched to see him come out. He tarried a long time. At length he appeared; he was weeping. I said, " Parker, what did he say to you?"

" Say?" said he, " he talked to me like a father. He told me about my standing in life, about my father, and how we should both feel in after-life if he should expel me. He said, 'Parker, you have but six weeks more to study,' and entreated me to behave *well* these six weeks; and *I will*."

This plain, feeling, personal conversation did Parker more good than all his three rustications of six months each. It was here that President Wayland showed his great power: as an eminent physician once said, "I was the greatest surgeon of my day, — not by *cutting off* limbs, but by *saving* them."

So, by impressing upon students the value of *character*, Dr. Wayland kept them in the path of rectitude. These were the two grand characteristics of that eminent man, — *the manner of his teaching, and the personal influence that he exerted over individuals.* He was truly pious, and sincerely aimed to do good.

Some curious incidents were developed in executing the plan of the officers, visiting the rooms of the students according to the new arrangements. One of them was near-sighted. He was accustomed to rap upon the door, open it a little, look in, and say, "Oh, you are here!" close it, and pass on. One of our class, knowing that he could not well see across the room, tried the following experiment one night. He used to sit with his back towards the door, and his hat on his head, the better to shade his eyes. The officer had seen him thus frequently. The student put his cane in the chair where he usually sat, and his hat and cloak upon it, and, when the visitor came, stepped back into his closet. The officer looked in as usual, and said, "Oh, you are here!" and passed on. After this, when he wished to go out, he left his hat and cane in this position. He never heard any fault found on account of his absence.

As the president often repeated in his autobiography, our class did all they could to sustain him in his new measures, and to advance the credit and honor of the college. We soon began to like the new way of reciting, because we found it the best mode to improve, expand, and develop the mind. It carried out the definition of the work *educo*, — to educate, to draw out, to lead forth; not "to pour in."

As an educator, Dr. Wayland was fifty years in advance of his time; and though our college course was nearly closed before he became our instructor, yet so great was our estimation of him for the interest he took in our personal welfare, that each one of our class could say of him what Cicero said of the poet Archæus: "Looking back upon past scenes, and calling to remembrance the earliest part of my life, I find it was he who prompted me first to engage in a course of study, and directed me in it." Though we thought we were studying *before* he came, yet afterwards we found we really commenced to *study* under him.

Still we had good professors in Tristam Burgess, DeWolf, and Park, each in his professorship. Many things, particularly to criticise a composition, I learned from Tristam Burgess. But I first learned *how to study* from President Wayland. The sons of Dr. Wayland have done a good thing for the Church and the world, and especially for all the lovers of learning, in writing, and Messrs. Sheldon & Co. in publishing, "Life of Dr. Wayland." No literary man, no library, and, above all, no professor or teacher, should do without these two volumes.

It was by the advice of President Wayland, that the writer, some years ago, engaged as a professor in two female medical colleges, one in Boston and the other in Philadelphia.

Just fifty years ago last September, our class graduated; and at this present writing just one-half of our number have passed away from this world. As President Wayland's pioneers, we have served our generation according to the ability given us, and those of us who still remain are old men among new faces.

CHAPTER XVIII.

RECOLLECTIONS OF CAPE COD.

CONTENTS. — The Name — Not to be altered — King Charles defeated — Early Settlement of — Marshpee Indians — Anecdotes of — Provincetown of Old — Improved — Churches and Ministers on the Cape Fifty Years ago — Progress in Union — Language peculiar to Themselves — Their Language — Good Citizens and Honest Men.

IN 1602, May 15, Bartholomew Gosnold, voyaging from Falmouth in England to Virginia, discovered a headland in the forty-second degree of north latitude, and anchored near it. They wanted fish; and, catching "great store of codfish," named it *Cape Cod*.

ATTEMPT TO CHANGE THE NAME.

Fourteen years after it was named Cape Cod, an unsuccessful attempt was made to change the name. Kings have never been successful in managing American affairs; and hence John Smith failed to change the name of this cape, and also Prince Charles, afterwards King Charles the First. This John Smith (I say this one, for there have been two or more of this name), the founder of Virginia, wrote an account of his voyages to this country, and dedicated the book "to the High Hopeful Prince Charles." In this dedicatory epistle, he implores his Royal Highness, that he would be gracious enough to change the barbarous names which had been given to the various places along the coast, and bestow upon them some more euphonious and elegant English appellations; "so that posterity might ever be able to say Prince Charles was their godfather." Having been thus solicited, Prince Charles tried his hand at changing names, but with partial success only, — so hard is it to get rid of an old name, be it good or bad.

Prince Charles gave the name of Cape Ann to the northern headland of Massachusetts Bay, which was called before, Fragabigranda, — surely a name barbarous enough, but one which Smith was probably unwilling to have changed, as circumstances had rendered it any thing but barbarous to his ear. To Cape Cod, the prince gave the name of royalty itself, and called it Cape *James*, after his father, the great and veritable and dreadful *King James*. But, as New-Englanders had had enough of King James, they refused to call it by that name; and so it has remained Cape *Cod* till the present time.

Nor was this the only case in which a king has been superseded or displaced by a *cod;* for in our Old State House there used to hang two full-length portraits, said to have been real Vandykes, of Charles II. and James II. Both these disappeared long since from our public halls; and in our present State House, in lieu of them, is a large and splendid *cod*, from which fish this cape originally received and still retains its name. So much for its name and efforts to change it before my remembrance.

> "Our Pilgrim Fathers started off,
>   Two hundred years ago, sir,
> To seek their fortune o'er the sea,
>   And anchored down below, sir.
> And, as they had no other food
>   Considered worth the dishing,
> They got their sinkers, hooks, and lines,
>   And went right out a-fishing.
> *Chorus.* — Yankee Doodle, keep it up,
>   Yankee Doodle dandy.
> At catching fish, or sailing ships,
>   Our Cape men are quite handy.
>
> "They pulled the cod and haddock in,
>   And fished without a rod, sir;
> And for the first big fish they caught,
>   They named the cape, Cape Cod, sir.
> And as they had amazing luck,
>   The fishing was so handy,
> They thought they'd settle on the Cape,
>   Although 'twas rather sandy. — *Chorus.*

The shore of Cape Cod was trodden by the Pilgrims before their feet pressed Plymouth Rock; and when the good seed began to be scattered the first handfuls fell upon Cape-Cod soil; and, though it was sandy, it bore fruit, as will be hereafter shown.

Pomet, now *Provincetown*, was the birthplace of popular constitutional liberty. Here the first written compact for "a government of just and equal laws" was made in "The Mayflower," Nov. 11, 1620, by John Carver and forty others, in the name of God, for "the general good," &c. Good for Provincetown!

Some parts of the Cape were settled very early in the history of our country. Indeed, a church was organized in Barnstable as early as 1639.

The 11th of October in that year, Rev. John Lothrop, with most of his church, removed from Scituate to Barnstable. Holmes says in his American Annals, Yarmouth and Barnstable were settled in 1639. Some of the most eminent and distinguished sons of Massachusetts were born on the Cape. From the town of Barnstable may be enumerated the Hon. Harrison Gray Otis, Prof. Palfrey, Chief-Justice Shaw, Attorney-Gen. Davis, with many others. Among the men who went with Mr. Lothrop from Scituate, were Anthony Annable, one of the first settlers of Scituate, Henry Cobb (who had lived some time before in Plymouth), George Lewis, J. Cooper, Isaac Robinson (son of the celebrated John Robinson, pastor of the Leyden church), B. Lombard, Henry Bourne, Samuel Hinckley (father of Gov. Thomas Hinckley), Thomas Dimmock, William Parker, John Allen, Henry Ewell, Robert Shelley, J. Crocker. Gov. Hinckley was an able chief magistrate, and governed the colony well; and, when Plymouth was united with Massachusetts in 1692, he was appointed one of the Council. He was also a member of Sir. Edmund Andros' Council in 1686–87. Gov. Hinckley died in 1706, at the age of eighty-five. He had the care of the Indians on the Cape, who were very numerous in those days, and was very anxious for their improvement.

These and their coadjutors were men of principle, and may well be classed among the best in these colonies. Thus the Cape was first settled by honorable men, and has ever since maintained its excellent character for raising men, — the noblest characteristic of any country.

My personal acquaintance with the Cape commenced early; for there I taught and lived three years. After studying theology with that remarkable man Rev. Thomas Andros of Berkeley, and Rev. Timothy Davis of Wellfleet, I was licensed by the Barnstable Association of Congregational ministers, at Chatham, Oct. 29, 1828. Their question for discussion was the resurrection of the body; and the subject of my sermon read at examination was, "Why should it be thought a thing incredible with you, that God should raise the dead?"

At that time there had been no separation in that association between the Unitarians and the Orthodox. I remember, however, but two Unitarian ministers then members of the association: Rev. Mr. Goodwin of Sandwich, and Rev. Mr. Hersey of Barnstable. Mr. Goodwin was a man of considerable ability; but Mr. Hersey said but little, and that little was usually comprised in one sentence: "Mr. Goodwin has spoken my opinion."

Mr. Goodwin asked me three questions: "Do you believe in one God? Do you believe Jesus Christ was the Son of God, and that God raised him from the dead?" I answered all these in the affirmative. He said, "That is my creed." Nevertheless, though I had assented to his full creed, yet he did not vote for my license. Mr. Davis asked him why he did not vote for me, as I believed all that he did; and he replied, "I believed too much heresy besides." I preached six months in Harwich. This was in the winter of 1828–29.

Everybody remembers Irving's description of Cape Cod in his "Sketch Book." But fifty years ago, at which time the writer taught school on the Cape, things and people had improved from what they were as Irving described them. Having been in every town in Barnstable County at that time, it may interest some to have a "bird's-eye view" of matters as they then appeared. Commencing, then, at the end, or Provincetown, it was then stated to the writer by Rev. Mr. Stone. This was the same Stone whom the Marshpee Indians requested might not be settled over them. The committee in Boston who had charge of the fund for support of the ministry in Marshpee had sent Mr. Stone to preach there; and, after him, Mr. Fish. The Indian deacon with one of the church was sent to Boston to see this committee. They wanted Mr. Fish. The Boston committee said, "We thought of settling Mr. Stone there." After a long plea the Indian deacon concluded, "Vel, if we ask a Fish will you give us a Stone?" It scarcely need be said Mr. Fish became their pastor; and an excellent man he was. And now, while I am with these Indians, let me tell one or two more anecdotes of them. In 1829, while preaching in Harwich, I exchanged with Mr. Fish. Mrs. Fish, a very lady-like woman, said, "Rev. Mr. —— preached here a few weeks since, and I asked our Indian deacon how he liked the sermon. 'Very vel,' said he: 'me always liked dat sermon.' — 'Always liked it! did you ever hear him preach it before?' — 'No marm, me never hear him preach it.' — 'Well, what do you mean by saying you always liked it?' — 'Me read it in Doddridge a good many times.'" One of them came to Harwich to sell his wares. It was at a time when there was considerable awakening among them, and a man whom they called "Blind Joe" was preaching there. Mr. Brooks asked him which was the better preacher, Blind Joe, or Mr. Fish? The Indian said, "Me no like to say." After a while, Mr. Brooks brought him round to the same question again; when he said, "Me must say, me think, you want a man to preach good sermons, you get Mr. Fish: you want a man to make good Christians, you get Blind Joe."

He said, "I do vish Mr. Fish would never preach any more about rum: only make me want some all de time. If Mr. Fish never say any ting about it, I go to meetin' and never tink of it; but he keep talking about it, only make my mouth water for it all the time."

To return to Mr. Stone, at Provincetown: he said, "Would you believe there is a town in Massachusetts of eighteen hundred inhabitants, with only one horse, and that horse with one eye only?"

The reply was, It may be so. "Yes," said he, "it is so. Our town has eighteen hundred people, and I own the only horse in it; and he is white, and has but one eye."

As Provincetown then had but one horse, so also it had but one street; and that ran along by the water in a straight line over a mile in length. It was, as may well be supposed, very sandy; and the ladies used to take to the boats, rather than the road, when they visited their neighbors. They could scull or row, or sail a boat in those days, as well as the Newport heroine, Ida Lewis, of our own more modern times; and often caught a mess of fish, as readily as would "an old salt." Instead of being like many of the ladies of these days, they could brave the roaring surge, as though they were the children of the deep; and many a shipwrecked sailor owed his life to these women.

Recently the writer visited Provincetown again. He had not been there for more than forty years. The place has much changed for the better. Instead of a single, sandy street, there are two beautiful macadamized streets of some two miles long; and, instead of a single horse, there are many owned by citizens, and one of the finest livery-stables to be found in the country, with some very fleet travellers, as I had proof of, by a gratuitous ride, through the kind invitation of the owner of the stable. Several new churches have been erected, a grand high-school-house, and many elegant dwellings. But off of the macadamized streets, the same old sands everywhere appeared. By the way, I once knew a sharp dispute between two little boys, one from the Cape (who was a visitor) and his little cousin in Bristol County. The Cape boy said it was *sand*, while the Bristol County boy stuck to it, it was *dirt*, — not an unapt representation of many controversies of "children of a larger growth."

Of *Truro*, the next town as we ascend the Cape, I never knew much, save that Rev. Mr. Turner in those old times built a meeting-house there, and preached to the people for several years. He was a fluent speaker, and could talk as long as any Methodist minister on the Cape in those days.

Naming the Methodists reminds me that great progress has been made towards Christian union during these fifty years. Then the good old sound Calvinistic ministers of the "standing order," as they were called, often preached against the "wild, ranting Methodists, running about and sowing discord, and breaking up churches;" and the Methodist ministers of those days felt it to be their duty to give old John Calvin a rap, and the Congregational ministers, the hirelings, and wolves in sheep's clothing, who were "twice dead, — blind leaders of the blind." But then the Methodists were comparatively few to what they are now. Their increase has been beyond all precedent. What glorious progress has since been made! Now we have a well-ordered, mutual loving association of the ministers of these old Congregationalists, Methodists, Baptists, Episcopalians, and some other denominations. It might almost have been said, fifty years ago, "If the Lord should make windows in heaven, might such a thing be."

Whatever some may say about the world's standing still, or retrograding, those of us who can look back fifty years or more, can see great progress in Christian brotherhood; and is it not matter of rejoicing, that professed Christians no longer "bite and devour one another," or *fight* for religion?

Rev. Timothy Davis was pastor of the church in Wellfleet. He remained there some forty years, and had the most extensive library, and was one of the most prominent ministers, on the Cape. I boarded in his family when I taught the high school in Wellfleet.

He used to relate some of the incidents of his early days, and among them was the following: "When I was a young man, I was a missionary in the then Province of Maine. Wild beasts then abounded in the province, and among them were many catamounts. Retiring to my log-cabin one night, in the twilight, I was accompanied by one of them. I looked him straight in the eye, as I had heard it stated that this beast would not attack a man while he thus eyed him. I went backwards, till I came to the door of the cabin, when I darted in, and closed the door. The animal, seeming to feel that he had lost his supper, threw himself against the door, with one of those peculiar yells which characterize this beast." This statement was made in the presence of his son, John, who was then about ten years old. The boy's eyes glistened as the father told the story. He slept in a room directly connected with my chamber, and retired about an hour earlier. When I went to my room, I had scarcely lain down, when the boy was at my door, screaming with all his might, "Mr. Cornell, the catamount is come!" I opened the door, and every nerve in the boy's frame trembled. A lesson from this is, never tell frightful stories to children in the evening.

Proceeding up the Cape, we next come to Eastham. At that time Rev. Mr. Shaw was the minister, and a good old Puritan he was, too. He had not then joined the Temperance Society; and, when father Davis exchanged with him, Mrs. Davis (though she had joined it) at noon presented the bottle for father Shaw; and, upon my lecturing her about it, she said, "Oh! Mr. Shaw wouldn't think he could preach in the afternoon, unless he had his dram."

Coming up still farther to Orleans, Mr. Johnson was the pastor, who had the finest orchard on the Cape, and was the greatest snuff-taker. Speaking of the orchards, the very trees seem to have a prescience that they have terrible winds on the Cape, for they rarely grow higher than a man's head.

Coming up still farther, we find the towns of Brewster and Chatham on the elbow. Mr. Pratt was then at Brewster, of whom I know nothing, save that his widow had a fine farm which she inspected every morning, and kept in the best order.

At Chatham Rev. Stetson Raymond was pastor. He studied theology with Rev. Otis Thompson of Rehoboth, and was a mild, kind gentleman.

Next comes Harwich, where I spent a winter, and boarded with Obed Brooks, Esq.; of which boarding-house I might say, if one was not satisfied there, he would not be anywhere this side heaven. Rev. Mr. Underwood had for many years been the pastor of the church in Harwich, but had now resigned. He had a number of sons who have since been active and prominent citizens, and one of them a member of the governor's council.

It was during the winter I spent in this town that I wrote my first article for publication. One of Mr. Underwood's sons had commenced publishing "The Barnstable Patriot." I had visited a school in Harwich, taught by an ignoramus, and gave a description of it for this paper, for which I came well-nigh losing my ears. Squire Brooks was besieged by a friend of the teacher, and finally settled him by saying, "I don't know whether Mr. Cornell wrote that article or not; but, if we have such a teacher as is therein described, somebody ought to write a more severe one than that."

Here I gave a "Dedicatory Address" of an academy, which was the second thing printed of my writing. Little did I then think I should live to scribble so much as I have since. Coming to the next town, Dennis, in the south part of which the minister was Rev. John Sanford, a very excellent man; and his remains now lie interred in the cemetery of that place, over which his son, late Speaker of our House of Representatives, has reared an appropriate monument.

Rev. Mr. Haven was pastor of the church in North Dennis; father of President Haven of the University of Wisconsin. Coming up to Yarmouth, fifty years ago, Rev. Nathaniel Cogswell was pastor of the church there. He married the eldest daughter of Esquire Doane, one of the rich men of the Cape. His son, Hon. J. B. D. Cogswell, is now president of the senate, a man of distinction and talents. Rev. Mr. Alden, the predecessor of Mr. Cogswell in the pastoral office in Yarmouth, was then living at a very advanced age. Mr. Cogswell built a large house which overlooked that of Mr. Alden, which was a low, one-story house; and on one occasion Mr. Cogswell said, "I can look right over your house, Mr. Alden." The old man replied, "Yes, the shepherd ought to look *over* the sheep." The retort seemed to be understood in those days, for some evil-minded persons thought Mr. Cogswell looked after money as much as he did over the flock. He was, however, a good pastor, and fed the flock well for many years. Mr. Alden loved a joke, as well as any other minister, and used to relate the following: "I was called to marry a couple one evening, and the groomsman handed me a five-dollar bill, having received his instruction to get the change back. I put the money in my pocket. By and by the man said, 'Mr. Alden, that was a five-dollar bill I gave you.' — 'Yes, sir, I received it as such.' A little later, as I was putting on my cloak, he stepped up to me, and said again, 'Mr. Alden, that was a *five-dollar bill* I handed you.' 'I replied, Yes, sir, I think your friend very liberal. Good-night, sir.'"

Coming up to Sandwich, they have had some dozen or more ministers during the last fifty years. This was the first town I ever visited on the Cape. I rode a little pony, bound to Dennis; was overtaken with a rain-storm, and stopped at "Swift's Tavern," — some two miles from the village towards Plymouth. This was then considered one of the best eating-houses in Massachusetts. I spent a comfortable sabbath there, though it rained all day. Mr. Swift was not only a good tavern-keeper, but also a good Universalist, and tried to convert me.

The people on the Cape are a plain, frank, open-hearted class, who live well, and are very hospitable.

They do all their marrying in the winter, because all the men are at sea in the summer.

The Cape Cod captains and seamen are the best in the world. They are competent, honest, and honorable in their dealings, and know the seas as the farmer does his field. They have a language somewhat peculiar to themselves, or a set of phrases of their own. Thus, fifty years ago, they called the youngest child *tortience;* but the derivation of this name I could never learn. They generally, like the Quakers, called each other by their Christian names, and often they had some other qualifying terms; as, for instance, in South Dennis, they had two men named Eliezer Nickerson; and as one lived near the church, and the other near a brook, they were characterized as "Meeting-house 'liezer" and "Brook 'liezer."

After spending three winters on the Cape, and often making other visits to it, I am fully satisfied, and feel confident, that the following may be truly said of them: Abating some peculiarities arising from their almost insular position, these people are as moral, industrious, honest, intelligent, hospitable, religious, and every way as good citizens, as can be found in New England or in any portion of the habitable globe.

CHAPTER XIX.

RECOLLECTIONS OF NEW HAMPSHIRE.

CONTENTS. — Newmarket — Mr. Broadhead — Bishop Heading — The Quaker — The Fat Man — The Coe Family — Boarding there — The Candle-Mould — Newington — John N. Maffit — Effect of his Preaching — Mrs. Maffit — Rev. Mr. Roland — Rev. Mr. Hurd — Mr. Belden and Judge Smith — Visit to Pembroke, and Rev. Mr. Burnham — Visit to Gilmanton — Gass's Hotel — Dr. Shattuck of Boston.

IN the summer of 1829, I took my flight from Harwich on the Cape, and lit in New Hampshire, that State so good "to emigrate from." I was employed by the Home Missionary Society of that State. I was sent to the town of Newmarket, the part called "New Fields;" why so called, I never knew. In the centre of the town was an old, dilapidated Congregational meeting-house, which nobody worshipped in, save the "moles and the bats," if they did. At the north end of the town was a manufacturing village, where Rev. David Sanford, of blessed memory, preached. At the part of the town I was in, there was an old academy building, in which I preached. Old Dr. Broadhead lived there. He had long been the Methodist minister; but now, in those days when the Democrats ruled that State, and Andrew Jackson the nation, he had left the pulpit for the forum, and was a member of Congress. He was a clever and genial old man as ever lived. But his wife! ah, "there's the rub!" She considered *that* Methodist ground. It mattered nothing that the Congregationalists occupied it long before the Methodists came. They now claimed it by possession. So good Mrs. Broadhead, when I called at their house, as I did by her husband's invitation, scarcely recognized me; and, when she passed me in the street, she used to remind me of one of the Baltimore clippers, which I had been accustomed to see when I was a cabin-boy. She would give me a wide berth, and go "by," like the wind, "on the other side;" but her daughters would come to hear me. I, however, enjoyed my visits there with the Hon. Congressman and old Bishop Heading, — as good a man as the Methodists or any other denomination ever had, — who spent the summer with Mr. Broadhead. They had a young Methodist minister there by the name of Lamb; and he seemed to have more of the lamb in him than of the tiger, and more gospel than politics. I boarded in the family of a Mr. Lovering some weeks, a kind of New-Hampshire Quaker: not of the good old orthodox Quakers (whom I always liked), for he never attended church; but his wife did. Mr. Lovering said the Bible was a strange book. I asked him why. He said it had a great many strange expressions in it. I asked him what they were. He said, such as, "cursed cows with short horns." I told him *that* was not in the Bible. He said he was sure it was. I told him to find it; so, one snowing day, he went to work to find it, and searched all the forenoon. At dinner, I asked him if he had found it. He said he had not. He had a copy of Bailey's Dictionary on the shelf. I told him he would find it in that, but not in the Bible; and he did.

There was a fat old gentleman by the name of Clarke, who came to hear me preach. He said he liked that young Cornell very well, but his sermons were too short. The fact was, the old man slept, and the sermon ended before his nap.

NEW-HAMPSHIRE ARISTOCRACY.

I don't know how it is now, but fifty years ago they had considerable of it. Perhaps the reader may wish to know how *I* came to get into such company. Well, it was on this wise: Old minister Coe, for many years pastor of the Congregational church in Durham, had left there, and bought a farm in Newmarket. He and his wife had gone to a better world. He had married into the family of old Gov. Gilman; and, of course, they were among the aristocracy.

Mr. Coe had given the house and farm to his two unmarried daughters, Mary and Ann. Their youngest brother, properly named Benjamin, lived with them. Providentially, I went into this family to board. It was a grand boarding-place. The Lord always provided for me in this respect, not on Cape Cod only, but elsewhere. These excellent ladies took the best care of me. The Coe family was large, and most of them prosperous. Eben Coe, one of them, then lived in Norwood, N.H. He was rich; had married a daughter of a Mr. Smith of Durham, who was also in the aristocratic line. This Mrs. Coe was one of the best women I ever knew. I went to Norwood, and she fixed me up with all the good things I could possibly want. She has now been in heaven forty years. She had a brother who was a minister, and, though he died young, did more good than many who have lived to be old. She had a sister Mary, whom the Rev. Mr. Young of Meredith Bridge, married.

Mary and Ann Coe were excellent women; and through them I was introduced to the rich and honorable families of New Hampshire.

THE CANDLE-MOULD.

I may tell one little story, the matter of which transpired while I boarded with the Misses Coe. One very cold day, when the wind was blowing a gale, and driving the snow before it like a hail-storm, the minister from Stratham, three miles away, came to our house; his face looked like a red beet; and, as soon as he could speak, he said to Miss Ann Coe, "My wife, when we took tea here last week, saw a large candle-mould; and, as she is going to have some company, she sent me over to see if you would lend it." Miss Ann gave him the candle-mould; and, as soon as he had passed out, with a merry twinkle of the eye, said to me, "There, I will never ask for a more obedient husband than that."—"Why?" said I. "Because any man who will go three miles such a day as this, to borrow a candle-mould, will never be wanting in obedience to his wife." Many times during the last forty years have I thought how many poor husbands go after candle-moulds all their days.

Newington, four miles from Portsmouth, was another field of my labors. Here I boarded with a Mr. Pickering, a fine family. There was a lovely young lady in this town, by the name of Mary Hill. She died early, too good to live in this world. The celebrated John N. Maffit was then in his glory. He was to preach at a "camp-meeting" in Kittery, just across the river. I asked Miss Hill, and Miss Lucy Pickering,—the only daughter and only child of "mine host,"—to accompany me to this meeting. Miss Pickering's father gave me a solemn charge to bring Lucy home before dark. Maffit preached from the text, "Is there no balm in Gilead," &c. He began by saying he was very feeble,—preached an hour. Everybody was carried away. Strong men, old women, young men, and maidens, were all subject to his will. They cried like children, or laughed like idiots, just as he pleased to have them. After him, an old Methodist minister preached, who tried to play Maffit; but, instead of crying, the audience only laughed at him. In the evening Maffit was to preach again. The girls were infatuated to stay and hear him; and it was almost by force that I got them into the chaise, in order to fulfil my promise to Lucy's father.

If Maffit ran away with the daughter of an Earl, — as was the current report in those days, — she paid him well for it, for she scathed him much. At one time, when he had told her he wanted a *light* supper, she put a dozen lighted candles on the table, and told him supper was ready; at another time, she found a nest of young mice, put them in the parlor, and sent for him, telling him some "young converts" wanted to see him; and, at still another, she locked him up in a room, and, after the bell had tolled and tolled, some of his people went for him and let him out.

While I was preaching at "New Fields," old Mr. Roland of Exeter was dismissed from the First Congregational Church in that town. The old man was well and active, and laid it to heart very much. His conscience would not let him attend church where he had preached forty years; so he came over to New Fields, every sabbath. I set him to preaching half of every Sunday, which pleased him. I had two reasons for doing this: one was, to comfort him, and the other to get some help, I being young. Little did I know then how an old man feels at being slighted.

How slow we old fellows are to learn that we are not wanted on earth! Dr. John Codman, spoken of elsewhere in these Recollections, once said to me, on giving a notice, "Tell the people he is the most popular young preacher in America." That man, though still in good health, has been laid on the shelf for some time, though long a popular pastor in Boston. No wonder Dr. Young, in his "Night Thoughts," said of the new race of his day, —

> "They come to push us from the stage,
> Or hiss us there."

We old fellows, however, have one consolation; to wit, This young craft occasionally have to dip into us, as into chronological tables, to know what happened before the flood.

While I was at "New Fields," the following incident occurred in Exeter. The church over which Rev. Mr. Hurd was settled was started as a Unitarian society, and Mr. Hurd had preached for them while he was a student in Cambridge. They gave him a call. He went to Scotland, and studied theology; and while there, became a Trinitarian. The society continued to write to him, asking him to come and be their pastor. At length he told them he had changed his belief, and, if they still wished him to become their pastor, he would. They wrote him to come, and he did. He was a prudent man, and the people all liked him.

At one time he exchanged with Rev. Mr. Belden, who was settled in Brentwood. Mr. Belden was an open-hearted, independent man, and not afraid to speak his mind. At the close of the service, he gave out the hymn, and added, "Sing it with the doxology." Judge Smith, a Unitarian, whose pew was near the pulpit, said, in a voice sufficiently loud to be heard by the preacher, "We don't sing doxologies here."

Belden was on his feet very soon, and said with some

emphasis, "When the judge is on the bench, he may conduct the case as he pleases; when I am in the pulpit, I shall conduct the service as *I* please. You will please sing the doxology." The congregation were delighted at this rebuke; for they thought the old judge was sometimes disposed to be a little dictatorial.

While at "New Fields," I had cause to visit Pembroke, to see Father Burnham, who was secretary of their Missionary Society, which then gave me my bread. I went there about the middle of the week, intending to leave the next day; but there came on one of those old-fashioned New-Hampshire snow-storms, which blocked up the roads, so that I had to remain over the sabbath. Mr. Burnham was a complete general, not to say, a Napoleon. Sabbath morning he said to me, "You'll preach to-day." I said, "I will preach half the day, and hear you the other half." — "No," said he: "you'll preach all day." I preached in the morning; and when we returned from the church, and had entered his study, he said, "As you are a young man, I want to give you some advice. It will do you good." I assented to this as all very nice, and thought it might be useful to me. He said, "There was one sentence in your sermon that I would advise you to leave out, as it don't mean any thing: 'The stone shall cry out of the wall, and the beam out of the timber shall answer it.' That don't mean any thing." I replied, "It is a Bible expression." — "No," said he, "that is not in the Bible." I replied, "It is in my Bible;" and, as he persisted in saying it was not in his Bible, I turned to the passage, and handed him *his* Bible. He pulled down his glasses, looked at it a moment, and then said, " Well, if all the world had told me that was in the Bible, I would not have believed it."

I preached in the afternoon, in obedience to orders. At the close of the services, he appointed two meetings, at the schoolhouses; and at supper, he said (he had two daughters) to one of them, " You will go with Mr. Cornell, and show him the schoolhouse;" and, to the other, " You will go with me."

At that period New Hampshire had been for some time under Democratic rule; but this year they had elected a Whig governor. Mr. Burnham was a Whig; and when he read the proclamation for Thanksgiving Day, and " God save the Commonwealth of New Hampshire," at the end of it, he added, with considerable zest, " And God *has* saved New Hampshire."

While in the " Granite State," I visited Gilmanton, and preached there a few sabbaths. This was a " right smart little place." They had an academy there, and were about establishing a theological seminary, in which they afterward succeeded. Here old Dr. and young Dr. Crosby resided at that time; and here were several families of note and of aristocratic proclivities. The young ladies, especially, gave evidence that they lived near the academy; for there was one, the daughter of a cashier, who lived a quarter of a mile from the church; and, though she was in good health, yet the horse must be harnessed to carry her there, lest " the timorously nice creature," like some in the days of Moses, " should set foot upon the ground." Then, there was another, an only child, with whom her rich and indulgent father had travelled all over Europe. He had bought her a splendid library. But language fails to describe this proud little village in those " olden times."

A party of us went to the White Mountains, and, on our return through Concord, stopped at the hotel kept by a Mr. Gass. He was lame with the gout, and kept hobbling from one end of the piazza of his house to the other. I said to him, " Mr. Gass, you have the gout." — " Yes, yes," said he: " I have the gout; but it pays me well." — " How do you make the gout pay you well?" said I. " Why, don't you see? I keep a public-house, and they keep a public-house over there " (pointing across the street) ; " but they have no custom there. Everybody sees me hobbling about here, and they know I have the gout; and they all say, ' There is good eating there ; ' and they all come here." This was the first time I had ever known the gout pay any one well, except the doctor.

I was ordained as an evangelist, at Exeter, by the Piscataqua Association, Jan. 19, 1830, Rev. Dr. French, of Northampton, preaching the sermon. He held much such a place among the ministers there as Washington did in the American army. I left New Hampshire in feeble health, and called on Dr. Shattuck, sen., in Boston, for medical advice. After a pretty thorough examination, he said, " If you have any friends, I think you had better go among them, and make yourself as comfortable as you can. This was equivalent to saying, "You won't live long;" yet I have lived fifty years since, wanting three.

CHAPTER XX.

HISTORY AND RECOLLECTIONS OF WOODSTOCK, CONN.

CONTENTS. — History of the Town — Settled by a Colony from Roxbury — King Philip's War — Rev. Mr. Lyman — The Old Major — My Advent to Woodstock — Four Quarts of Oats sent me there — Rev. Mr. Williams of Dudley — Muddy Brook — The Parish Quarrel — Capt. Walker and Daughters — Emily's Criticisms — Removal to South Woodstock — Father Lyman — His Settlement — Mr. Lyman's Kindness — Dr. Jedediah Morse — Dr. Abiel Holmes — William Bowen, Esq., and his Grandson Henry C. Bowen — Effects of Anti-Masonry — Deacon Chandler and Wife — Mr. Barsto laughing in Meeting — The Lions — Deacon Walter Paine — State of Religion in Woodstock — Protracted Meetings — How conducted — Results — Protracted meeting in Providence — Rev. Dr. Dow — Rev. Mr. Wilson — Rev. Charles G. Finney — His First Visit to New England — His Preaching — Rev. Dr. Wisner — Endurance of the Converts — The McClellan Family — Gen. George B. — Lorenzo Dow.

Little is known of Woodstock previous to the date of its settlement by the whites. We know, indeed, that it belonged to the Nipmuck Indians, who once numbered, in various villages in Massachusetts and Connecticut, some five thousand warriors. Woodstock was by them called Wabbaquasset, or Wapaquasset. From an early part of the seventeenth century to the time of King Philip's war, John Eliot, the "apostle to the Indians," was wont to preach upon these hills, and beside these lakes and streams, to that portion of the tribe who dwelt here and hereabouts. An interesting fact is related in this connection.

Uncas, the proud and crafty chief of the Mohegans, claimed sovereignty over not only his own tribe, but several others. He had heard, from one of his warriors, of the preaching of Eliot at Wabbaquasset, and that in the course of his sermon he had enunciated a radical doctrine, — which, indeed, was a favorite doctrine of that preacher, — viz., that there is no king but King Jesus, and that all others were usurpers; Jesus alone having a right to the homage of men, either temporally or spiritually.

The wrath of the savage was moved against this seditious doctrine, and against the preacher who had presumed to instil rebellious principles among his loyal adherents. He breathed out threatenings and slaughter against Eliot; but, while planning the accomplishment of his designs, a wise old sagamore of his tribe advised delay and caution, asking Uncas if it would not be right first to go in person to the preacher, or else to send some one in whom he had confidence, to hear the man, and afterwards, if need be, judge and punish. Uncas, pleased with this sagacious counsel, despatched the sagamore himself to attend at the next appointment, to listen and report. The messenger went and heard. It chanced that Eliot, who sometimes preached politics in the pulpit, gave his hearers that day in the woods nothing but pure gospel, so that the Indian returned with an answer very like that of Pilate to the accusing Jews, "I find no fault in this man. The kingdom he advocates is not a kingdom of this world, but the kingdom of the Great Spirit." Thereafter Uncas left the apostle to sow in peace the good seed of the kingdom. But the circumstance is a very early instance, and furnishes another notable warning of the imminent danger of those preachers who curdle the sweet milk of the word with the sour vinegar of politics.

In 1675 commenced King Philip's war, during which, nearly all the tribes of New England were banded together in a desperate effort to exterminate the hated Englishmen. In June of that year, Major John Talcott, with two hundred and fifty Englishmen and two hundred Mohegans and Pequots, marched from Norwich, and invaded the territory of the Nipmucks at Wabbaquasset. The Indians retired without accepting battle; and their fortifications in this township, made mostly of tree-tops, were destroyed, together with fifty acres of growing corn. This fort was situated on what is still called Fort Hill, a mile or two west of the village.

In 1683 the Governor and Company of Massachusetts Bay gave to the town of Roxbury, Mass., a tract of " land for the establishment of a village;" the conditions of the grant being that it should be settled by thirty families within three years, and that they should maintain among them "an able and orthodox godly minister." And in 1684 the town of Roxbury appointed Lieut. Samuel Ruggles, John Ruggles, John Curtis, and Isaac Morris, to view the wilderness, and find a convenient place to take up this grant; who, after a due time spent in searching, "found a convenient place in the Wapaquasset country, westward of Myannekesset river," i.e., the Quinebaug.

"April 5, 1686," says the oldest record, now in possession of Joseph McClellan, "several persons came as planters, and took actual possession (by breaking up land and planting corn) of the land granted to Roxbury for a village, called by the planters "New Roxbury," by the ancient nations Wapaquasset."

As we have seen, the town of Woodstock was first settled by a colony from "Newtowne" and Roxbury, from Massachusetts, principally by the names of Child, Holmes, Morse, and May. They were substantial, Orthodox, well-to-do farmers, whose word was as good as their bond; and from them descended many of the solid men of Boston and its vicinity. Rev. Abiel Holmes, D.D., of Cambridge, was born in Woodstock, and visited that town yearly as long as he lived and was able to do it: thus the present Oliver Wendell Holmes, lecturer, poet, professor, and no lover of Evangelical truth, came from a good Orthodox family. Rev. Jedediah Morse, D.D., the first geographer of New England, was a son of Deacon Morse of Woodstock.

The town was early divided into three parishes; the old now called South Woodstock, whence originated Henry C. Bowen, and where at his summer residence assembled President Grant and the other magnates of the land, some time since. *Muddy Brook* parish was in the north part of the town; and the third parish was called West Woodstock.

When the writer went there, in 1830, Father Lyman, then ex-pastor of the old, now south parish, was living. He was a good, substantial, straightforward, outspoken man, " who always said the thing he meant." Few idle words has he had to account for. He concealed nothing, even if by expressing his mind the case went against him: as on one occasion, when Deacon Morse, at the time of harvest, sent him a bushel of rye. When the boy returned Mr. Morse said, " Did you see Mr. Lyman?"—"Yes."— " What did he say?" — " He measured it, and said there wasn't enough by two quarts." Father Underwood was then pastor at West Woodstock. He was a good, but a very different man from Mr. Lyman, musical, social, jovial. He being of this cast, and Mr. Lyman solemn as the judgment, it used to be said, while the " Muddy Brook " parish was destitute of a pastor several years, Mr. Lyman was invited to attend all the funerals, and Mr. Underwood all the weddings.

My advent to Woodstock was remarkable, as it seemed to depend upon *four quarts of oats*. I had spent six months previous in missionary labors in New Hampshire. My health was miserable. But, after spending a few days in Taunton, I started with my old horse, a pretty decent one, but a carriage of home manufacture, which, as I journeyed, called forth the *irony* of old Father Williams of Dudley, on this wise: "A nice carriage, a fine carriage! I wish I had such an one; the horse very good." He was an excellent horse-jockey. I started with a view of returning to New Hampshire, but stopped at a country tavern (there were no *hotels* then) in Easton, and found Father Sheldon there. I had seen him before. He inquired where I was going; and on being told, going out as Abraham did, not knowing *where*, he said, "I wish you would go to Woodstock, Conn., for I agreed to supply them four sabbaths, and proposed to take my daughter to Woodstock Springs. But she is unable to go, and I want to send a substitute." I took a letter from him to Col. May of Woodstock, changed my course from north to south-west, and made for Woodstock. I passed the *toll-gate*, near what is now "Village Corners," in the dusk of the evening, which was kept and the road owned by a Mr. Clapp, an old man toward ninety. I gave him six cents toll. The next day, by some means, I don't know what, he discovered my clerical character, and on Monday morning, before breakfast, called to refund the six cents; which I declined. "But," said the old man, "you *must* take them, or you will spoil my story." — "How so?" — "Why, I have never taken toll of a minister for forty years, and I love to tell of it." So I took back the toll-money. I arrived at my destination in the evening, and was sent to Capt. Walker's, an uncle of our friend, the Hon. Amasa

Walker, to board. The next morning was bright and sunny. The village of old *Muddy Brook* looked well; good houses, apparently good livers, and good farms around. I went to the "meeting-house:" there were no *churches* in those days. It was an old-fashioned house, having as many doors as the "Old South," and one to spare. It had small windows, small glass, was two stories, and had a large gallery all round, and the entrance to the gallery was in the vestibule. The pews were square, and seats all round them, and tables to lay the hymn-books on, and also to sleep upon.

The congregation was immense, filling the whole house, galleries, aisles, and stairs.

At dinner, I said to Capt. Walker, "How is this? You seem to be rich, and good livers, and have a large congregation. How does it happen, that you have such an old dilapidated meeting-house?"—"Oh!" said Capt. Walker, "you do not know our history. We have been fighting seventy years about that old meeting-house. Seventy years ago, when that house was raised (it not being in the centre of the parish), when one party raised the timber, the other appeared to push down; and from that day to this, the quarrel has existed; and now one part of the parish are building a new house at Village Corners, about a mile west. This is the reason we have not had a better house of worship."

One thing which added much to the acrimony of the quarrel was, the people in the parish were all nearly related, having married and intermarried among themselves from the first settlement of the town, rarely going out of the neighborhood of "Muddy Brook" to form a family connection. They were one people, " of one heart and one mind," on all subjects except that of the location of the church. On this point they were sworn contestants, and they had brought up their children on each side of the brook with instruction, " Samuel, you fight for the removal of that meeting-house," and, " John, never suffer that house to be removed from its old location;" and they held on to this instruction as tenaciously as did the sons of Jonadab the Rechabite. Such was the condition of things, when the writer commenced preaching in the parish of " Muddy Brook;" so far as ill-will was concerned, it was *muddy* enough. But both parties seemed satisfied with the preaching; and so he remained for six months, till the new house, located at the " Village Corners," was completed; and, when a majority of the society, but not of the church, voted to worship at the new house the next sabbath, and the remainder determined to stay at the old house, a committee from each party waited upon the writer, to engage him to preach on each side of the brook the next sabbath. As he could not do this, he declined to preach on either side. Two brothers of Hon. Linus Child, late of Boston, were of the committee that wished him to preach in the new house, — Asa and Peleg Child. Asa did not then reside in the parish; but Peleg did, and was so active in the parish-quarrel that the meaning of the name originally might have applied to him: " His name was called Peleg, for in his days the earth was divided."

Strange as it may seem, it was afterwards reported by one of these committees, that Mr. Cornell remained with them as long as they wanted him. It was evident that the principle, "*tittila me, tittilabo te,*" ended with them, when they found their labor in vain.

This old "Muddy Brook" was one of the strong parishes of Connecticut. Rev. Mr. Backus had been pastor for many years. Mr. Backus was a good man, possessed of more than ordinary talent, but really indolent. One of the people, of more than ordinary intelligence, gave the following account of his ministry: "He was a good preacher, a thorough student when he would study; but he had some tact at extemporizing; and, when it was a rainy day, he would say, 'I had prepared a sermon, but as only few are present, I will expound a chapter.' On this rock he split. When he thus expounded, he was always half an hour longer than when he had a written sermon. This was so noticeable, that those who staid at home could always tell *when he preached*, and when he did *not*, as they called it. When he did *not* preach, he kept the people half an hour longer. They said they would not have found fault about his not having a sermon, if he would only tell them beforehand, so that they could calculate for dinner. But, as they were ignorant of this, they put the *pudding* in, at a given time; and, if he happened to have no sermon that day, it was all *spoiled*, being boiled to pieces. This really broke him up; for, though they were a sleepy people, yet they were more wakeful than their minister."

The result of this parish-quarrel was, they divided; built two houses of worship, settled two ministers; and for forty years have paid each of them a larger salary than they paid one, when they all went to the old house. Thus they have "*provoked* each other to love and good works."

A word should be said of Capt. Walker's two daughters, where the writer boarded six months. Emily, the elder of the two, was a young woman of bright parts, of sparkling wit, much intelligence, of an amiable disposition, and inflexible integrity. She was some thirty or thirty-five years old, and, consequently, had lost some of her maiden beauty. But she still possessed a black and sparkling eye, and a full share of wit. Her criticisms were keen, searching, and ever pertinent.

As specimens of her ready wit take the following: The minister was absent a sabbath, and they held a "deacons' meeting." On his return, he asked Emily how they got along. "First rate," said she. "Deacon Luther Child made the long prayer in the morning, and prayed just an hour. Deacon William Child made the long prayer in the afternoon, and seemed determined not to be outdone by Deacon Luther; so he prayed an hour and five minutes." Old Dr. Lyman Beecher was then in his glory in Boston. One day Emily took up a Boston paper in which it was said, Dr. Beecher said so and so, at a *temperance* meeting, and he was followed in a very appropriate address by Amasa Walker, Esq. "Well," she said, "my cousin Amasa is a great man down there among your Boston people. We always considered him a good fellow, but not so *great* as he is among your *Bostonians.*" Professor Walker was then a young man, and such a remark was perfectly natural upon the principle, " A prophet is not without honor save in his own country, and among his own kindred." How greatness diminishes as it comes nearer!

Nor did Miss Emily spare even the writer. He had not imitated Dr. Lyman Beecher, as many of the young ministers around Boston had, in using the blacksmith's hammer; but he had a habit, which has characterized some greater men than he, of using his hands as though he were fighting off mosquitoes, as used to be the case with that excellent minister Rev. Dr. Storrs of Braintree, and Rev. Dr. Wadsworth of Philadelphia. Something was said about his remaining the minister of the " Muddy Brook " parish after the " Village Corner " folks had gone off. Miss Emily addressing him said, " Well, you must learn to keep your hands still." It was an appropriate and well-timed criticism.

Miss Emily afterward married a mechanic by the name of Smith, and removed to New York. The writer visited them some years after her marriage, and found she had two fine boys, and was living in very comfortable circumstances. Miss Emily nearly ruined her health in nursing with the most tender care her sick sister Elvira, who died while I was in the family.

After the arrangement was made to have preaching regularly at both houses of the old " Muddy Brook " parish, and, after the interview with the two committees on the same evening, above named, I left that part of the town, and went to what is now called South Woodstock. It was the oldest part of the town, having been first settled, and was then called Woodstock; the other three Congregational societies being designated, "Muddy Brook," "Village Corners," and "West Woodstock."

I had negotiated an exchange with an old minister by the name of Rich, from New Hampshire, who was then supplying South Woodstock, for him to go to Muddy Brook, and I was to go there. This had been agreed upon by the committee of the parish, and by Mr. Rich and myself. So, when the division of Muddy Brook parish came, I went to the old part of the town. This was a weaker parish than either part of the Muddy Brook one. Over this first church of Woodstock, Conn., I was installed June 15, 1831. The sermon was by Rev. Mr. Maltby of Taunton. Father Lyman, the old minister, and his wife, were still living. He had been the pastor for nearly fifty years. But there had been another, Rev. Mr. Crampton, settled and left, before my settlement there. The parish had been somewhat broken. Mr. Lyman had been settled upon the old plan, for life, as it was called, his salary based upon articles at an estimated sum with a small amount of money.

For instance, he was to have so much wood at one dollar a cord, corn at fifty cents a bushel, &c., and for labor he was to allow fifty cents a day. During the long period of his ministry, prices changed very much, and this, among other things, created trouble. Mr. Lyman by laying out some money, which came by his wife, soon after his settlement, when land was cheap, became eventually one of the richest landholders of the parish; and, when labor became worth a dollar and a quarter a day, Mr. Lyman would say, "My contract allows me labor for fifty cents." Thus the man, who could have this sum, becoming provoked with Mr. Lyman, would labor for him no more. Finally, very unscrupulous means were used to get rid of Mr. Lyman. One man used to tell how he worked to get rid of Mr. Lyman. He went by the name of the "Old Major." The "Old Major" was a man of mind. He knew almost every thing and everybody. Young persons, hearing him speak for the first time, admired him. He reminded them (and everybody else who had never seen him before) of Goldsmith's village schoolmaster:—

> "Still they gazed, and still the wonder grew,
> That one small head could carry all he knew."

The "Old Major's" head, however, was very large. He was a moving man. He used to say, two years were enough for any man to live in one place: accordingly, as he owned a farm in two contiguous towns, he was accustomed to move from one to the other, and from the other to one, every two years.

The "Old Major" was a ministerial man. He was ever a great friend to his minister. If he had any product of his farm to sell, he would like to have the minister buy it. Unfortunately, often, for the poor minister, however, in trading with the Major, it turned out that he (the minister) "paid too dear for the whistle."

It happened, also, that in one of the towns from, and to, which the Major was accustomed to migrate, the minister, Father Lyman, was settled upon the good old New-England plan, for life; not, as in these modern times, on wheels. Now, it came to pass, in the course of human events, after this minister had been settled forty years, many of the people wished to turn him out to graze. But in accomplishing this several obstacles were to be overcome. In the first place, there were, in those days, several sturdy oaks on "the hill of Zion," who, adhering to grave principles, and walking in "the old paths," did not believe it right to serve an old, faithful minister, worse than a humane farmer would serve his old horse. This was the first obstacle in the way. But, as "Young America" was then coming up, a sturdy youth, of go-ahead character, and of break-shackle proclivity, and, as young Pompey told old Cæsar, "more worship the rising than the setting sun," more of this young craft was found than of the old settlers; so this first question was disposed of by popular vote of numbers against the minister. Then, next, there was the law, not having been made for the "righteous," but "for evil-doers." This presented to them a knotty question; for, if they dismissed him, they must, by law, still support him.

To get out of this dilemma, many expedients were devised. One was a somewhat new device, then, though since a very common one with corporations — those bodies without souls — for the society, an incorporated body, to put its property out of its hands. So its funds, left to support the gospel by the pious dead, and in this case chiefly by a pious old lady, were put beyond the reach of attachment as society property.

But, then, there remained the meeting-house. This could be taken for the minister's salary. Here was a tender spot. This difficulty was, however, proposed to be removed by a spruce young man who had recently become a member of the society. This young sprig proposed to sell the house at auction, and dispose of *that*, as they had of the other moneys. Some of the old men could not yet see that this would be exactly a very pious deed; nevertheless, it was carried, by a majority. In brief, the old minister was dismissed.

Now, what was a little remarkable, the "Old Major" was never seen at one of these society meetings. Not he: he was all the time a *ministerial* man. Many years after, however, he related the whole matter to the writer.

"I never appeared," said he, "at the meetings; but I worked like a beaver out of doors among the people."

The "Old Major" was a *repentant* man. He believed in asking forgiveness when he had done wrong: so, the day after the old minister was dismissed, he entered the study, and addressed (with hat in hand, and about to kneel before him) the ex-pastor, —

"Mr. ——, I have been very wicked; I've tried to get you dismissed: I'm very sorry; I hope you will forgive me," &c.

The "Old Major" was a *shrewd* man. He laid all the plans for the above-named result. But this was not all. He knew *where* to work. It was "from house to house;" and thus he always began where the squirrel puts out his dirt when he digs; viz., at the other end of the hole.

The "Old Major" was *an exhorter;* and hence, just before one of his two-year moves, he took occasion to exhort the people, and especially the young, to become good; and though he removed but a few miles, yet he always concluded his last exhortations (for he always had several *last* ones) with these words, —

"And now, my dear friends, and most precious youth, I shall never see you again," &c. The writer well remembers one of these last exhortations. The meeting was in the Academy Hall; and as the youth went out, one after another, one who remembered some former removals said, "Well, the 'Old Major' is on the move again."

The "Old Major," near the close of life, had a slight stroke of paralysis, which somewhat affected his speech. In this state he called on the widow of the clergyman above-named, — a woman of small stature, black eyes, bright intellect, of the age of eighty-five years, — and said, —

"Mrs. ——, I shall never *say* any more."

She quickly replied, —

"Well, Major, it is just as well, for you have *said* a great deal in your life."

The "Old Major" loved his family, as every good man should. He had two children by the last wife, children of his old age. There were no such children as these in the land. The son became a minister; and it would have done any one good to have looked at the "Old Major" when he preached.

From what has been said, and much more that might be said, the reader may infer that the "Old Major" filled a niche; that he had a good hull, was well built, finely rigged, and wanting in nothing, but ballast and a rudder. Query: Are there any niches in the church and the community now filled by men wanting both ballast and rudders?

From what has been said let no one infer that we considered the "Old Major" a bad man. By no manner of means. He was in many respects a good citizen.

Mr. Lyman's mind became very much impaired; and, while his bodily health was tolerably good, he finally lost his intellect. When he could not remember whether he had had family worship or not, and many such like items, his mind was clear on religious subjects, and he would expound difficult portions of Scripture (for which he was renowned) with great precision and clearness; thus showing the "ruling passion strong" to the last.

His desire to visit the house of God was strong, and he was always a punctual and regular attendant. He was exceedingly kind and tender to his successor, the writer. He is indebted to Mr. Lyman, also, for many critical remarks and corrections which were very useful to him, and some of them might be to young ministers of the present day.

He had a habit, when eating, of smacking his lips. Mr. Lyman said, "You smack;" and this remark broke up the habit.

A neighboring minister preached one day, and Mr. Lyman said, "You say 'beseech *of*' in your prayer. Just leave out the *of*." Many ministers of the present day might profitably take the same advice.

I remained pastor of this church until Aug. 13, 1834. About this time a considerable number were added to the church, and among them Henry C. Bowen, then a lad of sixteen years. I name Mr. Bowen because he has been a prominent man in getting up "The Independent," and in establishing Congregationalism in New York and vicinity.

His mother was like Eunice, the mother of young Timothy, one of the best women I ever knew; and his grandmother, like "Lois," truly "a mother in Israel." If ever a woman prayed earnestly for the conversion of her children, Mrs. Bowen, the mother of Henry C. Bowen, did; and she saw them all four united with the church, two sons and two daughters.

Old Squire Bowen, the grandfather, was a very peculiar man; a man of wealth, but not a church-going man for many years. Soon after I went to this parish, his wife, then an old lady, among others, was propounded to the church. News of it came to the ears of her husband. One evening he called on me, and said he had understood Mrs. Bowen had been propounded as a candidate for admission to the church. I said, "Yes, she has been." Squire Bowen said, he thought the thing was premature. I replied, "It has been said, she has desired to unite with the church for twenty years." — "Yes," he said, "but we were married early, and I never felt willing to give her up to Mr. Lyman," Mr. Lyman having been the former pastor. He said if I would put it off that communion, he would make no further objection. I told him she was propounded for admission to the church; and I could make no engagement about it, as coming forward rested wholly with her. Here the matter was left. She did not come at that communion; and at the next the old gentleman was as good as his word, for he came and brought her, and remained through the service.

He then desired me to appoint a lecture at his house, which I did. People were as much astonished as those were, who once said, "Is Saul also among the prophets?" or, as the disciples were at the conversion of Saul of Tarsus. The old Squire, however, though he often attended church, never made a profession of religion. His advice to his grandson H. C. Bowen, when he left for New York, was, "Well, Henry, if you will go, keep your ears open, and your mouth shut."

I once preached about sleeping in church. The next day, the old gentleman came jogging along, on his old horse; and, as he came up, said, "Well, I shall have to sleep one sabbath more, for I have not yet done haying."

Old Esquire McClellan (of whom more will be said hereafter) said, "Mr. Cornell, if people sleep in church hereafter, it will not be your fault."

This parish, at the time I went there, had been overrun by the anti-Masonic excitement, which began about William Morgan, and spread like wildfire through the country. The most wealthy men had left the parish, and refused to pay any parish tax. No man, who was a Mason, could be elected to any office in town. It was then supposed that Masonry was dead; and no man would have believed that in 1878 it would have been stronger than ever before.

One other little incident that transpired during the pastorate in Woodstock may be properly named. There was a colony in one part of the parish, of some half-dozen families who had moved up from Providence, R.I. Rhode Island people in those days had not been accustomed to attend church, and none of these families were regular attendants.

They did not like to be considered as having no regard for the sabbath, and professed to be Universalists. So, on one occasion they invited Rev. Mr. Pickering, who was then flourishing in Providence, to come up and preach to them. I had some personal acquaintance with Mr. Pickering, and knew him to be a very pleasant man. They applied to the committee for the use of our church. The committee asked my opinion. They wanted it on a weekday. I said, Yes, by all means. So they had the church. They made great preparations, — went to Southbridge,

Mass., and engaged a band of music for the occasion, and were to have a general gathering. The day came. Mr. Pickering appeared and preached. But the congregation was very small; for, though our people gave them the use of the church, yet they did not feel bound to attend. The result was, the leaders in getting up the meeting said they had been at all this trouble and expense, and the people would not attend, and they would never lift a finger again to get up a meeting. So the Universalists came no more into that land as long as we staid there; but, had we refused them the house, they would have built one, as, "If he hears you say Dublin, he'll sure take the road to Cork."

In the church at Woodstock we had some very curious people, some ignorant people, some strong, healthy people, and some very weak and feeble people.

Deacon Chandler was a large, strong, and apparently a very healthy and long-lived man. He was a Mason; and, at the time referred to, Masons were proscribed, as just said. As a consequence, Deacon Chandler had to resign his deaconship. He did so, and retired from the office. But he still attended church. This good man, whether worried out by the ill-will of his brethren, or by the trials arising from the feeble state of his wife's health, or from some cause to the writer unknown, did not live to old age.

But his wife (and herein is the pith of what I am now after) lived till about ninety years old, to verify the old adage, "Threatened people live long." Forty years ago she was so feeble she could not walk a quarter of a mile.

She could attend church but half a day, even when she had been carried there. She was so dyspeptic she could eat nothing, and kept her bed a large part of the time. Yet she lived. I could enumerate several instances of this kind, where the well, the strong, the healthy, have died, while the feeble have lived; verifying the declaration of Scripture, " It is not in man that walketh to direct his steps."

We had a man in this town who used to tell the following story : —

" When I was a young man I fell in love with a girl, and determined to have her. She and her mother were very good Baptists, and at one time I was afraid I should have to go into the water to get her. But I determined to have her, if I did. I so managed, however, that I got her without going into the water after her."

We had two families of Lyons in town. In its early settlement, one of them was quite superior to the other. But, after the old stock passed away, the scene changed. The prominent family left but one son; the other, four. These four held various offices, and did not hesitate to nominate and strive to elect each other, and to give each other all his titles. The *one* son came to me one day, and said, " It is strange to me, how all the honors seem to kind'r run in that are family. One is a colonel, another a squire, and another a deacon. It didn't use to be so in the days of our fathers." So indeed it was not. But things had changed " since the fathers fell asleep."

We had a man, a very worthy, good man, too, by the

name of Barsto; and one morning I read these lines of Watts's, in church, —

> "Lions and beasts of savage name
> Put on the nature of the lamb."

He laughed. On Monday, I met him, and he said, "Did you see me laugh in church yesterday?" I said, "Yes." — "Well," said he, " I was thinking what a change must have taken place since the evening previous, when we had a parish-meeting and a pretty smart quarrel, all the lions manifesting their peculiarly ferocious nature. If they had put on the nature of the lamb this morning, there must have been a wonderful *change* during the night." I could hardly blame the good man for smiling.

The following is an account of one of the worthy descendants of Woodstock, with whom we had a very happy acquaintance: —

Deacon Walter Paine was born in Woodstock, Conn., in 1776, and was the son of Amos, who was the son of Daniel, who was the son of Samuel, who was the son of Stephen, who came over in 1638 in the ship "Diligence," and settled in Rehoboth, Mass. Samuel, the grandfather of Walter, purchased wild land in Woodstock in 1694, and settled there. Amos, his father, married Priscilla Lyon; and Walter was the seventh of their thirteen children, who doubtless were a merry company when gathered round the spacious fireplace of the olden time.

Walter remained at home until he had gained his majority, contributing his share to the varied labors of the farm, and at one time seriously injuring himself through his ambition to mow as much grass in a given time as a strong hired man.

At the age of twenty-one he left the paternal roof for the great life struggle, and chose Troy, N.Y., as the place to test the entering wedge of fortune. He remained at Troy but a short time before he removed to Providence, R.I., where he entered on mercantile life, and became, also, largely engaged in manufacturing. His attachments in Providence were very strong, both in the church and in society; and his ardent temperament gained for him many friends. The latter portion of his life was spent in Pomfret, Conn., where he resided twenty years, and where he died at the age of eighty-four years. His seat in the church and at the prayer-meetings was seldom vacant, and his last years were peaceful and happy.

One who served as deacon more than fifty years, in the same church where he officiated, prepared an obituary notice, from which we extract the following: —

"Although the subject of this notice had not resided in this city (Providence, R.I.) for several years, yet formerly he was esteemed as one of our most prominent citizens, filling with honor several important offices, both civil and religious. He came to Providence when a youth, and by his industry and correct deportment he soon secured the confidence of those with whom he became associated. In early life he married a daughter of the late Daniel Snow, brother of the first minister of the Beneficent Church, by whom he had several children.

Two sons of this marriage are respected citizens of this place. His second wife was a sister of Judge Bacon of Canterbury, Conn., who, with an only daughter, have been his constant attendants in the closing period of his life, and who with the sons mourn the loss of a husband and father highly respected and dearly beloved.

"He early made a public profession of his faith in Christ, and in the year 1808 was elected to the office of deacon in the Beneficent Congregational Church, which he retained for more than thirty years, until he removed from the city.

"A short time previous to his decease he visited his former residence, and called on many friends of his earlier days, evincing to all that his faith was firm to the end. 'Blessed are the dead which die in the Lord, from henceforth; for they rest from their labors, and their works do follow them.'"

Some account of the religious revival in 1830 and 1831 may be interesting to the pastors and churches of the present day.

There were some wonderful conversions in Woodstock during my pastorate. There was a man by the name of J. P.,— a notoriously wicked man, and, withal, very profane. If good Deacon C., who lived near him, asked him if he would go to church, he would swear till the deacon was out of hearing.

This man's wife and eldest daughter were converted. Nothing had been said to him about religion, nor had he attended any of the meetings. He went into his garden, one evening, and saw two little vines just come up. The next morning he looked again, and one of them was gone. This text immediately came into his mind, "One shall be taken, and the other left."

He went into the woods to chop wood; but he could not work. "One shall be taken, and the other left," followed him. He went home to dinner, but could not eat. He was in an agony. Finally he appeared in the meeting. Every one was surprised, some utterly astonished. At last he was converted; and from that time there was no man more " ready to every good work," no man more ready to open his purse, and pay his money, when it was needed for a good cause, than this man. The conversion of Saul of Tarsus, or of John Bunyan, was not more striking, or the change more visible. That one sentence of Holy Writ fastened upon his mind, and, as an arrow from the Almighty, stuck fast. But the most remarkable thing in his conversion was, he had attended no meeting, and nothing had been said to him on the subject of religion. Christians had been praying for him; and He in whose hands are all hearts had heard and answered their prayers. Professor Tyndall, or any other professor, may account for such a conversion upon physical principles as they please. Such were the facts.

PROTRACTED MEETINGS IN 1831, IN WINDHAM COUNTY, CONN.

Such was the name given to the meetings held in 1831–32, in various parts of the country. One of the earliest of these was held in Western Connecticut, in March, 1831, at which the writer was present, of which the following is a description. It may be interesting to some who have since come upon the stage, to know how these meetings were conducted more than forty years ago, by which many hundreds were brought into the churches.

The first sermon was from the text, "Purifying their hearts by faith." The preacher opened the whole system of Christian theology, and brought to view the grand reason why Christ came into our world; to wit, that we might be saved through faith in him.

1. What is faith?
2. How shall we get it?
3. How does faith show itself?

Immediately before and after the sermon, a prayer-meeting was held by the church; and the prayers and exhortations were fervent and earnest.

The second sermon was from the text, "Ye are the light of the world."

Said the speaker, "Christians have been in all ages the lights in this dark world. Noah, Moses, David, Ezra, Nehemiah, and Daniel were the lights of their day. They shone in the old world, in the wilderness, in the captivities of Israel, as lights in a dark place. So 'in the fulness of time,' heralded by John the Baptist, a burning and shining light himself, the Messiah, the grand light and luminary of our world, made his appearance."

The third sermon was from the text, "Have I any pleasure at all that the wicked should die, saith the Lord God; and not that he should turn from his wicked way, and live?"

The former sermons had been addressed exclusively to the church. The usual course pursued in these meetings was, first, to address the church, —

1. From his sparing them so long.
2. From the ransom provided for them.
3. From the offer which He makes them of pardon.
4. From the earnestness with which He presses mercy upon them.

Then followed exhortations to the sinner to turn. It was said, "If you die, the throne of God will be clean from your blood. All holy beings will rejoice in God's justice."

The fourth sermon was from the text, "Except a man be born of water and of the Spirit, he cannot see the kingdom of heaven."

In this sermon was developed a little new-school theology, which about that time was considerably talked of, and which became more prominent; till, in 1837, the discussion culminated in the Presbyterian Church, by rending that great body in twain; and now, after thirty years separation, these two bodies have been made one again.

The ground taken in the sermon, from this text: "The Holy Spirit was necessary to renew the heart, not because man of himself had not sufficient ability to obey God, not because he had not sufficient powers and faculties to be an obedient subject, nor because God has not plainly told him his duty; but, simply, because *he is so bad*. All that renders the special influence of God's Spirit necessary to renew the hearts of men is, because they *will* not love God."

Then followed a relation of the state of religion in the various churches represented in the meeting. The work of the Lord was being revived all around us. Many very striking cases of conversion were related, such as thrilled the heart of every Christian. Sinners were awakened, crying for mercy. One old man, who had a good mother, ninety years old, said, " I can't go to my father, for he has been in heaven forty years; but 'I will arise and go to my' mother." He had been a drunkard for many years, and the only one of a large family who was out of Christ. He went, and, on bended knees, laid his head in the old lady's lap, and wept like a child. As the writer came down from the pulpit on one occasion, a lawyer, an ex-lieutenant governor of the State, trembling like an aspen-leaf, cried out, "What shall I do?" Such were the manifestations at these meetings. The Holy Spirit was present in a wonderful degree. After two sermons each day, and one in the evening, for four days, the Lord's Supper was administered; and with it the meeting closed.

They were sometimes called *Four Days' Meetings*, and sometimes *Protracted Meetings*, and were held more or less all over the New-England States, but chiefly in Connecticut.

While pastor at Woodstock in 1831, the writer attended a protracted meeting, in old Father Wilson's, the Beneficent Church, in Providence, R.I., elsewhere referred to.

Mr. Wilson kept Mr. Finney preaching so much that Rev. Dr. Dow, of Thompson, Conn., who had been invited to attend the meeting, but who had not been invited to preach, told us the following: "Mr. Wilson's keeping Mr. Finney preaching reminds me of the woman who named all her children *Molly*. When the first was born, they asked her what it should be called. She said *Molly;* and when, in process of time, she had another, and was asked what it should be called, she said that should be *Molly*, too." We could not blame Dr. Dow for the story, for he was an old man, and the best preacher in Connecticut; had been invited to attend the meeting, and Messrs. Finney and Wisner had done most of the preaching.

Let me here caution young ministers against overwork in seasons of revival. At those protracted meetings, I preached for several months, on an average, ten sermons a week. I was young, ardent, and if urgency to preach by my brethren, and full houses, were proof of popularity, popular; but I then laid the foundation for that disease of the vocal organs which afterwards compelled me to leave the pulpit.

TRUTH STRANGER THAN FICTION.

A good young lady of Connecticut, while I was in Woodstock, went through a singular experience. She left this world in 1830. She died of that peculiarly fatal disease, pulmonary consumption; especially so, in New England. In her sickness, she was the most patient, lovely being I ever saw, — always cheerful, always resigned, though constantly wasting with that incurable disease.

Rarely have I seen the following symptoms of this

disease so clearly developed as in her case: hectic fever, wasting of the body, cough, expectoration, perspiration, the nose sharp and drawn; the cheek-bones prominent, and a red spot in the middle, and apparently redder in contrast with the surrounding paleness; the lips retracted, and moulded into a bitter smile; the neck oblique, and impeded in its movements; the shoulder-blades projected like wings, the ribs prominent, and intercostal spaces sunk in; the nails crooked, and the joints of the fingers prominent. Such were the heart-rending symptoms daily presented to the agonizing friends, as the most amiable and lovely of creation hastened on to the grave.

Some time previous to her sickness, an event had happened that gave her serious trouble. There had been a revival, in which she and a cousin of hers had both experienced religion. The cousin had united with the church; but she had not. There was a young man in the neighborhood of ——. He was intelligent and active; but he was a nothingarian. He proposed marriage to her. She frankly and conscientiously told him, she could not marry a man with his religious views. He went directly to her friend, proposed marriage to her, and she accepted. They were married. He prospered in business; became one of, if not the most prominent man in the town. All the old maids and widows who had any spare money carried it to him. He graciously accepted it, but only to accommodate *them*. He had no need of it; and the interest and principal were always ready for them when wanted.

In addition to all this worldly prosperity, at one of those protracted meetings which characterized those days, he became a convert. He soon joined the church, became an active member. No man could exhort or pray like him. He was now almost adored by all. His family prospered. Sons and daughters were born unto him. His wife was praised by many of her acquaintances and relatives. Thus things went on swimmingly for several years.

The first-named lady lived to see it all. The thought often came to her innocent bosom, "*I* might have had all that. Had I not been too conscientious, I should have been where my cousin is." Then, she would think, "Well, I did what I then thought was for the best, and why should I regret it?"

She was comforted by being told, there was a "Divinity that shaped our course," — that God ordered all things wisely; and, in his wisdom, she acquiesced. She even went down to the grave, reconciled, and believing that "the Judge of all the earth would do right."

Some time after she died, and the writer had left the State, he saw in a paper the following: "Died in Connecticut, an old man. He had been a prominent citizen of the town for many years, and died honored and deeply regretted. All the nine clergymen of the town attended his funeral, and addresses were made by several of them. The whole town seemed in mourning."

But soon things put on a new face. The doctors who had been called to see him, knew, all the time, that great funeral was going on, that he had "shuffled off this mortal coil," by his own hand. They were well convinced by the *symptoms*, that his disease was "opium on the brain;" and, besides, in manipulating about the body, one of them had found an empty phial labelled *Laudanum*. Doctors don't always tell all they know; but it was a little too much to carry this farce quite so far.

These secret-keeping Esculapii might never have spoiled the character of this man, nor the grand funeral which followed his death, had not some outside "unpleasantness" been found to have a bearing upon the case; for as "Mammon" is an active god, and as those implements of his, called "banks," with their Argus-eyes are ever watching, it was soon discovered that there was a *deficit* in his account, which he left no money to pay. Moreover, it was also discovered, that he had been "robbing Peter to pay Paul," for several years; and that all the way he had kept his pecuniary head above water had been by forging the names of gentlemen, as indorsers, and then signing himself; and, before a note became due, getting the money from one bank to pay the note to the other. Thus, though carrying on a system of fraud for many years, he had managed so adroitly that he had never been caught until now. The Devil had got the noose so nicely adjusted about the neck of the poor victim, that, finding it impossible to meet his demands, he chose to take a short way of paying up.

But, as for the maiden ladies and widows who would have "plucked out their own eyes and given them to him," as well as their money, they lost all.

Were we disposed to moralize a little, many things might be said while contemplating the fate of these two friends.

It is necessary to wait sometimes for what Providence develops, even in this world. One went down to the grave lovely, and beloved, and with a conscience void of offence; and, with a hope of a glorious immortality, "entered into rest." The man had "that honor which cometh from men," while he lived; but "died as the fool dieth," as he lived; and the widows and orphans whom he defrauded will be swift witnesses against him at "the great day."

"God moves in a mysterious way
His wonders to perform."

His providence is a great deep.

God says, "What I do, thou knowest not now; but thou shalt know hereafter;" and this is found often to be the case in this world.

A novelist might make a tale of what is here clearly stated, without exaggeration, that would, indeed, make truth more marvellous than fiction.

THE CLERGYMAN BUYING A WATCH.

More than forty years have passed away since the writer went from the "land of steady habits," with a minister, to attend the anniversaries in the city of New York.

We lodged in Brooklyn, the bed-chamber of New York, with a mutual friend, and came over every morning to attend the meetings in the last-named city. One time, as we were walking up Broadway, we came to one of "Peter Funk's" dens which have always abounded in the great commercial metropolis; though I suppose neither Boston nor Philadelphia would tolerate such dens for a day. Hearing the ringing of "Peter's" bell, my friend said, —

"I am going to stop here, and buy a watch."

As he turned to go in, I said, —

"They will cheat you out of your eye-teeth there."

It was simply a parting remark, for I did not for a moment suppose but that he knew perfectly the character of those dens.

In the evening we met again at the house of our friend.

"Now," said he, "I will relate to you my success in buying a watch. As I entered, there were a number of persons standing around the door in the room, and one or two behind a little counter. The auctioneer was crying, '*Here's the good watches, — pure gold, six-jewelled,*' &c. I took the one he held up into my hand, and looked at it: it was bright, and looked well. Some one bid twenty-five dollars, and I bid thirty. I supposed it would go much higher than that, as the auctioneer had represented it worth a hundred dollars; but it was struck off to me. I thought I had made a good bargain, and secured such a watch as I wanted, at a much cheaper rate than I had expected. A man standing by, but not appearing to have any interest in the concern, said to me, —

"'Let me look at your watch.'

"I did so. He took it, opened it, and seemed to examine it very carefully for some time. At length, with a very serious look, he said, —

"'My friend, *they've cheated you.* That watch isn't worth five dollars. Now, I advise you to bid off a *good* watch, and make them take this one back as part pay at the price you gave for it.'

"'Will they do that?' said I.

"'Yes,' he replied, 'if you make them promise beforehand to do so. Ask them.'

"I did so, and they said, if I wanted a higher-priced and a better watch they would accommodate me, and take the other as part pay. Another watch was set up. The man who had so carefully examined mine, and pronounced it worthless, now seemed in good spirits, and said the watch now offered was a *good* one, and advised me to secure it by all means, saying, —

"'There was not often such a chance as this.'

"I bid upon it, and others did the same. When my bid reached sixty-five dollars, it was struck off to me. I now thought again, I had made a good bargain, and said to myself, 'Surely this is a first-rate place to buy watches.' I returned the other at the price I paid for it, and received my new purchase.

"Though well satisfied that I had now made a good bargain, and grateful to my stranger-friend who had advised me to this course, as I had an acquaintance, a watchmaker by trade, who had lately removed to the city from my parish, I thought I would go and consult him, and get his congratulations upon my fortunate trade. So I set off in good earnest, never once doubting but he would say, 'You have an excellent watch here.' Entering his shop, I presented to him the watch, I presume with somewhat of an air of triumph, and said, —

"'What is this watch worth?'

"He took it, looked at it for a moment, and then said, —

"'It isn't really *worth* any thing.'

"I was never more astounded in my life. I said, —

"'What will you give me for it?'

"'*Nothing*,' he replied.

"'What do you mean?' said I. 'What is the matter with the watch? Isn't it good gold?'

"To all these inquiries he merely shook his head, and laid down the watch. I persisted in my inquiries, when he finally said, —

"'You have been grossly imposed upon. It is nothing but burnished brass, and it is worth no more than its weight for old brass.'

"There was no more to be said, for I knew he spoke as he thought. I inquired, —

"'Have you any *silver* watches? I have had enough of gold ones.'

"'Yes,' said he.

"'Will you let me see them?'

"He handed out a number.

"'What is one of these worth?' said I.

"'Eighteen dollars,' he replied.

"'Will you give me one of these for mine?'

"'*No*,' said he.

"'How much must I give you in addition to my watch?'

"'Well, though your watch is not worth any thing, yet I will allow you five dollars for it in exchange for one of mine; *but it is merely as a favor to an old friend.*'

"So I paid him thirteen dollars and the gold watch; and here" (holding out the silver watch) " is the result of my day's experience in buying a watch."

My friend said that when the watchmaker told him his sixty-five dollar watch was worth nothing, he thought he felt very much as did the scribbler when Pope

"Dropped at length, but in unwilling ears,
 This saving counsel: Keep your piece nine years."

Since the period of my friend's purchase of this watch, then a young man, he has become old, and within a few years has passed away from earth.

THE M'CLELLAN FAMILY.

This sketch was written, and published in the "Public Ledger" in Philadelphia, in 1862, just after George B. M'Clellan was appointed general. The father of John and James M'Clellan, his grandfather and great-uncle, was a general in the war of the Revolution.

I have just read an article in the "Press" of June 25, entitled, "*Dr. George M·Clellan, by Dr. William Elder.*" It is an able article, and does justice to that eminent surgeon. My object, however, is not to find fault with it, nor specially to commend.

One end designed by the writer is, to correct some statements that have appeared from time to time in the papers, respecting the M'Clellan family. Having resided for several years in the same town, and same part of the town, with James M'Clellan, the father of Dr. George M'Clellan, and the grandfather of the present Gen. George B. M'Clellan, and having often visited the family, I claim to know what I state and " whereof I affirm."

The family of James M'Clellan was a very pleasant one to visit. He received his friends with great cordiality, and held them in high estimation. Often, by special invitation, have I visited the farmhouse, in the south-eastern part of Woodstock, surrounded by noble sycamores, looking as though they had stood there a thousand years. It stood on a level plat of land, bordering upon a branch of the Quinabaug, a little stream running through that section of the country, and emptying into the Thames, near Norwich.

James M'Clellan was more than sixty years old, when I first knew him; but he then had all the vigor, activity, and go-aheaditiveness of a Connecticut Yankee. His temperament was ardent; his thoughts flowed rapidly; his motions were quick; and his tongue was never at a loss for words. His residence was about a mile from the beautifully-located village of Woodstock; and we always knew when he was coming, by the swift galloping of the horse upon which he rode. Rarely was his horse seen to walk or trot when M'Clellan was on his back. The gallop was his usual mode of riding. Every one, who had business to transact with him, knew he must do it quickly; for he never seemed as though he could wait a moment. He was for several years the sheriff of the county of Windham, technically termed the "high sheriff;" and it was proverbial in the county, that if a rogue could escape M'Clellan he would never be caught, either by man or "devil." The people in the neighborhood used to tell a story of his crossing a pond, near his house, upon the ice, to catch a criminal that had eluded his grasp, when the ice could not have been much thicker than window-glass. Their theory was, that he went over it so quickly that it had not time to break before he was gone.

His general characteristics were quickness, resolution, perseverance, and unconquerable will.

I have already said, he was a warm friend; and it may be added, with equal truth, he was "a good hater."

Let me here leave James M'Clellan, the father of Dr. George, and grandfather of the general. The reason of referring to John will appear before I close. John was older than James. He was a lawyer, and married a daughter of Gov. Trumbull. John was just the opposite of James. He was calm, quiet, never in a hurry, but always as undisturbed as a "summer sea when not a breeze sweeps o'er its surface." I saw him when he was sixty-five, and often from that period till he was ninety-two, at which age he died.

He was famous for telling stories; but they were always related in a peculiarly moderate and considerate manner. There never were two men more perfectly antipodal than were John and James M'Clellan.

John kept up the old Puritanic, or, perhaps, it should be called the old "Levitical law,"—custom of giving the "first fruits" of the garden and the farm to "the priest:" thus you would see him with a little basket of the first ripe strawberries, or early cucumbers, or some nice early made butter, wending his way to the house of "the pastor," that he might share in these "first fruits" of all things.

Neither clergymen, nor their better halves, are always wise; and I suppose the squire (John M'Clellan always went by the name of squire, because, as already said, he was a lawyer) never forsook this custom, but in one case. It was on this wise:—

He had carried to his minister some very early nice butter. The wife of the good pastor, for some such reason as sometimes moves the ladies to speak before they have well considered exactly how the speech may sound, as soon as the squire had left, said to the servant, "Here, take this butter, and lay it aside: it will only do to eat on fish." The servant soon carried the speech to the squire's wife, who, being one of the best housekeepers in all the "land of steady habits," was distressed, most justly; and the squire carried no more butter to that pastor.

I could cover several pages with the stories with which

the squire was accustomed to amuse his visitors; but as the chief point for which reference has been had to him is, to show the contrast between him and his brother James, as to quickness and slowness, I will leave the squire, with relating one more item in which he acted a prominent part. The squire was accustomed to send the minister a cord of the best hickory wood every autumn. There was a man in the parish, not renowned for liberality, who owned a fine wood-lot. His heart having become opened at one time, " he said he would give the minister as large a load of wood as the parish would take to him." The squire proposed to get a sled built that would carry about ten cords, and, taking advantage of a good Connecticut sledding snow, gathered together all the oxen in the parish, and gave the minister a large load. This was so well managed that the pastor had wood enough to last all winter; and the donor was some time recovering from the shock produced by the breach made in his wood-lot.

I now come to *Dr. George M‘Clellan*, father of the general, and son of James.

He was born at Woodstock, and graduated at Yale College, studied medicine in Philadelphia, and became eminent in surgery. A volume might, and ought to, be written of this man. He possessed, in a remarkable degree, the quick perception and rapid action so conspicuous in his father. In him were concentrated many wonderful properties, which do not often meet in the same person. While he was quick to perceive, and prompt to execute, he was possessed of surprising perseverance. He never relinquished an object which he had undertaken; never "put his hand to the plough, and looked back." That he should have had enemies, ought to surprise no one. He entered the field of surgery in this city, the emporium of medical colleges and practice on this continent, and he came directly in competition with the first men in the profession. He was comparatively a stranger here, an exotic, born and educated in the manners, habits, and literature of New England. We do not intend to intimate by this, that the Pennsylvanians, or the citizens of Philadelphia, are reluctant to bestow the reward of merit upon any and every man, irrespective of his birth. To intimate such a thing, would be not only unjust in the abstract, but in contravention of many facts, — facts doing honor to the good sense, judgment, and universal and expansive benevolence, and unstinted largeness of intellect and purpose, which are ever willing to put "the right man in the right place." Such facts may be recognized, in many instances, in the honors and emoluments conferred in this city, upon many New-England men. It is necessary to refer to two of these only: the presidents of the two colleges, the old University and the Girard, are both New-England men.

It was not with the citizens generally, nor with politicians, that Dr. George M'Clellan had to contend. But it was with those of his own profession; and, with them, it was not only in competing with eminent surgeons, but also with the friends and patrons of medical schools.

Dr. Elder, in his graphic description of Dr. George M'Clellan, has well said, "Such a man was not to be repressed or matched. He must be treated with homage, or he must be denounced. I need not say to any one who has witnessed the rivalries of schools and sects, in medicine, which policy was adopted."

With this remark, I dismiss the unhappy controversy in which the doctor was engaged with his professional brethren. The writer was not then a resident of Philadelphia; and the time and the men have already too long passed away, to revive these unpleasant scenes.

My chief object is to show the power, activity, bold daring, and at the same time, the comprehension and discretion, of the Doctor. If it could be said, he operated fearlessly; if it should be contended, recklessly even, — it must be also added, he did it, in general, successfully. Had Dr. George M'Clellan lived to an advanced age, it is impossible to say what he would have been, or what he would have done. He died in the strength and vigor of manhood. Since his death, the college, which he labored hard to found, has sent out the largest graduating classes of any one in our land. He had little time to write, being engaged constantly in practice and lecturing. Still, he left notes upon a number of surgical subjects, which, after his decease, were collated and edited by his son, Dr. II. B. M'Clellan, of this city, and published in a beautiful volume octavo, of four hundred and thirty two pages. It was published in 1848; and the writer, then a medical practitioner in Boston, by the politeness of the son and editor of the work, received a copy. It is a very valuable work, and comprises, in a measure, the views and practice of the doctor. The notes as they appear, from Dr. George M'Clellan, are admirable. The articles upon Injuries, upon the System, Erysipelas, Abscesses, Ulcers, Burns and Scalds, Effects of Cold, Wounds, &c., are well written, contain excellent hints, both as to pathology and treatment of such patients. I never read this work but with admiration and profit; and it should be in the hands of all respectable surgeons of the present day.

In speaking of the M'Clellan family, I should not omit the name of Dr. James M'Clellan. He was a younger brother of Dr. George. He also came to this city, was for many years a successful practitioner of medicine, and married a daughter of the Rev. Dr. Ezra Stiles Ely, of Philadelphia. He did not give his attention so much to surgery, as to general practice; and in obstetrics, he had an excellent reputation and a large practice. He was very different from his brother, Dr. George. He was moderate, perhaps some would say slow; very careful and sedate. He was more like his uncle, the lawyer of Woodstock, than his father or brother. He had excellent characteristics for a practitioner of obstetrics, and showed his good judgment in selecting that, as the branch of the medical profession in which he might excel. He was an Elder of one of the Presbyterian churches of this city, and, I believe, universally esteemed. He also died in the strength of his manhood.

From what has been said above of the M'Clellan family, it will be seen that a peculiarity of it, running, at least, for two generations, was a mingling of the quick, daring, active, and of the slow, considerate, calculating character. This was, indeed, an idiosyncracy of the family. Scarcely will you find, in any one family, these two characteristics. They both had a place; both were necessary, both admirable, when properly blended. Neither may be said to be perfect alone.

A question may arise in the mind of my readers, How is it with the general, George B. M'Clellan? As he is a public man, now occupying one of the most prominent positions in the nation, looking at a genealogical chart of the family, as I have endeavored to draw it, it may well be asked, Does he most resemble his father and grandfather, or his uncle and great-uncle? The writer can only say, he has never seen the general since he was a babe, "mewling in his nurse's arms," and therefore the reader can answer the question as well as the writer. If the two general characteristics, to which reference is had above, are happily commingled in him, he would seem to be the right man in the right place. That they are not so commingled, I have no disposition to say.

That a most thorough general could be constructed out of the materials of the family, no one will doubt for a moment. Even an Alexander, a Cyrus, a Cæsar, a Napoleon, or a Washington, could be manufactured out of such ingredients.

The family has ever been one of the most honorable and respected in New England.

Lorenzo Dow, the only man in those days who wore a long beard, with Peggy his second wife, visited Woodstock Springs every year. He was an intelligent, gentlemanly man; and I allowed him to preach in our church, for which he thanked me very cordially. There are anecdotes enough of him to make a volume.

CHAPTER XXI.

AMOS LAWRENCE.

CONTENTS. — Birth, Death, Countenance, Manner of Giving, Contrast of Givers — Mother — Letter to Her — Delicate Constitution — Studying Astronomy — Education — Integrity — Temperance — Tobacco — Esquire Brazer's Store — Beginning just right — Recognition of Providence — Little Doctor — Catholicity — Debility — Diet — Letter to President Hopkins — Advice to One in pursuit of a Wife — Letter to his Daughter — Letter to his Sister — General Characteristics and Advice — His Sons.

"The righteous shall be in everlasting remembrance."

To young men especially, the life of such a man as Amos Lawrence, may be of signal service. Whether we consider him in the light of a man of business, as a citizen, a neighbor, as one of the benefactors of his age, or, as a man of high moral principle, and strict integrity and

piety, his life should lead every young man, and above all, every merchant, to admire and copy. It is not my purpose to write his life. That has been done, and well done, by his son William R. Lawrence, M.D.; and a life of him has just been published by D. Loring & Co. of this city.

My personal acquaintance with Mr. Lawrence was not intimate; and he lived but eleven years after my removal to the city. I knew him, however, as many other beggars did; for I have begged money for feeble churches, for Colonization and Anti-Slavery, for Temperance, Home Missionary, and Boston Provident Societies, as well as for many poor patients in a long medical practice.

I wish to speak particularly of the *manner* of Mr. Lawrence's giving; for there is as much difference in the manner in which different persons give, as in the amounts of their donations. Some give with such a patronizing air, and strive to make the recipient so feel his dependence, that one almost wishes they had not given at all. Others give with such a frowning countenance, and lugubrious looks, that one would think they were parting with their last dollar, or best friend. Mr. Lawrence always had a pleasant countenance; but when he gave, it seemed radiant with joy, so much did he seem delighted with doing good. On such occasions, he looked very much as a lady of taste, on beholding the engraving of him which accompanies this memoir, expressed herself, " What an angelic face!"

Things show best by contrast; or, as the poet says,

"Compare your bastard scarlet with the right:
The difference will appear, though both are bright."

This may be illustrated by the following: In one of my begging missions for a feeble church, I visited a parish not far from Boston, and called upon a deacon of the church. He gave me the names of three wealthy gentlemen, of whom he thought I should receive something. I visited them all, but obtained nothing; save sad details of poverty and distress. I returned to the deacon, and reported my ill success. "Well," said he, "we have no pastor, and to-night is our monthly concert. You stop and talk to us, and we will get some money out of these men." I did as he directed, and at the close of the concert, he stated that I wanted fifty dollars for what he considered a worthy object; and he came to the table, and gave me a five-dollar bill. Then a lady gave me three dollars, and so, others. Two of the men I had seen, but of whom I obtained nothing, were before me. Seeing others give, one of them began to twist about in his seat; and, finally, gave me a ten-dollar bill. This had a wonderful effect upon the other, and he came to the table, and gave me ten dollars. I went home with the deacon; and as soon as we entered the house, he said, "Didn't I tell you we would get some money out of them?" But how different was their manner of giving from that of Mr. Lawrence!

Mr. Lawrence was born in Groton, April 22, 1786.

"He fell asleep" on the early morning of the new year, 1853.

During the last twenty-three years of his life, he gave to charitable objects, six hundred and thirty-nine thousand dollars; and during his life, he gave away seven hundred thousand dollars. This was an immense sum for one man to give from his own private fortune.

The following items may be gathered from Recollections of this excellent man, and from what is recorded of him. I can only name, and let the reader expand, them.

1. In early life, like many other good men, he was much indebted to a mother's instruction. For this he gave the fullest credit; for late in life he wrote to her, "My dear and honored mother, my mind turns back to you almost as frequently as its powers are brought into separate action, and always with an interest that animates and quickens my pulse; for, under God, it is by your good influence and teachings, that I am prepared to enjoy those blessings which He has so richly scattered in my path in all my onward progress in life. How could it be otherwise than that your image should be with me, unless I should prove wholly unworthy of you? Your journey is so much of it performed, that those objects which interested you so greatly in its early stages, have lost their charms; and well it is that they have, for they now would prove *clogs* in the way; and it is to your children, to your Saviour, and your God, that your mind and heart now turn, as the natural sources of pleasure. The cheering promise that encouraged you, when your powers were the

highest, will not fail you when the weight of years and infirmities have made it more necessary to your comfort to get over the few remaining spans of your journey. To God I commend you, and pray him to make the path light, and your way confiding and joyful, until you shall reach that home prepared for the faithful."

2. His constitution was always delicate; yet, as has been seen by the date of his birth and death, he lived till his sixty-seventh year. His life was doubtless lengthened by his careful habits, which will be stated in the sequel.

3. He was an astronomer in early life; for he says, "The beautiful images of early life, come up in these bright moonlight nights, which I used to enjoy in the fields, below our old mansion, where I was sent to watch the cattle. There I studied astronomy, to more account than ever afterwards; for the heavens were impressive teachers of the goodness of that Father who is ever near to each of his children."

4. He was educated in a public school for a time, and afterwards, at Groton Academy; and not, as has sometimes been publicly stated, "in a grocery-store, where he sold rum by the glass." His education, though not collegiate, was sufficient for all business and social purposes; and to qualify him for a Christian gentleman, as well as a "merchant prince." I have the best authority for saying that Squire Brazer's store (where he was a clerk) was the rendezvous, and exchange, for half the county. It was a great institution. An entrance to it was coveted by every young man in town. It was considered equal to an

entrance to Harvard College, and was gained only by merit and great favor. The custom of entertaining the good customers with toddy, was universal; but no pay was taken.

Mr. Lawrence's industry, integrity, and honesty made his fortune.

6. Of his temperate habits, while in Mr. Brazer's store, Mr. Lawrence makes the following statement. He says, "The quantity of rum and brandy sold at this country store, would surprise the temperance men of modern times. Grog was dispensed every day at eleven and at four o'clock. For a short time, I drank with them; but, finding the desire for it increasing upon me, I made up my mind to stop drinking altogether. From this time forward, I never drank a spoonful, though I mixed gallons for my old master and his customers."

This liquor was not sold, as stated above; but given away to customers, as was the general practice at that time. In after-life, Mr. Lawrence used wine by the advice of his physicians. He decided not to be a slave to tobacco in any form; and he says, "I have in my drawer a superior Havana cigar, but only to smell of. I have never in my life smoked a cigar; never chewed but one quid, and that was before I was fifteen, and never took an ounce of snuff, though the scented rappee of forty years ago had great charms for me."

7. Mr. Lawrence ascribed all his "success in life, to the simple fact that he started just right."

8. He showed his wisdom in giving away his property *while he lived.*

9. He recognized the Divine hand in all events, both great and small.

In 1832, the health of Mr. Lawrence was quite feeble, and he was much strengthened by riding on horseback. He was accustomed to secure the company of a friend for his morning's ride. Sometimes this was one of his business acquaintance; but more frequently it was one of the city clergy. In this matter, no denominational distinction seemed to influence his choice; and there are now living in the city of Boston several clergymen, for whose benefit and company he kept a horse, and who still remember the long morning rides which they were accustomed to take with him.

So feeble was his health, that exercise alone would not render it tolerable. He was obliged to be watchful of his diet; his food was of the most simple kind, and was taken in small quantities, after having been weighed in a balance, which always stood before him upon his writing-table. He had a certain amount sent to him from the table, which he eat alone in his chamber, that he might have perfect quiet. For the last sixteen years, he sat down at no meal with his family. In a letter to President Hopkins of Williams College, he says: "If your young folks want to know the meaning of epicureanism, tell them to take some bits of coarse bread (one ounce and a little more), soak them in three gills of coarse meal gruel, and make their dinner of them and nothing else, beginning very hungry, and leaving off more hungry. The food is delicious, and such as no modern epicureanism can equal."

He wrote to his son in 1832, "My little doctor does wonders for me." His little doctor was his horse. "I want you to analyze more closely the tendency of principles, associations, and conduct, and strive to adopt such as will make it easier to go right than wrong. The moral taste, like the natural, is vitiated by abuse. Gluttony, tobacco, and intoxicating drink, are not less dangerous to the latter, than loose principles, bad associations, and profligate conduct, are to the former. Look well to all these things." His two surviving sons have so done.

To a young man, in 1832, he wrote: "There was a part of Boston which used to be visited out of curiosity, when I first came here, by young men, into which I never set foot for the whole time I remained a single man. I avoided it because I not only wished to keep clear of the temptation, common in that part, but to avoid the appearance of evil. I never regretted it; and I would advise all young men to strengthen their good resolutions, and to plant deep and strong the principles of right, and to avoid temptation." To a young friend about to select a companion, he wrote: "Take care that fancy does not beguile you of your understandng in making your choice. A mere picture is not all that is needful in the up-and-down hills of life. Be careful, when you pick, to get a heart, a soul, and a body."

To his daughter on her eighteenth birthday, he wrote: "Eighteen years of your life are now passed; and the events of this period have been deeply interesting to me, and have made such impressions on you, and have left such marks of progress, I hope, in the divine life, as will insure your onward and upward course, until you shall join that dear one whose home has been in heaven for nearly the whole period of your life. When I look upon you or think of your appearance, the image of your mother is before me; and then I feel that deep solicitude that your mind and heart may be influenced with those heavenly influences that gave a grace and charm to all she did."

Let young *ladies*, as well as young men, listen to the following: "If I were to select for you the richest portion (and what a portion of earthly wishes could not his millions have selected?) which a fond father could choose, it would be that you might have a mind and a heart to perform all those duties which your station and condition in life require, upon true Christian principles, so that at the day of account, you may receive the cheering sound of the Master's voice."

But I must cease to quote the admirable advice and beautiful sentiments of this excellent man. All his counsels, all his letters, all his intercourse with his partners and his clerks, all his rides on horseback with the clergy and ladies of Boston, all his longer journeys and tours with his companions, and all the counting-room and fireside chats with those who were privileged to be there, all speak forth the same kind of advice, — all have reference to being guided by that Christian principle which alone can secure confidence and honor among men, the approbation of our own conscience, and the favor of our final Judge.

To a sister, he wrote: "This morning seems almost like a foretaste of heaven; the sun shines bright, the air is soft; I am comfortable. I am the happiest man alive, and yet I would willingly exchange worlds this day, if it be the good pleasure of our best Friend and Father in heaven."

How happy must such a man have been! He had reached the zenith of human attainments, — rich in the goods of this world — rich in family and friends — rich in the blessing of him that was ready to perish, whom his bounty had fed and clothed — rich in "the alms-deeds" which, like "Dorcas," he did — rich in a good conscience; but richer still in faith, and an heir of the promised inheritance reserved in heaven for all who do the Saviour's will.

Of the sons (now living) of such a father, much may be expected; nor has such expectation been in vain, for they have proved worthy of their descent. They are Amos A. and William R., the former a well-known merchant, the latter a physician; both renowned for their benevolence and weight of character, and held in high estimation in this community. This is sufficient to say of them, as they still remain among us, and are known by their works.

INDEX.

A.

Abbott, 121.
Adams, C. F., 19, 20.
Adams, John, 257.
Adams, J. Q., 6, 9, 16, 18, 19, 21, 103, 137, 165.
Adams, E. E., Rev., 304.
Adams, Thomas, 118.
Adams Academy, 130.
Abstinence, 173.
Advent, Second, 223.
Aiken, Rev. Silas, 229.
Alden, Rev. Mr., 262.
Allen, William H., Dr., 306.
Allen, Rev. William, 121.
Antimasonic, 393.
Aristocracy, N.H., 366.
Andrews, E. T., 218.
Andros, Sir Edmund, 354.
Asbury, Bishop, 264.
Arnold, Ben., 176.
Aristotle, 143.
Association, A. Med., 248.
Association, S. S. Teachers', 283.

B.

Bacon, Judge, 398.
Backus, Rev. Mr., 382.
Baldwin, Matthias W., 304.
Baldwin, Rev. Dr., 77.
Barnes, Albert, 121, 263, 292, 293.
Bartlett, Ibrahim, 112.
Bank, Girard, 275.
Barstow, Mr., 396.
Bay, Back, 217, 222.
Baptists, Min., 78, 79, 80.

Baxter, Mrs. Mary, 59.
Beadle, Rev. Elias, Dr., 299.
Beal, Geo. W., 10.
Belden, Rev. Mr., 370.
Beecher, Dr. Lyman, 124, 176, 383.
Berkley, 90.
Bigelow, Dr. Jacob, 247.
Bible, 23.
Blagden, Rev. Dr., 229.
Blackwood, Rev. Wm., Dr., 197.
Blaine, Speaker, 225.
Boardman, Henry A., Dr., 295.
Bomberger, Rev. J. H. A., Dr., 299.
Bonaparte, Napoleon, 17.
Bowen, H. C., 391.
Bowen, Squire, 392.
Boston, 19, 20, 215, 280.
Braintree, 19.
Brackett, Lem., 133.
Brain, 151, 155, 162.
Brigham, Josiah, 100.
Breed, Rev. Dr., 301.
Bristow, Secretary, 325.
Brewster, 360.
Brodhead, Rev. Dr., 365.
Brooks, Obed, 356.
Brown, Rev. Oliver, 121.
Buckingham, J. T., 8.
Building, Main, 331.
Building, Agricultural, 332.
Burgess, Rev. Dr., 55, 210.
Burleigh, Mary, 82.
Burgess, Tristam, 104, 334, 338, 349.
Burgess, Bishop, 334.
Bumps, 145.
Butler, B. F., 230.
Burnham, Rev. Mr., 371.
Buying a Watch, 407.

431

C.

Calhoun, 32.
Cantata, 317.
Cady, Steward, 337.
Cape Cod, 350.
Carver, John, 350.
Catamount, 359.
Catechism, 77.
Channing, Dr. Walter, 246.
Channing, Rev. Dr., 230.
Chase, Secretary, 230.
Church, Clinton-street, 265.
Chandler, Deacon, 394.
Chambers, Rev. Dr., 300.
Charleston, S. C., 308.
Childs, George W., 305, 326.
Child, Peleg, 381.
Childs, Prof. H. H., 247.
Choate, Rufus, 257.
Church, Congregational, 53.
Church, Members of, 57.
Church, Methodist, 107.
Church, Universalist, 120.
Clapp, Mr., 379.
Clarke, Rev. Dr., 296.
Clergy, 16, 86.
Clay, H., 34, 38, 40.
Clark, Rev. Nelson, 121.
Clark, Rev. Daniel A., 201.
Cleveland, Rev. Charles, 235, 236, 238.
Clifford, Gov., 242.
Clock, Old South, 242.
Clergymen, 252.
Cleveland, Prof., 263, 266.
Cicero, 38.
Cobb, Rev. Alvin, 201.
Codman, Dr. John, 3, 55, 58, 184, 187, 225, 369.
Coats of Brain, 153.
Cobb, Rev. Dr., 346.
Coe, Rev. Mr., 366.
Coe, Mary and Ann, 366.
Coe, Benjamin, 366.
Coe, Eben, 367.
Coe, Mrs. Eben, 367.
Cogswell, Rev. Mr., 362.
Cogswell, Hon. J. B. D., 262.
College, Amherst, 340.
College, Harvard, 8.
College, Jefferson Med., 241, 247.
College, Williams, 194.
College, Woman's, 263.
Colver, Rev. Dr., 231.
Columbia, D. C., 41.
Colwell, Stephen, 304.
Colonies, 166.

Common, Boston, 226, 234, 235.
Congregationalist, 72.
Combe, 159.
Court, Central, 219.
Court, Supreme, 233.
Congress, 50.
Cowper, 107.
Crampton, Rev. Mr., 385.
Crane, Tutor, 337.
Cranch, Judge, 18.
Crowell, Rev. J. M., Dr., 300.
Cruden, 187.
Curtis, Adam, 114.
Curtis, Noah, 105.
Curtis, Samuel, 112.
Cutler, Rev. B. C., 54, 63, 101.
Crosby, Drs., 372.

D.

Dana, R. H., 26.
Davis, Rev. Timothy, 354, 359.
Demosthenes, 182.
Diary, 34, 102.
Dictionary, Entick's, 73, 74.
Dictionary, N. T., 87.
DeWolf, Prof., 334, 338.
Dickerman, Rev. Mr., 205.
Dilworths, S. B., 73.
Dimmock, Prof., 136.
Dimmock, Thomas, 353.
Diseases, Chronic, 151.
Dodd, Mr., 221.
Doctors, 257.
Dow, Rev. Dr., 3, 402, 403.
Dow, Lorenzo, 420.
Downes, B. R., 55.
Dunglison, Prof., 247, 273.

E.

Eastman, 360.
Edwards, Jona., Rev. Dr., 298.
Elder, Dr., 411, 417.
Eliot, the Apostle, 375.
Elm, Old, 234.
Ely, Rev. Dr., 418.
Emmons, Dr., 201.
England, 13.
Engine, Corliss, 326.
Everett, Edward, 287.
Expense, 167.
Exhibition, Centennial, 307.

F.

Fairmount, W. W., 270.
Faxon, H. H., 106, 119.

Father Taylor, 123, 124, 125.
Federalist, 16, 37.
Franklin, Benjamin, 21, 226, 228.
Francis, Sir Philip, 36.
France, 180.
Fish, Rev. Mr., 355.
Finney, Rev. C. G., 219, 220, 231, 402.
French, Daniel, 112.
French, Rev. Dr., 373.

G.

Gall, Dr., 142.
Gano, Dr., 79.
Gannett, Rev. Dr., 230.
Garrison, William L., 272.
Gallery, Art, 232.
Garland, A., 49.
Ghent Medical Society, 163.
Gilman, Gov., 166.
Gilmanton, 372.
Gile, Rev. Dr., 209.
Gillet, Mr., 130.
Girard, Stephen, 274.
Girard, Col., 274.
Girls' Grammar Schools, 279.
Glascock, Mr., 45.
Goodrich, S. G., 138.
Goodwin, Rev. Mr., 354.
Government, British, 42.
Grammar, Webster's, 73.
Grant, President, 323.
Grant, Mrs., 326.
Greeley, Horace, 261.
Gregory, Rev. John, 111, 115, 116, 117.
Griffin, Dr., 123.
Grounds, Exhibition, 329.
Groton, 422.
Groton Academy, 424.
Grow, Elder W., 78.

H.

Hall, Independence, 269.
Hall, Robert, 121, 293.
Hall, J. E., Rev., 123.
Hall, Jaynes, 288.
Hall, Machinery, 326.
Hall, Horticultural, 332.
Hague, Rev. Dr., 231.
Hancock, John, 4, 175, 226, 228, 269.
Hancock, Gen., 325.
Hathaway, Stephen, 94.

Hawley, Joseph R., 320.
Hayne, 33.
Hayward, Dr. George, 24.
Hayes, Dr., 264.
Health, 168.
Hedding, Bishop, 365.
Harwich, 356, 360, 361.
Harvard College, 425.
Haven, President, 361.
Haven, Rev. Mr., 361.
Hewitt, 176.
Herald, G. L., 87, 92.
Hersey, Rev. Mr., 354.
Hicks, Elder, 92.
Hill, Fort, 217.
Hill, H. A., 328.
Hill, Miss Mary, 373.
Holmes, Dr., 377.
Hospital, Insane, 251.
Hospital, Soldiers', 291.
Home, Old Ladies', 240.
Hotel, Marlboro', 216.
Hurd, Rev. Mr., 370.

I.

Ide, Rev. Dr., 207.
Indians, 267, 268, 355, 375.
Irishmen, 282.
Intellect, 170.
Ireland, 180.
Irony, 47.

J.

Jackson, Place, 225.
Jackson, Andrew, 39, 275.
James, Court of, 11.
Jefferson, President, 7, 16, 39, 42.
Jenks, William, Dr., 55, 229.
Jersey, New, 51, 262.
Johnson, Rev. Mr., 360.
Junius, 36.

K.

Kame's Elements, 341.
Keep, Dr., 218.
King, 12, 13, 14, 15.
King Charles I., 351.
King James, 351.
King Philip, 375, 376.
Kirk, Rev. Dr., 230.
Knapp, Rev. Jacob, 23.
Knox, John, 268.

L.

Ladies, Philadelphia, 291.
Ladies, Young, 428.
Lamb, Rev. Mr., 365.
Lathrop, Rev. John, 353.
Lanier, Sidney, 317.
Lawrence, A. A., 335.
Lawrence, Amos, 420, 421, 426.
Lawrence, W. R., Dr., 421
Lawyer, 17, 253, 256.
League, Union, 290.
Lewis, D. H., 46.
Lewis, Dr. Winslow, 249.
Lewis, Ida, 357.
License, 178.
Little, Dr., 427.
Lovering, Quaker, 365.
Lunt, W. P., 69.
Lowell, Rev. Dr., 230.
Lyceum, Quincy, 137.
Lyman, Father, 378.
Lyons, 395.

M.

Magazine, Christian, 86.
Magnetism, Animal, 221.
Maffit, J. N., 8, 368.
Maffit, Mrs., 369.
Maltby, Rev. Mr., 385.
Mason, Jeremiah, 256.
Massachusetts, 3, 7.
Massachusetts Building, 326.
Marshall, Tho., 32.
Marsh, Jonathan, 108.
Marsh, Elisha, 106.
Marsh, Mrs. Lucy, 59.
McCosh, Rev. Dr. James, 303.
McDowell, Rev. Dr., 294.
McLellan, James, 412. ✓
McLellan, George, Dr., 292, 411, 415, 416, 418.
McLellan, George B., Gen., 411, 412, 419.
McLellan, H. B., Dr., 418.
McLellan, John, 413, 414.
Merry, Mount, 3.
Medals, 232.
Messer, President, 333, 334, 335, 346.
Methodist, 287, 358.
Miller, Father, 223.
Mitchell, Prof., 247.
Milton, 27.
Ministers of Quincy, 4.
Ministers, Methodist, 256.

Morse, Rev. Jed., 84.
Morse, Rev. Dr., 377.
Mountains, White, 373.
Muddy Brook, 378.
Musgrave, Rev. Dr., 290.
Mutter, Prof., 247, 273.

N.

Neal, Rev. Dr., 231.
Nevin, Rev. A., Dr., 297.
Nevin, Rev. E. W., Dr., 299.
Newcomb, Jona., 122, 206.
New Fields, 370.
Newington, 368.
Newton, Rev. Richard, Dr., 300.
Newkirk, Matthew, 301.
Newmarket, 364.
Nightingale, Mrs. Susan, 59.
Nickerson, Eliezer, 363.
Niles, Judge, 10.

O.

Old State House, 229.
Old Major, 386.
Oliver, Elder, 227.
Orleans, New, 2.
Otis, H. G., 353.

P.

Paddock Elms, 228.
Paine, Walter, 396.
Palfrey, Prof., 353.
Parkman, Dr., 246.
Park, Calvin, Dr., 334.
Parker, Fred., 346, 347.
Paris, 18, 20.
Parr, Old, 27.
Parker, S. D., 331.
Patriot, Barnstable, 361.
Patriots, 172.
Penn, William, 266, 267, 329.
Peace, 168.
Perkins, Benjamin, 261, 263.
Pembroke, 371.
Perkins, Rev. Jonas, 201.
Perkins, Mrs., 205.
Perry, Dr. M. S., 245, 250.
Peter Funk, 408.
Phrenology, 140, 146, 148, 149, 150, 157.
Philadelphia, 261, 262, 270, 271, 274, 276, 279, 309.

INDEX.   435

Phillips, Rev. John, 210.
Phillips, Wendell, 359.
Physician, 252.
Pierce, Dutty J., 38.
Pierpont, Rev. Dr., 230, 140.
Pilgrims, 181, 196, 352.
Pickering, Mr., 368.
Pickering, Rev. Mr., 393.
Plymouth, 354.
Popery, 83.
Poetry, Mr. Adams's, 28, 31, 53.
Pomet, 353.
Pratt, Mrs. Sarah, 59.
Prayer, Bishop Simpson's, 310.
Prayer, 30.
Practice, Medical, 259.
Providence, R.I., 397.
Protracted Meetings, 399.
Preston, 32.

Q.

Quaker, 264.
Quincy Family, 5.
Quincy, Josiah, jun., 129.
Quincy, 1, 8, 53, 210.
Quincy Patriot, 127.

R.

Randolph, John, 339.
Rantoul, R., jun., 131.
Raymond, Rev. Stetson, 360.
Reed, Dr., 179.
Recorder, Boston, 196.
Ransom, Elisha, 73.
Republicans, 16.
Road, Old Colony, 2, 129.
Rings, 44.
Rogers, Rev. W. M., 189, 211, 212, 222.
Ruggles, Samuel, 377.
Russell, Benjamin, 219.
Rum, Jamaica, 254.

S.

Sabbath, 29.
Saltonstall, Col., 328.
Sandwich, 362.
Sanford, Rev. Mr., 364.
Sanford, Rev. John, 361.
Sanford, Rev. David, 207.
Sargent, Lucius M., 258.
School, Boarding, 111.
School, Farm, 112.

School Committee, 233.
School, Public, 232.
School, Private, 276, 277.
Seminary, Andover, 208.
Seaver, Master, 105.
Select Men, 227.
Sharp, Rev. Dr., 231, 278.
Shaw, C. J., 353.
Shaw, Rev. Mr., 360.
Shattuck, Dr., 373.
Sheldon, Rev. Dr., 379.
Sheridan, Gen., 325.
Shields, Rev. Dr., 296.
Simpson, Bishop, 310.
Sketch-Book, 355.
Skull, 152.
Smith, Miss, 10, 18.
Smith, D. D., 69, 100.
Smith, Elias, 69, 70.
Smith's Sermons, 89.
Smith, M. H., 99, 108, 110.
Smith, Prof., 121.
Smith, Jesse, 216.
Smith, Judge, 370.
Smith, Rev. S. S., 122.
Snow, Deacon, 220.
Society, N. E. S. Aid, 289.
Society, Medical, 258.
Spear, Deacon, 54.
Spooner, B. J., 74.
Spectacles, 75.
Springfield, Mass., 76.
Sprague, Rev. Dr., 295.
Spurzheim, 142, 144.
State House, 252.
Stone, Rev. Mr., 355.
Stone, Rev. Dr., 265.
Storrs, Rev. Dr., 55, 63, 184, 190.
Stuart, George H., 124.
Storrs, Dr. R. S., jun., 198, 199.
Street, Park, 220.
Stillman, Dr., 84.
Stetson, Dr., 133.
Struthers, William, 291.
Swift's Tavern, 363.

T.

Tabernacle, 224.
Tappan, John, 132.
Taylor, Gen., 112.
Tavern, Lamb, 216.
Tavern, Shepard's, 216.
Temple Place, 224.
Temperance Address, 165, 174, 177.
Thayer, Rev. J. H., 121.
Thacher, 6.

Thompson, 48.
Thompson, Samuel, 93.
Thompson, Rev. Otis, 360.
Thwing, Rev. E. P., 122.
Tories, 71.
Tully, 182.
Turner, Rev. Mr., 358.
Truro, 358.
Trumbull, Gov., 413.
Type, 208.

U.

Unitarians, 54, 206.
Universalist, 93.
Underwood, Rev. Mr., 361.
Uncas, Chief, 375.
Underwood, Father, 378.
University, Brown, 207, 333.
University, Vermont, 211.

V.

Village Corners, 379, 385.
Volume, 157.

W.

Wadsworth, Rev. Dr., 272, 298.
Ware, Dr. John, 245.
Walker, Captain, 379.
Walker, Amasa, Prof., 380, 384.
Warren, Dr. J. C., 161, 241, 243, 254.
Warren, Dr. J. M., 245.
Watts's Psalms, 73.

Wayland, President, 333, 336, 338, 340, 343, 348.
Wayland, Sen., 344.
Webster, Daniel, 33, 256.
Webster, Noah, 255.
West Point, 104, 342.
Welch, John, 315.
Wesley, John, 128.
Whitefield, 80, 86.
Willard, President, 185.
Whitney, Rev. Peter, 53, 209.
Winslow, Rev. H., Dr., 229.
Whig, 37.
Whittier's Centennial Hymn, 313, 314.
Whilldin, Alex., 303.
Whitney, Myron W., 317.
White, Nathaniel, 112.
Williams, Rev. Mr., 379.
Wilson, Father, 402.
Williams College, 426.
Wisner, Rev. Dr., 403.
Witherspoon, John, 268.
Wise, Rev. Dr., 125.
Wise, H. A., 36, 52.
Windsor, 75.
Wood, Prof., 147, 273.
Wollaston Heights, 135.
Woburn, 85.
Woodstock, 374.
Woodward, Dr., 133, 134.
Worms, Span, 285.
Wylie, Rev. Dr., 291.

Y.

Young, Mrs. Mary W., 367.

www.ingramcontent.com/pod-product-compliance
Lightning Source LLC
Chambersburg PA
CBHW022103300426
44117CB00007B/572